Choice

In memory of Christina Harper and Ted Cuff,
different people loved in different ways but loved all the same

Choice

The Sciences of Reason in the 21st Century:
A Critical Assessment

Richard Harper, Dave Randall and Wes Sharrock

polity

First published in 2016 by Polity Press

Polity Press
65 Bridge Street
Cambridge CB2 1UR, UK

Polity Press
350 Main Street
Malden, MA 02148, USA

ISBN-13: 978-0-7456-8386-7
ISBN-13: 978-0-7456-8387-4 (pb)

A catalogue record for this book is available from the British Library.

Library of Congress Cataloging-in-Publication Data

Harper, Richard, 1960–
    Choice : the sciences of reason in the 21st century : a critical assessment / Richard Harper, Dave Randall, Wes Sharrock.
        pages cm
    Includes bibliographical references and index.
    ISBN 978-0-7456-8386-7 (hardcover : alk. paper) -- ISBN 0-7456-8386-X (hardcover : alk. paper) -- ISBN 978-0-7456-8387-4 (pbk. : alk. paper) -- ISBN 0-7456-8387-8 (pbk. : alk. paper) 1. Choice (Psychology) 2. Decision making. I. Randall, Dave. II. Sharrock, W. W. (Wes W.) III. Title.
    BF611.H375 2015
    153.8'3--dc23
                                                                    2015016787

Typeset in 10.5 on 12 pt Times NR MT by
Servis Filmsetting Ltd, Stockport, Cheshire
Printed and bound in the United Kingdom by Clays Ltd, St Ives PLC

For further information on Polity, visit our website: politybooks.com

Contents

Acknowledgements

This book has been written on the back of opportunities provided by Microsoft Research, Cambridge. Wes Sharrock joined Richard Harper at Cambridge for a sabbatical, and this in turn resulted in some funding on the role of rational action models in predictive analytics that involved Dave Randall. Throughout this time, Microsoft Research allowed Richard to indulge in the general topic of 'choice', which led to the focused work presented here. Microsoft Research was an unusual corporate establishment for fostering such inquiries, but all three of us, even if we have been recipients of this boon in different ways, are grateful for it.

At the same time, the University of Manchester, and in particular the Sociology Department, has been home to Wes Sharrock. He expresses his gratitude to many long-standing colleagues – as well as some who have moved on to more leisurely pursuits (retirement) – during the creation of this book. Sadly, one of his much loved colleagues passed away suddenly during the period this manuscript was being prepared. Ted Cuff will be missed by many in the common rooms of the universities in Manchester, as will his written work by the world at large. Dave Randall, too, was close to Ted and will miss him greatly. As it happens, a second colleague, also from the North West, passed away too, though his was more expected since he had been ill some time. John Hughes will be missed by many, not just us.

Dave Randall wishes to express his gratitude to the Dipartimento di Scienze Umane e Sociali at the University of Bergamo, and to Fabio Dovigo in particular, for facilitating two productive and enjoyable visits to the lovely city of Bergamo, where much of the work for this book was undertaken. He would also very much like to thank Volker Wulf and colleagues at the University of Siegen for their continued support and engagement. Mark Rouncefield, at Lancaster University, also offered some good-tempered comparisons that helped calm him down.

Richard Harper would like to thank his immediate colleagues in the Human Experience and Design group who put up with his absence while this book was done. Whether this was something they were grateful for is of course for them to decide. Lastly, Richard would like to honour his mother, Christina Harper (née Nolan), who passed away while the manuscript was being finished. Like Ted, but for obviously different reasons, she will be missed.

1

CHOICE: A TWENTY-FIRST CENTURY SCIENCE?

People make decisions every day; indeed, we all make lots of decisions. And yet decisions can seem difficult to comprehend. Others' decisions especially, but even our own, can sometimes seem inexplicable. When we make a choice we cannot account for, we say that we were 'irrational' or were driven by our gut feelings; sometimes it was 'instinct'. That we all make decisions is then a fact of life, just as is their occasional ineffability. Being perplexed about choice is a feature of the human condition. This is hardly a new concern. Historically, cultural techniques have been used to explore this topic. Greek plays made hubris the cornerstone of their narratives about choice; Shakespeare put muddles about identity as the centrepiece of his comedies about choice in love, and he put prejudice as the source of decisions – ones that turn out to be cruel – in his tragedies. In the early twentieth century, the 'death of God' led to the existential turn, and the need to decide – to make decisions – became a 'moral imperative'. In this view, To Be was To Decide, to paraphrase. Much writing on this angst appeared. Sartre's *Roads to Freedom* trilogy comes to mind.[1]

Recently, however, the ineffability of choice has become something that we are at once celebrating and admitting, and yet, even as we do this, treating as a concern we can unpack and better understand. There is, however, a curious paradox about this new understanding of choice – or, rather, how we are thinking about choice and the tension between the ineffable and the analysable. On the one hand, cultural theorists are arguing that people are no longer willing to make choices. This is not because a credo of 'unreason' is coming into the ascendancy, as the cultural theorist-cum-philosopher Slavoj Žižek might put it (1989); it is, rather, because the amount of

---

[1] Consisting of *The Age of Reason* (*L'Âge de raison*, 1945), *The Reprieve* (*Le Sursis*, also 1945) and *Iron in the Soul* (*Le Mort dans l'âme*, 1949).

information now being produced by computer-based systems is so great that it is overpowering the capacity of the human mind to digest (Andrejevic, 2013). The term cloud-computing evokes not how new technology is helping people reason but how, on the contrary, it is only computing on a massive scale that is capable of making the analysis that leads to right choices. This shift is supposedly visible in the performance of US presidents: 'Reagan, being uninformed, could be utterly clear about his goals. Clinton, being exceedingly informed, sometimes got lost in his facts' (Shenk, 1997: 78, cited by Andrejevic, 2013). After Clinton, the next president didn't even bother with evidence: Andrejevic quotes Laura Bush: 'He [President Bush] has good instincts, and he goes with them. He doesn't need to evaluate and re-evaluate a decision. He doesn't try to overthink. He likes action.' The basis of his choices, according to Laura, was 'gut feel'. In short, we turn to the inner, to our instincts, because we are confronted with 'Infoglut'.[2]

The view from cultural theory turns on the ineffability of choice. But there is another side to the debates about choice. If the cultural theorists are claiming that we are losing our desire to choose, being confronted by an all too awesome amount of information upon which to make up our minds, those within the social sciences, economics and psychology, particularly, are beginning to claim that this most essential of human characteristics – the ability to choose – is being made palpable to experimental dissection and, thus, scientific comprehension. A 'science of choice' is appearing (though this particular nomenclature goes some way back, well before the kinds of arguments we are thinking of came to the fore). This is creating considerable excitement in some parts of the academic world and, indeed, in the press.

This shift has its roots in old debates, as well as in the emergence of new thinking and techniques in the area. The long-standing dissatisfaction with economists' classical views of rationality, a notion that people made all their choices on the basis of what was optimum for them, has resulted in a gradual but now almost irresistible turn to new notions of reason. For one thing, the classical notion did not describe the 'real world', nor could one find actual instances of

---

[2] The trouble with these arguments, though they articulate strongly held views about the competence of a sequence of political leaders, as well as a critique of the mystique of technology (Žižek, 1989), is the difficulty with which one would know whether this approach to decision-making and choice is widespread. How a president reasons in his or her White House office may be a long way from reasoning on the street, in the world of ordinary affairs. It doesn't help that Andrejevic uses *Wired* magazine for his evidence; Žižek, Andrejevic's inspiration, doesn't seem to use evidence at all.

persons making choices in economics books. It was, as economists themselves readily admitted, an idealised notion of choice. Over the years, and in an effort to allay this over-idealised view, economists have explored, for instance, the different 'conditions' that influence choice, where conditions label the form and constraints on information available to a chooser. Some of these conditions sound very like sociological phenomena, such as how the cargo of skills and social connection that people build up comes to frame their decision-making and hence their capacity to choose at any moment in time. Indeed, the work of Gary Becker, who was the first economist to develop fully the notion of 'social capital', is illustrative of this attempt to link the basic idea of rational action to stocks of knowledge, to the things people know when they act.

At the same time, and within the social sciences more generally, in sociology and anthropology particularly, there has been an equally long-standing and continually vigorous debate about what matters beyond the economic; rationality cannot be, in this view, only about money matters but about all things. Here, the answers offered emphasise both moral uniformity and systems of exchange and obligation that are not economically motivated but socially driven. Experimental techniques are not valued when exploring these concerns. What might be the 'right' way to proceed is rather less clear, and many of the arguments, as we shall see, turn out to be about methodological appropriateness.

Even so, the pull of the basic economic model of rationality has remained central to nearly all these debates, and it has done so by being the measure against which all new ideas are placed. Daniel Kahneman's Nobel Prize for economics in 2002, and the subsequent publication of his book *Thinking, Fast and Slow* in 2011, has led to an interest in the possibility that the picture of human rationality in economics is substantially wrong for reasons that are psychological. People's reasoning is, in some sense, irrational, he claims. In his view, it is not an economic model that lies within the mind (i.e., a capacity to identify maximum utility) but psychological mechanisms that govern choice. Along with his colleagues, Kahneman claims to have shown that there are *systematic, mentally derived* deviations from the traditional standard of rational decision-making in real instances of action. People not only misjudge their options, they misjudge them repeatedly and in specifiable ways. While Kahneman's view starts with the economic one (the view that action is governed by some notion of rationality), his claim is constructed on the basis of something that economists (and not sociologists or anthropologists) hadn't always entertained: the traditional laboratory experiment. He argues that the business of decision-making, or choice, can be subjected to an empirical description of a scientific kind, and in his view this means experimentally. This is, of course, a very limited notion of what is science, even if it is commonly held.

These are not by any means the only views on reasoning and choice being articulated at the moment, even if they are currently the most cited – Kahneman especially. There are plenty of other approaches which see themselves as investigating how the mind works and comes to make decisions or choices, and some of these seek to expand the case of economic choice (irrational constraints notwithstanding) into a wider set of topics. Here the question of method is only partially material. In recent decades a return to the notion that human action can be explained *causally* has been revised in philosophy, for example. For many years this idea was largely dismissed, but it has gradually come to prominence again, though, as with economists and their notion of rational action, philosophers have various notions of what cause might be (for an introduction, see Sandis, 2012). Many within philosophy want to treat cause as merely a logical fact; in this view, something must have led someone to undertake such and such and the relationship between one and the other must be causal, even if it is not clear in any instance just how. After all, accounts of reasons and causes do not necessarily lead one to a true understanding of cause, so Davidson (1963) argued long ago. But some have advanced causal explanations of a particular kind. Daniel Dennett in his *Darwin's Dangerous Idea* (1995), as a case in point, attempts to explain *why* people make their choices through reference to evolution. In his view, even if one's choices are typically made through a process of maximising utility, as economists suppose, there is still a need to explain why people's motives for making certain kinds of choice are fairly consistent through time – indeed, in Dennett's view, over the ages. Understanding what disposes people to value and desire the things they do is to be provided through Darwin's ideas, unlikely though it may seem on the face of it.

There are, also, other notions founded in cognitive and evolutionary psychology which suppose that the mind operates through logically structured computational procedures; these are causal too, but in a subtle sense. John Duncan claims, in *How Intelligence Happens* (2010: 116), that many psychologists are coming to believe they are 'demystify[ing] thought' by combining insights from observation of brain processes with those derived from mental acuity tests of various kinds. This combination of evidence implies that certain sorts of computational powers operate in the brain. We choose algorithmically, this perspective holds. According to Duncan, human reasoning is made up of logical processing elements, analogous to a computer program. Not only is intelligence to be thus explained, but so too are character and personality, as well as the more mundane facts of choice, of everyday reason, he would have us believe. Some philosophers of science have offered similar arguments, though each with a different nuance. If Duncan emphasises pattern-matching then Skyrms, in *Signals* (2010), following Dennett, models the way systems capable of performing logical operations can evolve from very simple signalling behaviour. In this view, choice is merely (though complicatedly) a function of entropy versus strength, the evolutionary development from strictly biological signals to linguistic ones. The work of Norbert Weiner in his seminal book *Cybernetics* (1948) comes to mind.

The topic

This is only to highlight some of the reasons why choice is of such interest at the moment. From the view of cultural theory to the more arcane views of experimental psychology, from economics to philosophy, how people choose, why they choose and how it is to be explained is now treated as open territory for investigation. What was once the ineffability of the human condition is now being tamed, rendered explicable through new tools and techniques, new concepts and starting places. At least this is the hope.

In this book, we cover as many of the perspectives on this topic as we reasonably can, and our goal, also, is to offer reasonable assessments of these claims. As with all new sciences and territories for investigation, there is much excitement, but along with the excitement comes hyperbole and exaggeration. We want to sort these out from the facts.

Five elements will be central to our musings. The first is conceptual. A simple way of viewing our topic is to ask the question 'What are we talking about when we talk about [motive, reason, decisions, the individual]?' We will show that there are conceptual difficulties to do with definitions about these matters that are much more profound than sometimes thought. A second theme has to do with a topic beloved of the social and human sciences – the question of methods. This pertains not so much to what evidence can be marshalled to support the various explanations on offer as to how that evidence is *produced*. We will not say that some methods produce false data but that, rather, different methods cast evidence in different sorts of ways. This can make comparison between the output of one set of methods difficult to compare with the output of another, or at least can make it a very hard thing to do. Besides, and as we shall see, some of the methods that are deployed when addressing the topic of choice are simply not handled very well. It is not always clear why these errors are made, but made they are. Kahneman's experiments are a notorious and high-profile example of this.

A third concern is obviously related to both methods and definitions, and this has to do with boundaries. For, when one examines choice, it is not just a question of defining what one means or coming up with a method to capture evidence about it; we also have to come to a view about what to include and what to exclude from our deliberations. In this regard, human choice is radically different from other types of phenomena subject to empirical inquiry, for it really is unclear where choice ends and something else begins. As we shall see, it is not wise to assume that human reasoning is made up of chains of thought, each determinate, logical and easily specifiable; reasoning is more a set of interconnected concerns that makes separation of one line of thought from the larger context of which they are a part quite difficult. Indeed, and given this, one can sometimes come to doubt whether there is a class of 'decision-making', such as, say, related to 'economic life', which can be separated from other forms of decision-making behaviour – indeed from behaviour in the general. Without this kind of distinction, claims about the right tools for the analysis of choice behaviour can become contentious – are experiments good for everyday decision-making, for example? If not, what are? Ethnographic techniques? Modelling or other abstractions?

The fourth element relates to what is right and what is wrong, or, rather, what is the right kind of behaviour presupposed in our perspective. This is typically called the question of *normativity*. Many of those concerned with choice, most obviously sociologists but of course economists too, have never feared to step into debates about how the world ought to be. Describing choice is only the preface to that concern, in their view. A whole range of correctives are implied in their various methods and topics. Experiments such as the 'Prisoner's Dilemma', as we shall see, purport to tell us something about the conditions under which we might be selfish or, alternatively, cooperate with others. They suggest how the world ought to be when cooperativeness is clearly better than the selfish view. The notion of what is better and what is worse, even though it is often unstated, allows contrasts and critique of the world as it is. Models about choice in economics don't just invoke rationality but also imply a more 'economic' future, where rationality can be more effectively undertaken, and so on.

The fifth element concerns changes in the modern world which might entail changes in human nature, thus shifting the foundations of choice-making. As we noted, some cultural theorists claim we are being driven from choice towards our gut feelings by the weight of information. We are overloaded and so can't choose. Others, meanwhile, have developed pragmatic techniques that seek to encourage decisions of one kind over another. These 'nudge' people to choose, as it has been put (see Thaler and Sunstein, 2008). Others have suggested that essential or motivational aspects of choice behaviour are altering because of the Web. Yochai Benkler's celebrated work *The Penguin and the Leviathan: How Cooperation Triumphs over Self-Interest* (2011) comes to mind. This proposes that online behaviour is creating a new social psychology, where cooperation begins to displace self-interest. This is clearly different from Andrejevic's view, though echoes can be found in the starting place of each. Information production is affecting choice, either making it more freely available, as in the case of Benkler, or in overloading us, as in the case of the author of *Infoglut*.

Our goal: a view across disciplines

Claims about the science of choice, then, and despite some indication of inter-disciplinary approaches emerging, need to be seen as of distinct and possibly incommensurate kinds. There is considerable difference between, say, Taddeo's (2009) logical model of trust, which might help explain choice in game theoretic behaviours, and the use of trust by people to make choices in everyday action as described by Watson (2009), for example. One is not a reduction of the other. They offer different accounts of the basis of decision-making. The differences cannot be summarised by triangulation or some other view of integration in scientific reasoning, for they are predicated on different assumptions about the phenomenon in view. The empirical adequacies of these and many similar arguments has to do with their pragmatic goals, what they were trying to answer and why. Put simply, disciplinary purposes largely underpin questions of concept, method and theory when it comes to the question of choice (as indeed they will with any topic). These 'logics', as Winch (1958) pointed out long ago, define how one ought to judge each.

Beyond this, there is the question of the relationship between the explanation offered and individual instances of choice. Accounts such as those of Duncan and of Kahneman offer *models* of reasoning and not accounts of particular choices. This raises important issues in respect of the relationship between the (often abstract) models produced in classical or rational action (and hence choice) and revised accounts of rational choice and actual cases of decision-making. The connection between gross notions of choice and inherently particularised individual choice is still obscure. Is the model an abstraction, a distillation of these particulars, or a heuristic that seeks to characterise them at the expense, to some degree, of accuracy, of verisimilitude?

Developing these themes, we will begin with a brief history of the idea of 'rational choice' and the different things it might mean. An important part of this has to do with the fault lines dividing the way social and human scientists consider why and how people choose and what implications this has for understanding the nature of economic behaviour and social behaviour more generally. Arguments about free will and determinism will not be central to our interests, though consideration of the ways in which people make choices might be seen as begging the question of whether there are any choices for people to make. After all, the idea that anyone has personal control over what they do next presupposes that they have, in some sense, free will. Unfortunately, there is no settled answer to the question of whether they do (indeed, one of the reasons we do not wish to sail upon this particular boat is that there are few settled answers to any philosophical questions at all, this one included!). To the extent that we engage with problems of this kind, we do so strictly and only insofar as they arise *after* the assumption that people do in fact make choices has been accepted and treated as allowing evidence of various kinds to be gathered. It is important to bear in mind that the notion of choice we will focus on is strongly connected to the idea of 'decision', because the idea of choice, as we will see, is most often understood from the perspectives we deal with as a matter of electing to do one thing rather than another – as an empirical matter. The problem of 'free will' is not.

As we shall explain, most of the disciplines identify an activity as choice-making if people face a situation composed of discrete alternatives, a situation affording the possibility of doing lots of different things but in which, at a given point in time, they could choose only one. Of course, one of the questions we can pose for the science of choice is whether and how we can delimit the number of choices the decision-maker can be said to face, since, in the real world, there are normally lots of choices to be made. In experimental conditions, in contrast, choices will be artificially limited, to A, B or C. And, moreover, choice has to be made in the experiment, making it all the more easy for the researcher. Subjects can hardly say, 'I'm fed up with this, I'm going to the pub' – even though they might wish to do so.

Though the real-world character of decision-making is elided in the experimental context, nevertheless the tidiness with which the experiment sets up choice has its echoes outside of the perspective of experiments. The relative simplicity of experimental conditions is, broadly speaking, matched by how economists think about making choices, for example. In their picture, they create situations of choice that have that kind of organisation – where choice is between this and that and is not bound up with a multitude of concerns (the question of marginal utility, judgements between choices of similar and dissimilar goods notwithstanding at the moment). Along with this, they emphasise how decision-making in the real world is confounded by limitations in understanding, in what those who make choice know about the relative merits of the alternatives in front of them.

This way of treating choice glosses much that is of importance. Take as an illustration the following somewhat playful (and certainly English) scenario. There are fish and chips and a sponge cake on the table. An individual sits beside the table and is confronted with a choice. They can eat the fish and chips or the cake but not the fish and chips and the cake together (at least, not within the conventions of seemly dining). Thus the diner's eating the cake is a matter of eating the cake first *rather* than the fish and chips *or* vice versa. The fact that there are, theoretically, alternatives that entail choosing both, the question really being one of order, can therefore be considered unimportant in explaining how the diner comes to choose what they do and what should be subject of inquiries into that choice. Choice here is not, then, a logical choice between independent acts A and B. The two acts are interdependent and defined in part by conventions (i.e., don't eat cake with fish and chips; eat them as separate entities, first one, then the other). One might add that conventions such as this are sometimes so taken for granted that they can lead one to forget, or at least fail to see clearly, how they frame choice situations. Choices subject to any inquiry need to be understood carefully before any attempt to explain them is made – their conventional features recognised, the particular logical relationship between acts deriving from choices determined.

There are other issues. Not only are these choices bound to each other but the selection of one or the other is also, obviously, a matter of *what* to choose. The preferences of the persons in question are self-evidently pertinent. To inquire into the nature of choice presupposes, then, that the diner be assumed to be a reasoning creature where that reasoning needs some explanation – all the more so if those reasons might be said to be constrained, inhibited or even irrational to some degree. *Explaining* choice consequently turns out to be quite an encompassing task, whether one is taken with the experimental method or is focused on real-world sites of action. Choice is rarely if ever simply between things, but has to do both with the character of that choice (that it might require serial ordering, say) and with who makes the choice. What starts out as something that looks like a question of logic and information processing turns into a question about the nature of the creature that makes the choices – a creature with preferences, habits, a capacity to process information, perhaps, but also a creature that might be wilful, deceitful or simply lazy.

It is in these ways that 'choice' quite often ends up pointing towards the ineffable – and thereby something that needs explaining, something that needs inquiry, that deserves a 'science'. To say that people reason and that they choose is not, in itself, enough. The trouble is that, when the word 'explaining' is brought into play, a raft of other considerations result. The fish, chips and cake example is conceived of in very simple terms indeed, but the point of studying choices isn't to go around finding out what *specific* reasons people have for choosing one thing over another – at least it most often isn't. More commonly, studies of choice try to identify *general* principles on the basis of which people make any and all choices. This is not an easy undertaking. And if this is the goal of understanding (to generalise, say), then there is a requirement that the resulting level of generalisation satisfy the conditions that those making the study set out as acceptable, proper explanations, at the right level, with the right methodological proofs of evidence and justification.

Generalisation has various forms, of course, but if it is a label for an effort to systematise knowledge there is still a distinction of considerable importance between this and what one might call scientific knowledge. Philosophers seek to generalise, and this is not the same as what scientists do; their generalisations are of another order. The key difference – and of course this is simplifying but sufficient for the point we are making – is the relationship between evidence and explanation. This is, to say the least, a tricky and delicate affair and can distinguish many of the disciplines from each other and not just those that cast themselves as either scientific or philosophical.

Consider: a scientific approach seeks (or claims) to discover the truth about why people choose one thing or another, but, if it does this, are these reasons, the ones that science uncovers, different from the ones that people themselves avow? What does it mean to say that the reasons for an action are *not* the ones that the parties in question think they have? It seems very reasonable to say that some kinds of explanation of human conduct don't entail looking at the reasons people themselves have, but not in all cases. The contrast between when one would want science and when one would want another order of explanation is not then so simply made. It becomes even more complex if it is the case that the way people organise their affairs is through conscious recognition of the role their own and others' choices make on the situation in question: *where it is reasons that both oneself and others have* that determine what gets done in a particular situation. Whether these reasons are good or bad, right or wrong, is moot; what needs to be recognised is that it is this – reasons as understood and acted upon – that is to some degree constitutive of the behaviour in question. What then of scientific inquiry? Is it offering something that is to compete with this role of reasons in action? How would it compete? Could one have a revised notion of scientific inquiry which made reasons as so conceived the topic? Wouldn't this be best described as more like an empirical philosophy anyway? Why the need for the label 'science'? And thus we end up having to reflect on disciplinary views about science and other evidence-based social sciences and humanities, about the relationship between evidence and explanation, the role of method and generalisation, and much else besides.

As we end our introductory sketch of the topic, we can see then that, when one asks 'What is a decision?' and 'What does it mean to "make" one?', these questions are less trivial than they appear. As should be clear, the first question is to do with what a decision is and has a number of different and competing answers depending upon where one approaches the topic and, as part of that, what one assumes and how one wants to measure 'success' – what a good answer looks like. The second question, to do with what it means to make a choice, is equally complex. When we ask what a decision might be, are we referring to an outcome, to a particular kind of process which applies in limited circumstances, or to a categorisation of human activity which can be universally applied?

As is obvious from what has already been said, the answers to these questions can lie in the disciplines and the purposes they lay out for themselves. But however hard one tries there will be dispute between disciplines, each claiming to be the best, and this will turn out to be a dispute about what the purposes of different disciplines might be and the appropriateness of the concepts, methods and theories deployed by each in pursuit of these goals. If one is bold enough to seek an approach that is not constrained by disciplinarity, one needs to ask who might be interested – not the trades that have built a business by having a view, a stance on choice already. Choices about choice, about what it is, how it might be examined, what one seeks thereby, are far from easy. One needs to take a view from 'here', this discipline, or 'there', that discipline, and, if not from these places, from an alternative that needs to justify its starting point. One cannot view choice from anywhere at all. It really isn't like choosing between fish and chips and cake.

Who is this book for?

The nature of what is implied with the word 'choice' is, we are saying, quite wide and is subject to already well-defined disciplinary framings. Consequently, we think that the appeal of this book will be wide too. But we have to be careful as we say this – for, while this very breadth might excite some, it puts others off. The book is certainly for people schooled in the various disciplines constitutive of the social sciences and the humanities, sociology, economics, philosophy, psychology, and so on, and it will be especially appealing to those who wonder whether there are things they might learn from outside the landscape with which they are familiar. It is for those, in other words, who feel themselves sensitive to the kind of conceptual assumptions made in such inquiries, the reasons for those assumptions and how that frames answers to what choice 'is'.

To be absolutely clear, however, we are not wanting to demolish the arguments one finds in this space through seeking a view that looks at them dispassionately, and from afar. Though disciplines can treat the topic of choice so differently that it can at times seem as if the disciplines in question view the reality of choice quite differently too, this doesn't meant that some views must therefore be wrong. As should be clear by now, we have to accept, and will indeed show, that there are good reasons for the variety of perspectives one can have on choice. But this doesn't preclude observing that sometimes the reasons offered for some view are not sufficient to justify it. One has to separate legitimate differences in perspective from what might turn out to be quite grandiose empirical claims, for example, which neither credit the discipline in question nor fairly represent other views – views which might be criticised in the campaign to justify the aggrandising discipline. We should be plain, consequently, that our audience is not for those who are interested only in the disciplinary views. We are writing for those who seek to look at the disciplines for the ways they offer and, through considering this, hope to benefit by seeing all these views as legitimate alternatives about how to look at choice. With that perspective – a view of the wood for the trees, if you like – we think the reader of the book will find themselves better able to navigate their way around the subject of choice.

Something about us, the authors, might help explain the conviction we have that this view has merits. Though we were all trained primarily as sociologists, our careers have developed in *interdiscipli-*

nary inquiry. Variously, we have been interested in social philosophy and, more specifically, the philosophy of Ludwig Wittgenstein, in methodological issues surrounding the way in which human beings make use of technology, in how the mind works and whether this has anything to do with computation, in the design of computational artefacts of one kind or another, and so on. As such, our research has ranged over a vast territory. Included in this have been studies of the way classic economic thought is based on a notion of 'revealed preference' and what kind of work is done with this; of the way some sociologists have tried to use conceptions of rationality to explain what kinds of choices people make in society; and of the way biology has intervened in philosophical debates to suggest means of understanding human motivations. Our inquiries have been widespread as a consequence.[3] What we have learned, if anything at all, is a kind of modest scepticism about the idea that any *individual discipline* can provide anything that looks like a universal explanation of human behaviour. For one thing, the evidence seems to us to make that enterprise – singularity in explanation – look unwise. As should be clear from our sketch above, choice is not anything except an exemplar of a topic that can be looked at in a variety ways. To impose one view is simply narrowing the topic, not exploring it.

Besides, allowing any one discipline some imperial-like status runs the risks of pastiche. Back in the 1970s, for instance, Leijonhufvud observed,

> They [the Econ] are not without some genuine and sometimes even fierce attachment to their ancestral grounds, and their young are brought up to feel contempt for the softer living in the warmer lands of their neighbours, such as the Polscis and the Sociogs. Despite a common genetical heritage, relations with these tribes are strained – the distrust and contempt that the average Econ feels for these neighbours being heartily reciprocated by the latter – and social intercourse between them is inhibited by numerous taboos. (1973: 327)

This satiric comment on the attitudes of economists would, of course, apply equally well to those working in any discipline (and

---

[3] Books that we have published variously together and with other colleagues that are representative of this range include *The Myth of the Paperless Office* (A. Sellen and R. Harper; Cambridge, MA: MIT Press, 2002); *Brain, Mind, and Human Behaviour in Contemporary Cognitive Science* (J. Coulter and W. Sharrock; Lewiston, NY: Edwin Mellen Press, 2007); *Fieldwork for Design* (D. Randall, R. Harper and M. Rouncefield; New York: Springer, 2007).

reflects the fact that many cross-disciplinary exchanges are dialogues of the not-listening-very-carefully). As Crowley and Zentall observe, however, these developments take place 'to date with surprisingly limited trading of ideas across disciplinary boundaries' (2013: 1). Of course, answering why this is could make for a book in itself. One would need to ask what limits the disciplines set for themselves such that this trade is so difficult to establish and maintain; one would have to ask too why it is that, where such attempts are made at interdisciplinary exchange, they are routinely challenged or, worse, ignored by those entrenched within particular frameworks.

Though this is not the book we present here, nevertheless the history of the concepts that the disciplines hold so dear and the reasons for their persistence is very much at the heart of what we are about. This is because these questions (and others) inform the topic of choice itself. For the evidently human capacity to reason and decide is at once a crucible for muddles about data and disputes about method; it is also rife with opportunities for researchers to make claims that treat choice and its nature very differently. As a result of this, researchers in this area, we have found, too often choose to talk past each other – and frequently don't realise that they are doing it.

Our plan with this book is to help explain, at least in some substantive cases, why this happens and why those who study choice sometimes choose to ignore other approaches to the topic. As we explore this, we want to show that, despite these troubles, there is evidence about how people choose, why they choose and what they choose that can be subject to rigorous, insightful or at least perspicacious inquiry. This book is not for those academicians who are happy to run with their professional starting points, then, but for those who wonder what might be learned if they look at those starting points themselves and consider, as they do so, where else they might get even before the standard disciplinary enterprises begin. It turns out, as we shall see, that we can make choices about choice even before we start to say what choice is or how we might look at it, or, better still, how we might learn to make our choices better given where we start from.

2

THE ORIGINS: CHOICE IN ECONOMICS

In this, the first substantive chapter, we will explore some of the starting assumptions that are found in perhaps the most dominant of the social sciences, and certainly the one evoked as the source of ideas about reason and choice being a logical, rational matter. This is the discipline of economics, which has often been thought of as the most 'scientific' of the social science trades, doubtless because of its insistence on rigorous mathematical modelling. Perhaps more importantly for us, this modelling is based on what looks like simple assumptions – that people are motivated by self-interest, and specifically by money. Something that is less often stated is that the simplifying assumptions are precisely what allow models to be built in the first place. When these assumptions are described in detail (something we shall do shortly), many people would (rightly) observe that real people aren't like that, and that they are more complex than the picture the economists paint, but they would be wrong to conclude that economists aren't aware of this. The very fact that economists term their assumptions 'simplifying' indicates their awareness that actual situations in the lives of individuals – even when confined to the economic sphere – are much more complex than can be captured by the economic perspective. But part of the reason why this doesn't worry economists is that their problem is not to understand how individual *minds* work; it is to understand how *economies* work. It is not what the model starts with (or consists in) that matters – the individual, the actor, the subject; it is what this ends with – the imagined economy. The basic model of *homo economicus* is provided not so as to draw non-economists into accepting a thoroughly misleading idea of what people are like – though this almost certainly is a consequence it can have – but in order to provide initial traction in working out how economies considered as an ensemble of innumerable economic choices organise themselves.

Having said that, the starting place of economics, though simple and regarded as such by economists themselves, as we say, needs some examination. If we recall the fish, chips and cake example from the first chapter, what we see is that economists make decisions about what choice looks like that preclude other apparently just as simple and reasonable starting places. They do this under the umbrella terms 'rationality' and 'rational action' in such a fashion that it is all too easy to forget quite how consequential their choice about choice can turn out to be.

To be economically rational

One can begin to explore this by recalling that the term 'rational' is often used in everyday language to describe the quality of people's reasoning, typically in reference to some situation. 'They think about it logically', one might say. But this usage doesn't imply that that person so described is therefore making the right decision; they may or they may not. What the phrase labels is merely the character of the reasoning process: it was or is logical. In this view, rational action originates in rational thought. Whether that is 'good' thought or appropriate action is another question.

For economists, the use of the term means something much more particular – something that relates to the ordering of preferences. At the most basic level, it implies that people choose on the basis of preferences which are hierarchical. When economists use the term 'rational' they also take for granted that this ordering is consistent through time – otherwise it would not be possible to predict people's actions on the basis of their preferences. Basically, how people act today will be how they act tomorrow. In addition, though this is not necessarily implied when they say 'rational' (it being more a question of hope), economists treat people's preferences as being mostly organised in pairs: if one prefers A to B, and one prefers B to C, then C to D, and D to E, then one prefers A to E. If, in other words, one's preferences are paired in this way, then one would – one *does* – choose the first of the pair over the other, and that order of preference extends throughout the sequence so that it covers also the various other paired alternatives featuring those same items. One's preferences are assumed to be consistently ordered and thus *transitive*. Finally, when economists use the term 'rational', they also imply its opposite. That is to say, given their definition, it would be by definition irrational, when offered a choice between A and E, to pick E. This is consequential, because it turns out that the definition of one, of rationality, by default creates a set of actions that is a contrast pair with the first: the rational goes with the irrational. It is no wonder then that, when economists look for rationality, they often find irrationality. And these categories are not necessarily related to how the persons in question – the rational actors, so to speak – think of their own actions; this contrast pair is a construct of economics.

Some economists question whether people's rationality has all these features – its logical shape, its opposite, and so forth. (Those from other disciplines do so as well – something we shall come to much later.) Queries are made about whether there are cases of *reverse* preference, for example, when people at one time choose A over B but at another time choose B (this leads to stochastic models, among other things). Doubts are also raised as to whether behaviour that does not fit the starting model needs be described as 'irrational' or whether it should be labelled a different kind of rationality (and, if this is so, how one might label it). Since we are here exploring these things only at a fairly basic level, there is no need to go into these matters when our point is only that this basic notion of rationality, this view from economics, doesn't really apply to the *quality* of reasoning at all but simply to the way in which (at least supposedly) people's *preferences* operate. And, furthermore, this notion is somewhat generalising about human nature, insofar as it assumes that all people act this way – there are no odd bods choosing their preferences randomly, for example.

All these assumptions sound reasonable, and indeed they certainly afford a place to start about which few would dispute. But before we go further to examine what consequences follow on from this, consider by way of contrast an alternative starting description of rationality. Karl Popper, the great philosopher of science, argued that 'situational rationality' should be the basis of what is perceived as reasoned behaviour for the social sciences, and in this he wanted to include economics.[1] This is not a rationality in terms of preference ordering but one which applies the standard of effectiveness to the choice of means for a particular end. It's not choice between objects that matters, in other words, but how to get to one of those objects when they are treated as goals. Others too have suggested this contrast between types of rationality; the sociologist Max Weber explored this issue well before Popper.[2] The point is that both views do seem reasonable starting places – simple, to be sure, and probably a good way to capture a lot of human action. But

---

[1] This is not something for which Popper is most famous – his notions about the character of science being better known. But, for a good introduction to this aspect of his various works, see Notturno (1988).
[2] See in particular Weber ([1949] 2011).

already one can see some of the consequences that follow on. Let us focus on Popper's view to continue this.

There are, according to Popper, at least two ways of considering means–ends rationality in the social sciences. One adopts current scientific knowledge as the standard of assessment of people's actions towards some end. Science is used to judge whether some actions are rational in effectively achieving the actor's end. Typically, this view is illustrated by comparing those who consult an oracle or a witch doctor to cure their illness against those who use something like standard Western medical treatments to cure themselves. The latter are viewed as being more rational – much more rational – in this matter than the former. Both have a goal in mind, but, with regard to means – witchcraft or science – one is logically more likely to deliver that goal than the other.

The second view focuses on understanding the choices from the chooser's point of view. As it happens, this is a concern that Popper had, though whether he quite understood what all this implies is moot. But, from that starting point, a rational choice is one which entails picking an end which is appropriate, given the chooser's goals, where 'appropriate' may feature means which are conventionally considered appropriate in the situation. The point is not, in this view, to determine whether the chooser got the choice objectively right – i.e., by reference to, say, a scientific measure of what is right – but to understand, in the terms of the chooser's own reasoning, whether they selected the means they did because they supposed that these were the best for *their* ends. That is where the question of rightness fits. If one figures the measure of that rightness out, one has a better understanding of why the individual used one means rather than possible alternatives, Popper argued. As it happens, he placed great emphasis on the importance of 'unintended consequences' and so didn't build into his ideas the supposition that the choices that people make would always yield the best result for the chooser or for society as a whole. His view is intended to draw attention to how means might be chosen; choice is relative to a situation is his starting premise.

From starting points to persons

There are, then, a range of notions of rationality available even when we start at the most elemental, extremely simple, level. As we see already, some treatments are much more likely to produce judgements of irrationality than others; to assume there is an objective measure of 'rational' implies what is not rational. By the same token, irrespective of which starting premise one has, one should begin to see, also, that these starting points imply other matters that one can grossly describe as to do with 'perfection'.

Key to the salience of this issue – perfection – is the relationship between this notion and reality itself or, more particularly, various emphasised aspects of reality. If we confine ourselves to economics, the assumption of 'perfection' is most often connected to considerations about markets and not to how some individual is confronted with information and choice, perfect or otherwise. In the market emphasising view, it is assumed that markets in which there are many buyers and sellers can be not unrealistically considered as pretty much all in the same position. None of them can, through their individual action, affect the price level – they are too small a part of the whole to have an effect on it. Thus, for a large market with many buyers and sellers, it can be assumed that everyone in the market knows more or less the same as everyone else and, for the purposes of optimising preferences, each and every actor knows all they need to know. Here lies perfection, as economists understand it.

Considered this way, the idea is less a way of endowing market participants with seemingly superhuman powers than it is a way of rendering the distribution of information in the market *irrelevant* to the economists' deliberations. This simplifies the calculation of market behaviour. But this is not done by falsifying what individuals know; assumptions about what they know and will do seem quite acceptable – realistic, one might say. This can stand as the reasoned and empirical justification for the 'perfect' assumption.

The perfection assumption is not always good enough to work with, however, even for economists. Some ways in which features of economies work require more care as regards what is meant. The situation in question demands it, one might say, though, as we shall see in a moment, the cases in question turn out to be economic ones. This is important to bear in mind, since the revisions the economists seek are still intended to enable them to inquire into imagined things – economies – and not to offer empirical insight into individual acts whose specific properties are not required to imagine (or test) those economies, even though these individuals are, in a loose sense, the assumed elements within these constructs. It is the behaviours of these individuals which have to be recast to fit the adjusted notion of perfection in such instances.

When economists assert that businesses have a 'logical' tendency to maximise profit, for example, it implies that a company is persistently and exclusively directed towards the pursuit of the greatest level of profit. But, so conceived, rationality, the selection of the most profitable options, is unbounded in the sense that it is applied exhaustively, so that every possible opportunity will be exploited, and there will be no 'time out' from searching for and exploiting opportunities for profit. Perfection here lies in the knowledge of the market. It also refers to the (relentless) pursuit of profit. But this affords such an unrealistic picture of what businesses are like, and how business managers act, that refinements of these treatments are often made. Two main criticisms drive these correctives. Firstly, unbounded rationality implies that ends to a particular means will be chosen only after a review of all the alternative possible means to a given end has been conducted. All the alternatives will be examined and the most effective – i.e., the one that provides the most profit – will be chosen. But people in business, it is argued, do not really engage in this kind of comprehensive, alternative testing behaviour and often select the most plausible option from a set they can easily comprehend; they don't exhaustively explore all possible options, with all that means in terms of labour and difficulty. Secondly, business people are not always motivated to maximise profit in some crude and absolute sense, but sometimes set themselves a level of profit which they think is 'good enough' when viewed against other, as it were, more local concerns, such as whether the shareholders and markets will be happy with that level. Managers more often than not attempt to reach that 'compromised' target and consequently don't strive for every ounce of possible profit. Their rationality is thus bounded, applied within pre-set limits, allowing those in the firm to realise aims other than that of yielding the greatest possible profit. This has all sorts of marginal benefits for the actors in question, of course, such as being able to enjoy a less stressed working life. If they are able to achieve the 'good enough' level of profit, then they won't have to discipline themselves into relentlessly seeking greater profit. In the jargon, they are not maximising but 'satisficing'.

These refinements in the starting assumptions are made so as to allow economists to get further with their inquiries. It is not that economists working from the assumptions of, say, bounded rationality suppose that actual people in businesses are really, in every respect, operating in this way, or even that people are necessarily behaving *as if* they were applying bounded rationality all the time. It is rather that economists can deploy a characterisation of *bounded* actions as no more than a first approximation of some relationship being modelled that allows them to see how the extent of boundedness plays out in real measures – profit margins, organisational investment strategy, and so on. We are saying then that, in setting out simplifying assumptions, economists can be attentive

to the ways in which they are 'unrealistic' and that they are aware
of the manner and extent in which actual cases differ from the
assumptions in the model. Economists are happy to qualify or com-
plicate the initial assumptions, to introduce elements deemed 'more
realistic'.

One should not forget, however, that economists have to start,
and they have to start somewhere. And, as we say, most start with
the idea of sequential, ordered patterns of choice as regards identifiable preferences; and this assumes certain orders of perfection
about information, and so forth, and, in some cases, requires some
adjusting as to what is being sought from an ideal notion towards a
satisficing one. With these very modest refinements to basic assumptions, economists can get down to business: making models. But
– and as our opening remarks pointed out – models are the economists' tools rather than their end product, and they are used in turn
as part of their central effort to work out, deductively, how elements
of economic organisation are connected with one another, in service
of which they can introduce all sorts of variants into their existing
models about the economy – but not (at least until recently) about
the psychology of individuals. The models are attempts to get to a
particular view of reality, one that we are calling, somewhat teas-
ingly, the imagined reality of the economy. We mean only that the
economy manifests itself through indices that are, in effect, the only
real things that economists can grapple with – prices and such like –
but through them they can come to see the thing they are after. This,
though we use the word 'imagined', is very real. Our point is that
one can start with some 'reasonable fiction' so as to get to the truth
about even a fictional thing, the 'imagined economy', and this can
lead to some real truths – testable, scientifically derived, evidentially
– about an entity that is otherwise difficult to grasp.

Rational choice in general

Having pointed to some of the different basic assumptions underscoring the label 'rational action' and suggested how these are at
once unrealistic but not therefore unreasonable, we should not
be thought of as defending economics, though by the end of this
chapter, having spent some time recounting complaints about
economics, we will find ourselves in that position. At this moment,
our focus is on how economists' concepts and the models are to be
judged *with particular regard to* the purposes that economists have.
This is not to say that disagreements among economists do not exist.
Nor is it to say that other social sciences might want to do different

things. But, importantly, these different things might be vulnerable to criticisms that won't apply to economists.

One needs, always, to examine exactly what is being asserted in the social and human sciences, whether assertions made can be accepted given the empirical results that derive from them. As we have forewarned, one of our concerns is the way empirical results, based on pragmatically simple starting premises, are frequently accompanied by large and sometimes excessive claims that elide those premises and starting points. In this regard, we don't wish to determine here whether all the purposes of economists are worth having, and whether they succeed in all cases, since what we are wanting to convey is what kind of structural form they have and how the assumptions underscoring these purposes allow certain sorts of sensible empirical inquiries. Whether these get pushed too far by economists themselves, or to places that may be of little interest even within the discipline, is not really our concern, though recent complaints by undergraduate students that their economics curriculum lacks relevance suggests it is of concern to some.

Be that as it may, what should be clear is that the so-called gloomy science has always been and persists in being interested in the notion of *preference*. Why should we choose one thing over another, given that whatever we choose comes with a cost? The cost, of course, need not be only in terms of money. Put bluntly, if we choose to spend our money on one thing, we cannot then spend it on another. The money has, after all, gone. Exactly the same is logically true of *activity*. If one accepts this 'preference' proposition – that one chooses between preferences and does so in ordered, consistent ways – then the same would be true of non-monetary choices. If we choose to do one thing, we cannot do a different thing at the same time.

That this is so is of course old hat in economics, and hardly needs any contemporary theoretical comment from economists or from us – it's taken for granted. But while we have been noting the ease with which economists ride on this assumption, an ease that is bound to what they do with it, one should note also, and perhaps with more concern, how versions of this have been adopted and elaborated by other disciplines that want to ride in different directions. The goals of these other disciplines are often distinct from those of economics; some of the questions that slip out of view from the perspective of economics come back into sight and turn out to be important when these other directions are taken.

In psychology, for example, at least by the 1950s, this notion of rationality, of preference, transivity, and so forth, what one might call a theory of rational action, though designed for economics, was gaining currency. Ward Edwards (1954), as a case in point, was one of the first to develop what he called a *theory of decision-making* for psychology – basically a renaming of rational action theory.

Edwards intentionally echoed economists in saying that, if one can put the expectations associated with making a choice in some kind of order ('if I do this, then that will result') and then make a choice based on which result confers most advantage, then one can be said to be rational – psychologically rational. He is saying, in other words, that 'utility maximisation' – making the choices that produce the best outcomes, which in turn evokes a notion of the perfect market – has something to do with psychology. And the trick here is to move from the market to the individual. In Edwards's view, it is the human that is a perfect decision-making entity, not the market (or, rather, whether the market is or is not no longer comes to matter). Edwards is saying that these notions of perfection could hold true for the topics of psychology – for the things that psychologists are interested in – and this is not the imagined entity – economies – that economists are interested in. So while it might be the case that Edwards might agree with economists that perfect markets do not exist in reality, and even though he might also agree that there is no such thing as perfect information, something about the actions in question that produce markets, something about the mechanics of preference that produce prices, something about the bodies in question – the human actors doing their individual acts – manifests a specifiable order of reasoning – mental reasoning.

If economists imagine the economy, and use as a starting place to get to their imaginations a simply cast individual actor, one that reasons 'rationally', Edwards, and his discipline's imagination, is focused on that starting point as its end point. In so doing it transforms the way that phenomena should be treated. It can no longer be something with which one gets going, no longer a simple view of reasoning, but instead the object, crudely speaking, of a particular scientific attention. In the view of psychology, as Edwards would have it, rationality, rational processing, identifying choice and then acting on a preference, is the topic of that discipline's imagination; it anchors all it does and all that follows. There is, if you like (and to remind ourselves of Popper), an inversion of means–ends in rational actor theory. When Edwards uses the theory, he puts that actor at the end, not in the starting place. What follows is quite consequential in ways that we shall pick up throughout later chapters.

That simple, even gross, assumptions may gloss actual actions doesn't prohibit the use of various starting points from which to investigate that action. We have seen that economists have their own solutions to dealing with some of the residues of their starting point and the problems to which it leads. One way out of these difficulties, a way that is familiar to macro- or large-scale economics in particular but indeed to all economics, is to ignore individual particularities and look only at statistical tendencies, assuming the so-called law of large numbers – that individual variation is ironed out across a big enough population. No need, given that approach, to worry about why a person might decide to opt for one thing rather than another – one can simply read off that there is a *tendency* for people to behave this way rather than that – and no need either to concern oneself too much with why that is, what things are being preferred. Nor is there any need to consider how local conditions and constraints might affect individual behaviour. There need not be, in other words, a concern with 'actual instances of action'. In sum, if these solutions are taken, along with other tweaks and refinements, such as the move to allow more bounded forms of rationality, the result is that there is no need for *economists* to concern themselves with any *psychological* underpinnings because, given all this, preferences are revealed in the consistent decisions that people can be presumed to make. These can be demonstrated through the residues of real economic actions – the sales volumes and prices of some objects, the profits of companies. This version of rationality – 'revealed preference', as it is called – requires only that preferences are ordered in a consistent way and that they are manifest – what is chosen is revealed. Given this way of thinking, the psychological is made irrelevant.

Why then did Edwards offer what constitutes the basis of this view to psychology? Is it because he was unaware that, when economists undertook their inquiries, such matters of psychology are of no significance? Or was he seeking something different? Was he wanting to stretch and extend the rational action view into a stronger thesis, a view that is not merely a starting place but a topic in its own right?

A much stronger version of rational action could involve claims about motivation linked to or manifested in revealed preferences. To give some flavour of this, this view might lead one to argue that something 'in our heads', an engine if you will, enables us to do the calculations allowing us to decide that one choice is better than another. Such a conception of rationality requires a psychological foundation, and, if one takes this line, one can see how this might initiate a whole industry that links the modelling of economics to the experimentalism of psychology. Indeed, this is the move that Edwards makes in *The Theory of Decision Making*. This is what he reports – tentative attempts to describe experimentally the machine inside the head. As it happens, and irony notwithstanding, it is not just psychology that was altered as a result, but economics too.

Years after Edwards wrote, behavioural economics has emerged, and, as we shall see, this is merely a descendant of that move.

The properties of rationality

Thus far, then, the rationality we have considered consists of two basic versions, a weak view, the standard one, used in economics, and a derivative, stronger view, taken up outside economics, at least initially.

For the economist, someone not behaving in ways that reflect the basic tenets of standard rational action would, needless to say, be irrational, though whether this happens in any particular case is immaterial. Though the economist might not care too much about real people, his or her notion of rationality implies something like a natural state for the human being. Yet, if we have a natural tendency to act in the way rational choice predicts – that is to say, if there is a natural state – it is not unreasonable then to ask whether there must be something that makes us do so, and this leads us to the strong view. One such input presumes a 'reasoning engine' in our heads to calculate the costs and benefits so as to identify maximum utility. This is the province of psychology and its affiliates, cognitive science especially.

At this point, we can give only a crude idea of what psychology says about this 'engine' (and, indeed, there are many different versions of the engine). Roughly speaking, the engine takes an input, our motivations or reasons, and through a calculative or computational process, which entails assessing the means available to us, produces outputs which are behaviours. Something – in our heads, in our bodies – causes us to desire certain outcomes, and our engine works out how best to achieve them.[3]

We have only scratched the surface. Nevertheless, if we presume the existence of this calculating engine, why should we believe that its calculations are limited to purely economic choices? All social action, it could be argued, is rationally motivated and is mainly a form of instrumental action, however irrational or non-rational it may appear to the outsider. That is, once we understand the

---

[3] It should be apparent that rationality predicated on this view entails some very sophisticated calculative abilities and, moreover, abilities which we cannot produce consciously, since few of us – generations of social science undergraduates included – demonstrate the statistical abilities that are implied when we seek to calculate consciously and deliberately. If that were not true, there would be very few bookmakers, and the whole discipline of behavioural economics (see below) would not exist. We leave you to decide which would be the bigger loss.

motivations of the actor, the choices available to them and the information they have available, we could start assuming that all human behaviour is consistently geared towards getting the best deal available.

At this point, two different views come into play:

- *either* there is a distinctive form of human behaviour which we can call 'decision-making' – behaviour for which 'rational choice' is an appropriate explanation;
- *or* all behaviour can be seen as decision-making – this view under-pinning what we will call the strong version of 'rational choice' that seems to echo across economics and much of psychology.

Here, if one takes the second view, the crucial question is whether decisions are made consciously or whether there are underlying psychological mechanisms operating as an 'unconscious rationality'. We should note that universality is implied here. If all behaviour can be thought of in this way, then all behaviour everywhere can be thought of in this way independent of cultural values or beliefs. Thus it would seem reasonable to assert that an engine of this sophistication would be capable of applying to non-economic information and making similar calculations about decisions that are not about economic well-being. It can be assumed to allow us, also, to maximise well-being across the board – from the boardroom to the bedroom, from saving to spending, and all things in between.

Take a simple example: trying to understand why people do or do not commit crime. All you need to do, if you assume the strong rational action starting point, is understand the costs and benefits attaching to any criminal act. People will (or will not) commit crimes if they have a preference for a certain outcome (more money) and see that there is a way of actually achieving it (robbing a shop) while other ways – such as working – are more difficult. They are seen as motivated by the wants or goals that express their 'preferences'. They act on the basis of the information (or, at least, beliefs) that they have about the conditions under which they are acting.

The rationality engine for everyday life

Can this view really be defended? If these assumptions and models seem, when we look carefully, more or less plausible, that doesn't mean they are immune from criticism. We are all familiar with the inability of economists to predict complex futures, after all. The 2008 crash, as so many before, is often referred to as proof of their failures to predict well. Whether this is a fault in the economic reasoning, however, or to do with, for instance, an absence of adequate data, is open to question. It could be that economists might have done a better job at predicting the crash with better data, though not all would agree.[4] In any case, it might have been that economists were predicting it, their voices being drowned out by the needs of politicians. Votes don't get bought with bad news.

Be that as it may, the philosopher John Dupre alludes to ways in which one ought to criticise economics for its starting premises:

> Economists, of course, have interesting and sometimes successful models for dealing with heterogeneous markets, imperfect information, monopoly, oligopoly, and so on. I do not intend to make any negative (or, for that matter, positive) evaluation of their efforts in analysing these various market conditions. What I do want to emphasize from these elementary observations about markets is that markets are highly diverse; and the various features that differentiate markets lead to quite diverse behaviour; and in contrast with the orderly equilibration that makes the theory of perfect competition so appealing, these various imperfections may lead to indeterminate and disorderly behaviour. The point of this ... is not to discourage economists from attempting to extend their theoretical treatment of markets into these more difficult areas, but rather to note that as the subject matter gets further removed from the central model of perfect competition, the relevance of basic [economic] insights becomes increasingly questionable. Thus, finally, to attempt to apply the concept of a market to aspects of human behaviour far removed from even the exchange of commodities for money is to invite confusion. (Dupre, 2003: 122–3)

What he is asking is whether the simple model of rational self-interest can be applied outside the context of monetary considerations. For him, and numerous others we don't need to cite here, the answer is no.

Others are equally convinced that the answer is yes. Examples of the latter are numerous. We can find them in the admittedly populist work of Harford (2008), for example, and Frank (1998, 2008), where claims about the rational foundations of a vast range of behaviours are confidently asserted. Such commentators typically try to reinvigorate rational choice theory by providing new examples of how it

---

[4] Madrick (2014) is far from the first person to assert that the problems of mainstream economics are as much conceptual as empirical.

can explain human activities of all kinds. Harford uses the example of sexual behaviour to show this. He suggests that the increasing propensity for oral sex among American teenagers can be explained in terms of cost–benefit calculation. A similar argument is made about the behaviour of Mexican prostitutes, as follows:

> Interviews with over a thousand Mexican prostitutes, most from the Morelia area, suggested that one in six was suffering from a sexually transmitted infection, while a prostitute can expect to be attacked by a client every couple of months. On the other hand, the wages are better than these women could otherwise expect. Prostitutes work long hours but they make over half as much again as their peers with more conventional jobs, even before the commissions they get from bar owners by encouraging clients to drink. That's not to say that prostitutes are motivated only by money and don't care about the dangers and humiliations of the job. But they are hardly doing the job because of its prospects for promotion. . . . Prostitutes are well informed, have condoms, and negotiate cannily. Nevertheless, [efforts] at empowerment have not prevented widespread sexually transmitted infection, and they never will. 'Empowered' prostitutes don't always use condoms. Why not? Because they're a useful bargaining chip. The client will . . . pay more if he sets conditions on the use of condoms. If he insists on using a condom, he'll pay nearly 10 percent more. If he insists on 'bareback' sex – no condom – he'll pay a premium of nearly a quarter. The prostitute uses the client's declaration of a preference as a bargaining chip, and she gets more money either way. Obviously the negotiating workshops laid on by local health projects are paying dividends . . . It's tempting to argue that the prostitutes do not understand the risks. That's patronizing: Even without the efforts of the health and development organizations, prostitutes probably know more about the risks of sexually transmitted infections than anyone who thinks of them as simpleminded victims. In fact, the prostitutes know that while the risks are real, they are modest. Only one in eight hundred Mexicans carries HIV, and even among prostitutes it afflicts just one in three hundred. Even if a prostitute is unlucky enough that one of her unprotected jobs is with a man who is HIV-positive, the risk that she will catch it is less than 2 percent if one of them is carrying some other sexual infection and less than 1 percent otherwise. None of the prostitutes wants to catch HIV, but the risks of catching it because of one instance of unprotected sex are small, while the pay is substantially

higher. Wouldn't you notice a pay increase of 25 percent? (Harford 2008: 27–8)

Now, we might make a number of points about such a case (and indeed many of the others used by Harford). That teenagers, prostitutes and pretty much all human beings are capable of making judgements is not at issue. All of us can and do at various times. The issue here is whether the behaviour of these prostitutes in fact involves *any* cost–benefit calculation. It is one thing to assert that there is a certain statistical risk associated with AIDS in Mexico, and quite another to assert that prostitutes both know what the risk is and calculate on the basis of it. Harford provides no evidence at all that 'decisions' are being made; he simply assumes that they are.

Finding examples which appear to show that there are rational foundations to behaviours outside of the economic nexus, or present what might on the surface look like some unreasonable behaviours, does not answer the question of whether *all* intentional behaviour can best be understood in terms of cost–benefit rationality, nor does it provide evidence of calculating behaviour that is required for rational action. Examples all too often suggest that this is so but don't often prove it.

The trouble is that commentators in the field are tempted to assert so and worry too little about how to demonstrate this carefully and evidentially. Take the following claim by Harford about calculation:

I do not argue that we have the conscious calculating mind of a Spock. We do make complex calculations of costs and benefits when we act rationally, but we often do it unconsciously, just as when someone throws a ball for us to catch we aren't conscious of our brain solving differential equations to work out where it's going to land. Most of us couldn't work out the calculations behind catching a ball if you gave us a pen and paper, yet the brain carries them out unconsciously. (2008: 10)

This is an odd claim. It is not at all clear one can find any evidence for it – though one might treat it as an assertion. The only evidence that can be produced to support such an assertion is that we are able to do things like catch a cricket ball or baseball which, if one chooses to use maths to describe it, can be shown to travel in a typical arc (largely a function of the effects of gravity). The earth goes round the sun in an equally predictable way, but no one has (to our knowledge – doubtless someone has in a public house) ever wanted to argue that the sun is engaged in this kind of calculation. There is, we are noting, an assumption in Harford's work that turns into an assertion. It is that the person calculates unconsciously. Hence the affinity between economics and its notion of rational action and some variants of psychology.

These assumptions can be challenged by the simple fact that we do not appear to be very good at the very things that supposedly make us rational. Thaler and Sunstein say:

> If you look at economics textbooks, you will learn that *homo economicus* can think like Albert Einstein, store as much memory as IBM's Big Blue, and exercise the willpower of Mahatma Gandhi. Really. But the folks we know are not like that. Real people have trouble with long division if they don't have a calculator, sometimes forget their spouse's birthday, and have a hangover on New Year's Day. (2008: 15)

Might there be other, better (or at least alternative) explanations of 'reasons'? Might there be considerations – empirical, theoretical – which mean that we must modify our assumptions of rationality? The 'strongest' form of rational choice theory, after all, would deny the existence of any kinds of intentional action other than the purely rational and calculative.

One possibility is that we fall short of these strong standards of rationality because of one undisputed fact of social life – the information we have may be incomplete and/or unreliable – that there might be, as Kahneman, Slovic and Tversky (1982) put it, 'conditions of uncertainty'. Given various uncertainties, it might be, they argue, that human minds employ heuristics or are subject to biases. Another possibility is that other factors intervene in our decision-making, factors best described as 'social', 'normative' or 'cultural'. A third is that our actions are often merely habitual, and some proportion of those habits (like catching a ball) are simply a function of the way our bodies and minds learn. It is to these possibilities we now turn.

From economic to sociological rationalities

We cannot emphasise forcefully enough how willing many economists are to adjust their traditional way of doing business. If they are challenged by critics who insist that there are important matters which decisively affect the organisation of economic activity but which are excluded from economic consideration, then economists will respond by wondering whether and how to model these considerations, how to revise, reconstruct or add to the stock of models they already have. Even so, economists won't alter their basic *modus operandi* – to model. This never waivers, nor do economists alter the rational creature that lives in their models. This happens even when they look at matters that seem somewhat distant from their normal purview.

Gary Becker, with his 1996 book *Accounting for Tastes*, is probably the best-known 'rational choice' theorist who was prepared to recognise that there was a need to address the sorts of things people used to complain that economics couldn't deal with – important influences on choice such as advertising, for example – and hence it is with Becker that we can best make the move from economics as traditionally conceived to sociological topics. The complaint that economics didn't deal with advertising and ideological influences on choice was one often made by sociologists, and Becker was prepared to agree with them. Becker's idea was not to adjust economics in the direction of sociology, but to continue the modelling framework used in economics – not unreasonably, since the kind of discursive work sociologists themselves do can't easily be fed into economic models. If we use advertising as an example, Becker's problem was not 'How are consumer choices shaped by advertising's influence?' (the kind of thing that might exercise the sociologist) but, instead, 'Why are consumers prepared to meet (as they do through the prices of goods they purchase) the costs which suppliers incur by providing advertising?' and 'Can we model the resulting behaviours?'

Once one has accepted such an idea, it is a logical step to ask why the same thing shouldn't be done with all sorts of topics that disciplines other than economics had thought their own. To apply the basic form of choice modelling, in terms of optimising the relation between costs and benefits, Becker therefore launched a programme to explain a large part of social activity through the choice mechanism. But this didn't mean adopting the tools and perspectives of other disciplines; it meant, in contrast, extending the scope of economic inquiry.

For Becker, the main modification to traditional economics that was required resulted from the fact that it fails to account for people's reasons for doing what they do (we will come to this again when we look at evolutionary psychology). At the outset of his book *Accounting for Tastes*, he suggests: 'Much of modern economics still proceeds on the implicit assumption that the main determinants of preferences are the basic biological needs' (Becker 1996: 1). Preference curves, the main vehicle for analysing utility maximisation, provide no explanation, he says, for why we make the choices we do. His solution is to add two key (and economic-sounding) concepts to economists' model building – personal and social capital – which can both be included in the resources that choosers access.

Personal capital refers to personal experiences – biographical factors, if you will – that affect current and future utilities. Diet and other health-related activities are things we put into practice because we expect a future benefit. Further, these often become habitual because experience of their benefits reinforces the behaviour. Becker argues that this can explain harmful addictive behaviours as much as self-evidently beneficial behaviours. Social capital refers to the influence of our peers, the people in our social networks, on our preferences. This is important because it means that what is 'rational' will vary according to the networks we are part of – a teenager at school will build social capital in a very different way from a middle-aged academic. The concept of social capital, along with its cognate, cultural capital, has latterly become extraordinarily influential in the social sciences. There is no need to believe that, in making decisions which are meant to add to our personal or social capital, we are necessarily right. People, as Becker puts it, 'are not omnipotent'. It is enough that we expect the future benefits. Thus Becker allows belief to intrude and sees prior experience, social networks, and so on, as powerful forces in forming the preference we have.

As it happens, the result of the developing interest in social capital has not led to a convergence between economics and sociology; there has not been an 'economisation of sociology' or, conversely, a 'sociologicalisation of economics', despite complaints by some that this has indeed happened. The different disciplines, even where they share an interest in 'rational choice', do not see the landscape of choice in the same way. That they do not do so provides evidence for our general claim in this chapter – namely, that the apparent simplicity of starting assumptions should not lead one to think that these assumptions can easily be shared or that the ways in which their simplicities (and hence apparent distances from reality) can be corrected or managed.

Differences in methodology are crucially important. Economists' reasoning operates overwhelmingly through models, although experimental work is increasingly common. Sociologists, by way of contrast, overwhelmingly avoid and commonly disparage precisely these methods, tending either to analyse samples statistically or to rely on single cases of 'real-world' data captured through first-hand observation. Besides this, there can be differences in the 'level' of interest that the different disciplines take. Classical economics tends towards the view that rationality is universal and, if so, assumes that individual behaviours can be aggregated and modelled. Insofar as sociologists have models of social agents at all, these tend to be 'all-in' models, with sociologists trying to include all the characteristics of individuals they think can influence the behaviour of those individuals – their beliefs, attitudes, social positions, relational networks, etc. – seeing these as varying across certain dimensions (much as configurations of personal, social and cultural capital).[5]

In any case, some of the starting points are profoundly different. If economists presuppose, through their rational action notions, that the start of their inquiries is choice, sociologists, on the other hand, are much less inclined to start with people as choosers, being much keener to ask how individuals come to be in a position where they are confronted with the alternatives they have and how their preferences for these have been shaped by their social circumstances. As Hedstrom and Stern (2008: 1414) put it,

> Typically this entails explicating three causal links: (a) how individuals' orientations to action – their beliefs, preferences, and so on – are influenced by the social environments in which they are embedded (A → B); (b) how these orientations to action influence how they act (B → C); and (c) how these actions bring about the social outcomes to be explained (C → D) . . . sociologists tend to pay more attention to the macro-to-micro link (A → B) than to the latter two links . . . Sociologists tend to focus on how networks, social norms, socialization processes, and so on influence how individuals act by shaping their preferences, beliefs, opportunities, and so on.

There are different attitudes towards 'realism' too. To repeat our characterisation of economics, and, as Camerer and Fehr (2006) argue, that individuals can be assumed both to form correct beliefs about their choices and, given these beliefs, to maximise utility by choosing those actions that best satisfy their preferences is adopted only on 'instrumental' grounds in that discipline. Correcting these assumptions might occur only if they affect the models that derive; often they don't. Sociologists are often concerned with realism at the expense of the instrumentation that might derive. This doesn't mean that they avoid modelling, say, but it does mean that it is not the models that craft the exactitude of the starting evidence. Even those within sociology who espouse some kind of kinship with rational choice theory in economics (and even some that don't, such as Hedstrom, 2005) tend to be more interested in the empirical realism that underscores models. They complain about 'false assumptions'

---

[5] As a way of introduction, see, for example, Squazzoni (2012).

or starting 'fictions' and ignore what derives from modelling. This is the core to the disagreement between sociology and economics.

The critique of rational choice

As we have already indicated with reference to Becker, and as we will explore, the extent to which, and the ways in which, plausible objections to economics actually affect economics varies. In chapter 4, we will consider the development of particular forms of 'institutional' economics and new rationalist sociologies, founded on ideas about 'social capital' that seem to imply some kind of convergence, since they make institutions, norms, values, etc., part of economics as a discipline.

Thus far, we have pointed out that the economists' model of rational choice – one in terms of consistent choices on the basis of ordered preferences – can easily be regarded as a general model of choice. Most of human activity, after all, can be seen as involving choices in some sense. It can then be supposed that rational choice models can be exported into the territories of other social sciences, sociology being the one we have just explored, but others spring to mind as well (political science, for example). The same kinds of thoughts as occur to economists such as Becker also occur to those in other disciplines, and attempts have been made to introduce rational choice models into these disciplines. If the modelling of economic choice is well founded, one needs good reasons to argue that this would not be the case with the modelling of other kinds of choice. Nevertheless, it is fair to say that the economic notion of rational action has not had great impact in other disciplines and often gets sceptical reaction.

Ian Shapiro, for instance, in a strong polemic against the use of rational action theory in political science, regards it as part of a wider 'flight from reality'. This flight has spread across the academic world, particularly in social science, and starts with basic assumptions. In Shapiro's view, 'In discipline after discipline, the flight from reality has been so complete that the academics have all but lost sight of what they claim is their object of study' (2005: 2). This has to do with a variety of causes, Shapiro supposes, one of which might be the search for a spurious scientific rigour. Indeed, he insists that the flight from reality happens in part because of an obsession with method which is seen as inseparable from good science. But this doesn't produce good science, merely 'good method'. He criticises particularly those who seek to emulate the highly general and abstract deductive theories that are successful in natural science, for, he argues, adopting the *form* of those theories has not enabled many other trades in the social sciences to do their trade, it not being necessarily appropriate to the phenomenon of these other trades. This is especially so in his own discipline, political science. He goes on:

> Such [general, abstract] theories often rest on simplifying assumptions about reality, or even 'as if' assumptions that are not valid empirically at all. It is conventional to defend this practice on the grounds that these theories do a good predictive job in accounting for empirical reality. This might sound reasonable in principle, but in practice [those concerned] often formulate their claims so generally that they turn out to be compatible with all possible empirical results. (Ibid.: 3)

One might add that Shapiro is averse to *many* modes of inquiry in the social sciences, and not just those informed by rationality notions. He is equally (but, in our view, less convincingly) critical of other supposedly misguided approaches such as 'interpretivism', Marxism, linguistic philosophy and postmodernism. All these are but varied strands of 'relativism' and are hostile to the 'realism' that Shapiro commends (see, e.g., Archer et al., 1998; Bhaskar, 2011).

We are concerned not with Shapiro's attack across all fronts, only with the case against rational action theory. His criticism on this front is that,

> Taken on their own terms, rational choice theories have, for the most part, degenerated into elaborate exercises geared towards saving universalist theory from discordant encounters with reality. Belying the fanfare about theoretical rigour that often accompanies their claims ... rational choice theorists play fast and loose with the definition of rationality in developing hypotheses, in specifying their empirical implications, and in testing them against the evidence. (2005: 10)

He further points to the more than somewhat confused nature of the various views on rational theory found by those who claim to abide by it: 'variants of rational choice theory impose different assumptions about the sorts of utilities people maximise, the nature of the beliefs they possess, and the manner in which they acquire and process information' (ibid.).

If modelling activities are to be valued as formal, and if that is all they aim at, then there is relatively little reason to be concerned with them, Shapiro says. In his view, rational choice theorists are often

engaged in somewhat abstruse reasoning about the formal properties of models and have little to say about the real world. Shapiro
continues:

> One of the most frequent reactions to our book among those
> with whom we have spoken is, 'Why isn't this book Pathologies
> of Social Science? Why pick on rational choice?' Our answer
> is twofold. It is our impression, first, that traditional research
> in political science, although often trivial, uninspired, and ill-
> conceived, is more flatfooted than tendentious. . . . Second,
> traditional political science, for all its defects, is not similarly
> bereft of empirical accomplishments. (2005: 54)

The analytic advances of rational action theory, as against its empirical banalities, is a function of the method-driven character of the
endeavours that result from this view. Not least, this entails ignoring alternative explanations[6] (cf. Durkheim's *Rules of Sociological
Method*) and making 'slippery' predictions. One way in which this
is done, Shapiro explains in *The Flight from Reality*, is to imply
the universal validity of the rational action approach by showing
that *some variant* of it can accommodate every fact. In his view, the
rational action approach is not only no better than other starting
points for general theory in social science but possibly even worse,
though this does not amount to a positive commendation of those
other starting points of view.

Together with Donald Green, Shapiro points out that *all* social
science theories have proven disappointing, and the approach from
economics, when applied outside the setting of that discipline's traditional domain, has effectively produced just more failed schemes
for the systematic explanation of human behaviour. Hence:

> The social sciences were founded amid high expectations about
> what could be learned through systematic study of human
> affairs, and perhaps as a result social scientists are periodi-
> cally beset by intellectual crises. Each generation of scholars
> expresses disappointment with the rate at which knowledge
> accumulates and yearns for a new, more promising form of
> social science. The complexity of most social phenomena,
> the crudeness with which explanatory variables can be meas-
> ured, and the inability to perform controlled experiments may

---

[6] See, for example, M. Gilbert's book *On Social Facts* (1989), which suggests that
rational action might be based on facts produced by society, not by individuals. This
obviously derives from Durkheim's *Rules*.

severely constrain what any form of social science can deliver. (Green and Shapiro 1994: 51–2)

Shapiro and his co-author are at pains to emphasise that they are not wanting to deny that people are rational but disputing the notion that people are rational *in the sense that* can be captured by economics-style thinking. It is always possible to light on one of the various senses of the word 'rational' that will apply to an episode of human behaviour – that is why they complain that rational choice theorists 'save' their position by shifting between senses of the word.

It is hardly disputable that there is a broad sense of 'rational' in which we could all – certainly most of us – agree that people are more or less rational; people often act in terms of their self-interest (likewise broadly construed) and are largely effective in their everyday combination of means to ends when engaged in activities which might require it. This is a long way, however, from asserting that their behaviour is utility maximising, that 'perfect' knowledge describes any – let alone most – forms of human interaction, or that there are good empirical methods (once the conceptual problems have been cleared away) for determining preference.

The tenor of Shapiro's book, as well as that with Green, does verge towards the tendentious in one sense – the belief that there are superior theoretical alternatives. It is, even so, fairly representative of the general tenor of debates in the area. One can be sympathetic to this tone if one considers the apparent appeal of rational actor theory to political science; it would claim to allow accurate (or at least more accurate) predictions about behaviour. As Shapiro argues, the assumption that, *given what they know or believe*, people vote for rational reasons is hardly absurd. It would seem sensible too to hope that one could model the connection between what people are confronted with in terms of political choice and their actual preferences – what (or who) they choose to vote for. One might accept as well that voting can be seen as some kind of an analogue of monetary action – an index, if you like, of preferences that political science wants to dissect. For all these reasons the turn to rational actor theory in political science must have induced a degree of expectation as well as excitement: new insights will be obtained through what looks like scientific method – or at least the economists' sort of method.

All the more heartfelt must have been the discovery that this route didn't actually get political science very far. What that discipline has found when it has tried to deploy rational actor theory, hardly surprisingly, is that there isn't any imagined thing, the economy of voting, that is the equivalent to the imagined economy. Voting for one party doesn't affect the value of voting for another, not in the way that economists imagine it, in terms of exchange value.

That voting can be predicted with some degree of success is not the issue – after all, Nate Silver has made a reputation out of doing so in books such as *The Signal and the Noise* (2012). But Silver isn't interested in human nature: he is concerned with statistical (Bayesian) technique. For the likes of Shapiro, and those whom he critiques, getting to human nature is the goal of their inquiries. Or, at least, the presumption of a human nature implies a strong notion of what that nature might be: that it is rational and that therefore the choices that human nature makes will be explicable through rational choice theory. What the political scientist can define as choices in the political realm should be choices that the human actor in voting situations should make on the basis of preference ordering. Whether voters vote this way, however, remains up for grabs. Their motives and the way that these can be explored may well be far more diverse and subtle than is allowed for by rational choice theory. Perhaps it has been in vain attempts to preserve a semblance of rational actor theory that leads those whom Shapiro criticises into bending their claims and empirical proofs into shapes that no longer make them consistent with one or other of the basic tenets of rational actor theory. Maybe it is this which leads them to use evidence in such arbitrary ways as to make proper evaluation all but impossible. It is certainly these consequences that Shapiro mocks.

Causality, rational choice and rules

One can sympathise readily enough with Shapiro's point of view as applied to an arena such as voting behaviour. Almost anything goes from the rational theory perspective, one feels like saying. Rejecting rational choice as a means to predict voting behaviour does not necessarily mean that it is an inadequate device for understanding (modelling) the way that markets might work, however. We need to remind ourselves that economic choices viewed at a macro-level may be a different order of problem – a concern for economies, not persons – a technique to assess aggregate economic actions. This does not mean that effort should be placed into confining it to this domain, but it does mean that considerable care needs to be invested when taking it elsewhere – much more care than is always applied, it seems.

We will be saying much more about precisely this last point through the book. What we have been wanting to do is sketch the main landscape on which an important element of the science of choice and reasoning operates: a landscape that turns around rational choice theory. Whatever take one has on this perspective, most if not all are at one in treating the purpose of their inquiries as similar. Theirs is a discovering science, a science that might look at human affairs but assumes those affairs to be a version of natural phenomena. In this view, investigations seek the antecedents of events, the causal histories of happenings.

There is an important distinction that has been elided in all the above: the distinction between ideas and material things, between what people reflect upon and use to guide their action and the physiology of their brains. To say an idea causes an action is to delimit the kinds of ideas one is interested in as well as to confine what actions one might be trying to explain; not all action can be said to be caused by an idea, after all. Indeed, it seems odd to separate some ideas from actions, since some actions seem to embody the ideas in question. The relationship between ideas and action is, then, a delicate and nuanced one. To say that some kind of mechanical process causes a body to react in a certain sort of way is to point towards a distinct subject matter – in this view ideas may be irrelevant. There is a fault line between these two notions that is not always clear in rational actor theory. Edwards seems to want physiology, the brain; Shapiro the world of ideas, the mind. They are best not conflated.

Dupre (2003) makes the point that there is a 'scientistic' illusion contained in the various versions of rational choice. With specific reference to evolutionary psychology (but exactly the same point can be made about all rational choice approaches), he argues that there is a dependence on a 'weak' version of culture against a 'strong' version of decision-making or genetic influence or rationality. Hence:

> While there may be something to the view of cultural influences as ephemeral, an inevitable corollary of their ability to evolve rapidly, I want to suggest that far from being (comparatively) weak influences, there is good reason to think that they are often much more potent than genetic influences on behaviour. There is a perfectly straightforward reason why cultural forces are more potent in determining the fine structure of human behaviour than are internal, biological forces, namely that culture is typically normative. Since there is a tendency to think that rules are made to be broken, proven by exceptions, and so on, whereas causation reflects the iron rule of law, this point may be less than obvious. (2003: 96)

Dupre is pointing out that, when we refer to cultural laws or rules, we are speaking of a particular kind of rule – the normative kind:

Of course, rules or laws are seldom or never completely effective. For a variety of reasons they may be violated or, in some
cases, overruled. Some rules, such as those enforcing speed
limits, are largely ignored. None of this, however, undermines
the contrast between a cause, that works only if all the atten-
dant circumstances are correct, and a rule that applies unless
some specific factor overrides it. When a rule is not commonly
overridden and is considered legitimate and appropriate by a
community, it will often be extremely effective in determining
behaviour. The parallel that may still seem compelling is not
that with an isolated causal factor, but with a piece of machinery. Machines are designed with great efforts made to ensure
that other things are equal and interfering forces are excluded.
I will not rehearse here the arguments for doubting that there
are machine-like generators of particular kinds of behaviour.
The point is rather that rules often do function in an almost
machine-like way to determine behaviour from the outside.
Think of the countless people driving on the correct side of the
road, stopping at traffic lights, eating with cutlery, and so on.
Such behaviour is, of course, done unthinkingly, and it is done
so largely because any thought would immediately confirm that
there was no reason for violating the rule. The conscientious
rule-follower, when confronted with a difficulty in following the rule, may go to some trouble to conform nonetheless.
It is tempting to see this as closely parallel to the kinds of
mechanisms that ensure that a machine works even when some
unwanted factor threatens to interfere. In some cases social
rules achieve conformity less easily, by imposing sanctions or
occasionally rewards. Rules are successful, presumably, to the
extent that they provide individuals with compelling motivations for acting in conformity with them; and perhaps most
successful to the extent that such conformity is seen as something that should be done simply because there is a rule. (Ibid.:
97)

Rules, put simply, can be of many different kinds – ones related to
mechanical relations, crudely speaking, and ones related to more disputed and delicate relations – ideational ones. This illustrates a wider
theme in our book. This is something which is not appreciated by
many who take sides in the dispute over whether standard economics or some other social science (even a natural science such as brain
science) gives a better explanation of human behaviour, namely that
rival disciplines don't just differ over which explanation is best, but
may differ over what kind of thing comprises an acceptable topic in

the first place. Economists are convinced that explanation is done through mathematical – at least, formal – reasoning, and therefore decline to take an interest in things that either aren't treated in that way or apparently cannot be – that are too connected to relations between ideas, say. Many of their sociological competitors don't have much competence in the mathematical and logical tools of formal reasoning and so make very limited use of them anyway. In any case, many demonstrate a continued scepticism about whether those tools are well suited to understanding how social life works, which is, in their view, better understood as a nexus of ideas, not mathematical relations. What can be a studied indifference to each other's perspectives, even so, can dissolve as the 'greedy' theorising of rational choice advocates infringes on the 'normative' territories of sociology. The use of economics-style models has been, as we see above, extended to the study of phenomena that have traditionally been those of other social sciences, such as politics and sociology. We should point out, however, that, for the most part, and until the rise of so-called behavioural economics, this extension of modelling activity has been a minority sport. Most economists remain engaged with what has been their traditional and central concern – analysing how markets work; this is still a matter in which sociology and political science, among other disciplines, have had only limited interest.

Conclusion

The supposition that there is a single, general, specifiable human nature is, we are seeing, a starting point for one social science, economics, just as it is for another, psychology, though just what is meant by the characteristics we have noted also turns out to depend upon the assumptions that these disciplines make about their starting point. We have noted too, though only in passing, that both these views treat the phenomena of human action similarly, as being explicable through causal models, and hence treat their respective social sciences as essentially like the natural sciences, with all that implies about the relationship between explanation and evidence. We cited Dupre, who noted that this is a kind of scientism, not allowing another view about the phenomena of human action to come into play, one that emphasises especially the role of ideas and the salience of 'normativity' with regard to them. We shall come back to this argument much later on in the book.

Leaving these issues aside for the moment, and disregarding also the problems that ensue when the view of one discipline is adopted by another (as in the case of Edwards and economics), that there is a generalised human nature seemingly implied by both economists and psychologists is fiercely denied by some. Those who oppose the notion argue that individual human development shows a great deal of plasticity, so that there is effectively no chance that saying what human beings are *all* like could be achieved. It is, in this view, so empirically unlikely as to be best treated as impossible. In their view, the individual is 'a blank slate' on which local circumstances and culture write the content.

Thus the question of human nature versus blank slates comes to the fore. The human nature that economics implies, even if it doesn't explicitly state this, is one which makes individuals selfish and materialistic. All that the 'economists' chooser' (so to speak) is interested in is satisfying their own wants, which, given that it operates under a condition of scarcity – there aren't enough preferred resources to go round – means that it does so at other people's expense. If this is true, then perhaps we need to understand *why*. Economics, as we have seen, is broadly indifferent to why human beings might be, at least very generally, the way it assumes them to be. If human beings have a general character – largely selfish and materialistic – then something presumably causes them to be like that. There must, that is to say, be a set of rules embedded somewhere in our psychology or biology which impel us in these directions, or there must be a set of universal cultural features such that we all learn in much the same way.

As we will see, various accounts concern themselves with exactly this kind of problem. The idea that *homo economicus* is dedicated to his or her satisfaction alone, to the complete exclusion of others, involving total indifference to another's preferences, takes us back to the fact that the basic economic model neither says what preferences people have nor gives us reasons for why they have them. The theorist *assigns* preferences to the model – under the aegis of the clause 'Let us assume that . . .' – and one can assign preferences that, by any ordinary standards, would result in acts we would consider selfish, but there is *absolutely no reason* to refrain from assigning preferences that are, so to speak, other regarding.

One can point out, for example, that any assessment of rationality or otherwise can depend on the judgement of an evaluator. More precisely, if we cannot demonstrate absolutely clearly that the maximisation of utility in economic terms is what is going on in someone's head, then we have to infer the reasons, and we do so by assuming that they are rational ones, even if this includes the possibility that these are focused not on the benefits to the chooser but to someone else or some others. Otherwise, why would anybody buy presents, and why would they make their choices on the basis of whether the intended recipient would like a certain gift or not? One chooses to buy, let us say, the enormously popular computer game *Super Mario Double Dash* rather than the alternative *Power Rangers Overdrive* not because one is cheaper than the other but because the recipient will – at least in the buyer's estimate – get more pleasure out of the first than the second. One can optimise one's own satisfaction by adding to someone else's satisfaction. In other words, if the question is not about money, then rationality or otherwise is a judgement made by the onlooker. This, of course, brings us back to a set of broadly non-economic questions, and it is to those we now turn.

3

AN EXPERIMENTAL CHOICE

The view of the human being making choices is constantly subject to challenge from within and across the disciplines. It is also constructed in ways that reflect disciplinary starting places – even as they evolve, fix and change again. We have pointed out how the rational creature presumed to exist in the classical economics perspective is one that is somehow perfect – perfect in its capacity to understand what choices are to be preferred, perfect in its ability to undertake the mathematical procedures for computing optimum outcomes. This creature is evidently unreal, but anyone with a sympathy for economics will agree that starting with it can allow explanations of the relationships between choice outcomes when viewed as the aggregates of individual economic actions.

Given this, it would seem an unlikely starting place for characterising the particular processes actually at work when real individuals make choices. The perfections that economists assume turn into a black box for these concerns, concerns that point towards the question of human competence and motivation – inside the black box, if you will. When we say competence, we are alluding to how people come to understand, say, some market place and the choices that confront them in that domain; we are thinking too of their competence at assessing and calculating between the choices they perceive. With regard to motivation, we are thinking of what might lead people to make the choices they do, assuming their competence. Here questions of desire and need come to the fore, as well as more subtle notions about 'reasons' and 'causes'. Why people choose one thing over another cannot always be reduced to some elemental need. Passions are not the same as reasons.

A concern with motive and human competence in judgement is, we are forewarning, quite complex and demands careful examination, certainly more so than might appear at first glance. Their importance is such that we will return to them throughout the book.

For the purposes of this chapter, let us commence with a largely uncontroversial statement: sociologists, psychologists and economists, all in those disciplines concerned to understand 'choice', will want to distinguish their analyses from the 'common-sense' viewpoint. This isn't merely a contrast between science and everyday knowledge; it is also a contrast in technique. The main way in which the social sciences distinguish their thinking from the thinking of everyday life is through specialised methods. Controversies between the disciplines reside in what methods are the 'right' ones.

As we shall see, most of the recent attempts to deal with competence and motive as regards the specific question of 'choice', with respect to how people reason about some alternatives, have been based on an experimental method, one which derives in the main from psychology. Psychology is, of course, a very broad church in terms of its topics – it encompasses aspects of physiology right the way through to topics of morality and 'joint action'. But psychology has for a long time – and for good or ill – based its work on the experimental method, whatever its empirical topic. On methods, psychology is not so catholic.

In recent years a new conjunction of economic assumptions and this form of inquiry as instantiated in psychology has begun to merge around the topic of choice; this has become known as *behavioural economics*, something we have alluded to several times already. The literature on behavioural economics is huge despite its recent provenance; indeed, its very size and current popularity are reasons among others why we chose to undertake the study reported here. We do not propose to deal with this literature in its entirety, however. Instead, we want to use this chapter to address the methodological and conceptual foundations of this approach (though, as we do so, we shall venture into experimental psychology itself, even if for the purposes of this chapter we won't be too particular about separating the two).

If behavioural economics uses a basic experimental procedure to investigate 'rationality', doing so implies certain other more conceptual assumptions. One is that rationality is a universal, and thus the use of the experimental method is bound up with a contrast class, 'irrationality' (though, as we see, this is more often put as some kind of 'systematic bias'). Underscoring this and other notions is the more basic idea that the human brain is a calculating 'engine'. But, and as we shall also see, given the salience of the contrast class in its conceptual framework, behavioural economics comes to explore not how the human creature at the heart of its inquiries is rational but, rather, its opposite, or, more precisely, how this creature is none too good at its tasks. The experimental method is used to show that the human brain is subject to various problems that make the output of its calculations less than perfect. People are flawed in their rational reasoning, behavioural economics asserts.

Having explored the grounds upon which this approach makes this claim, we will then look at the method itself and ask whether this method is used well. It often isn't. We will also reflect on whether this is the right method for inquiring into choice anyway. Whether or not the experimental technique pays off in terms of providing us with explanations of behaviour is an open question. We remain dubious as to its merits in predicting choice behaviours. To begin with, there are questions of what an experiment might compare: the old adage about apples and pears is apposite here, since it alludes to the problem of how one selects the things people choose between in an experiment. At the same time, the adage also points towards the problem of extrapolation: what can one learn about choice in the general if we have evidence only about how people deal with apples and pears? In any case, it might be that some choices are better examined in their natural milieu, in the flow of life, not in the tidy world of the experiment. This, in turn, will lead us to reflect on what is being sought when researchers use experiments to examine choice. Is it the robustness of technique so central to the more physiological concerns of psychology that they aspire to, or is it to demonstrate, through the manner of science, something else – rhetorical power, for example? This seems an odd thing to suggest, but, as we shall see, much of the studies reported under the aegis of 'experimental' seem to be more about the latter than anything to do with science. As Brannigan (2004) puts it, they want *theatre*. What are the researchers in question seeking through drama? Pedagogy? Surely it must be more than entertainment.

People reasoning badly: the case from behavioural economics

Perhaps the best-known of the writers on behavioural economics is Dan Ariely.[1] He is not necessarily the most advanced or subtle exponent of this view, but his arguments are clear and neatly illustrate the typical form they take. While undoubtably entertaining, the faults in method and ambiguities about claims they present will allow us to recognise some potential difficulties with apparently more sophisticated arguments, even those that have resulted in Nobel awards. As we shall see, at times it is hard to make out what behavioural economists are trying to achieve.

---

[1] He can be viewed on numerous YouTube clips, for example.

Ariely's book *Predictably Irrational* (2008) reports a number of examples of how people choose. What his examples demonstrate is the way in which biases affect decision-making. They demonstrate how choices might be 'irrational', and predictably so, in his view. For instance, in referring to advertisements in which readers/viewers are offered alternatives, he points to the way that choices are made according to the manner in which one piece of information is presented relative to other pieces of information in adverts.

As a case in point, Ariely reports an experiment he conducted that uses an advertisement for the *Economist* magazine. MIT students are given three choices:

Internet-only subscription	$59
Print-only subscription	$125
Print and Internet	$125

He found that 84 out of 100 subjects opted for the print and Internet subscription. He then explains that, when what he terms the 'decoy' (the middle choice) is removed, 68 students chose the Internet-only subscription. Of course, what such evidence shows is that people – even MIT students – can be misled. Ariely is aiming, though, to use experiments such as this to critique the notion of a universal rationality in the human creature. It is above all common-sense assumptions about human nature he wants to assault. As he puts it:

> From this perspective, and to the extent that we all believe in human rationality, we are all economists. I don't mean that each of us can intuitively develop complex game-theoretical models or understand the generalised axiom of revealed preference . . . rather, I mean that we hold basic beliefs about human nature on which economics is built . . . I refer to the basic assumption that most economists and many of us hold about human nature – the simple and compelling idea that we are capable of making the right decisions for ourselves. (Ariely, 2008: xix)

In other words, the perspective of behavioural economics, represented here, doesn't describe decision-making processes at all. It presupposes they are faulty and seeks ways of demonstrating this to a public which may believe otherwise. Ariely's research starts from the inverse premise to economists; he wants to argue that we are *irrational.*

The twist Ariely gives this is that this irrationality has predictable forms. There are patterns to the way we are irrational, and we should understand and acknowledge this in our everyday thinking.

The kinds of irrationalities he is thinking of include, for brief mention, the 'asymmetrical dominance' effect, which holds that people are likely to choose one of two comparable options rather than a third which is less directly comparable; the 'anchor' effect, which holds that the price we are currently willing to pay for something appears to depend on previous prices charged for it; a bias towards 'free' articles rather than ones that cost (irrespective of the 'utility value' in question); the role of emotion and 'arousal'; the role of time (deadlines); the tendency to overvalue things we already own and our unwillingness to accept losses; and our preference for 'winning'.

Such patterns, if they exist, beg a series of questions. Even before we test what their features are, we might ask why we should presume that any deviation from an 'ideal' constitutes irrationality, predictable or otherwise, in the first place. Is it possible that people are aware of how they are subject to biases of one sort or another? Don't they make the choice, sometimes, to go with their biases anyway? Everyone knows a tired body leads to tired decision-making, but sometimes people will make a tired decision even so. Are they rational when they let such 'facts about their nature' control them? Can one be rationally irrational? If they are aware, rational to their irrationalities, are they aware as well of how some of their biases are more likely to operate in some contexts than others, and aware too of the extent of a bias? Do they allow themselves to be more irrational in some places rather than others?

It would be odd to argue that human beings don't show biases of some kind. Bias is a very encompassing term and doesn't allude merely to the capacity to calculate. Sexism is hardly a matter of computation after all, but is a bias even so. The examples that Ariely presents are perhaps ones that are more expressly related to calculation, but surely they are variously well known even if common knowledge doesn't label them. The advertising industry works at exploiting many of them already, such as how people choose between the easily comparable more willingly than between complexly presented options. This is called, as we noted above, the dominance effect, but at a common-sense level we are all familiar with saying we chose between things that were easy to compare and left aside another option because the effort of understanding that was 'too much hassle' – it was too dissimilar.

What we think is at stake here is the difference between some fairly common-sense assertions about people having biases and the idea that some kind of better, more evidential scheme can be established which suggests that our everyday knowledge is not good enough. And the difference here is not merely that one is more evidentially based than the other; for one seems to uncover the systematic features in question, whereas the other may (or may not) recognise bias in a more ad hoc, improvised way, and as a result has less capacity to identify the systematic and may, indeed, be error strewn.

In the case of Ariely, and for most behavioural economists, the method that delivers the corrective to common-sense is experimental; it is thus also, in this view, scientific. It is not merely different from common sense in being evidentially based and made so through special technique – experiments; it is an explanation of a different order altogether – one that should replace common sense *tout court*, displacing the ad hoc with the organised.

So, what is the relationship between people's common sense and scientific knowledge? Can people understand scientific insights about reasoning? After all, with regard to how people choose, if they can come to understand the insights of science, does that then result in the scientific knowledge making for better decision-making? It certainly seems that is what Ariely wants to claim. Given this, we are then confronted with a problem of what is meant by rational and the different sorts of ways in which we describe rational actions – reasoned action. We have already wondered whether people can be rational about their irrationalities. Now we are asking, if Ariely's experiments produce insights that get people to understand their biases better, does that mean the people who learn about these biases are even more rational afterwards? In what sense more rational? Or does it make them, so to speak, more conscious of the ways they don't always attain a perfect notion of rational? What does the phrase 'more conscious' mean in this context? After all, experiments of the kind that behavioural psychologists typically do are always predicated on statistical outcomes. They infer some psychological characteristic only from aggregate results. There remains the question of where these systematic biases reside. One can put this another way: is there an implication in the way Ariely works the scientific method such that it comes to uncover the *unconscious*? This seems to be what is implied if the method produces knowledge that the *conscious* mind can then act upon. Regardless, the important point is that it is people themselves who 'own' their sense of rational action in the end. After reading Freud's *The Interpretation of Dreams* ([1913] 1990), some might say, 'I did this because I came to understand my unconscious was telling me'; after reading Ariely's *The Upside of Irrationality* (2010), they might say, 'I did this because I came to understand the biases I have'. Another point that is seldom made is that any possible benefits which might accrue from recognising one's biases will be maximised only if other people do not behave like that. In the case of the well-known phenomenon of 'loss aversion' in investment practices, the benefits of being willing to take a loss will be maximised only when other people do not act in the same way (for, if they do, the loss will be much greater).

What methods imply

What is at stake when we look at these special methods for identifying 'failures' of rationality is not whether they discover that people are sometimes less than perfect, since everybody already knows that. The question is whether the *methods* are successful in telling us *how much* less than perfectly rational people are and the *systematic forms* these take – the science of it, if you like. Unfortunately, too often behavioural economics – and Ariely exemplifies this – offers very little evidence that these effects are consistent and systematic – even across the experimental contexts provided, let alone in the world at large. We would need to know more than that there is a tendency for us to show some bias when, for instance, we choose what beer to drink under experimental conditions. We would need to know, as well, that the same or similar degree of bias is present to the same degree in a range of different beer-consuming contexts;[2] only then would we say that the bias is something more than a caprice and chance, that it is systematic. In addition, if there is a systematicity to our biases, we should expect to be able to demonstrate the same biases in all comparable circumstances or, conversely, find exceptions and be able to account for those exceptions in a similarly systematic way.

Ariely, for instance, spends some time discussing the so-called placebo effect and a number of cases where it seems to operate. Now, we don't wish to dispute the idea that people can sometimes be persuaded that they feel better when given sugar tablets instead of an effective medicine. The evidence seems fairly convincing – though this doesn't mean one can be sure precisely why they work or that these effects are systematic. It is entirely possible that it has something to do with our confidence in drugs/caregivers, and it is equally plausible that it has something to do with the release of endorphins as a conditioned response to the prospect of improvement.[3] What

---

[2] The call for an 'ecological psychology', one which seeks to pin down how far results established in experiments apply in activities 'in the wild', is long standing and regularly made, but not much responded to by behavioural economists, though there has been some interest in the 'ethnographic'. See, for example, Henrich et al. (2001) – but here ethnography is treated not so much as a mode of inquiry as a label for geographic location.

[3] Although how this release of endorphins is maintained over twelve months – the period of some reported experiences of pain relief – might need further explanation.

is not explained is whether the *power* of these effects is *consistently* experienced in a range of contexts. If not, all we are really left with, despite the numbers quoted from experimental or statistical reports, is a common-sense proposition: that placebos sometimes work. Ariely, indeed, gives us a good example of how the expectations generated by caregivers (and, presumably, the release of endorphins) do not always work (2008: 191–4). Are we entitled to ask why the placebo effect didn't operate in this instance? Would we be entitled to ask other questions as well, such as how many biases there might be, and which supersede others in which circumstances or whether they all aggregate? Just how powerful are the effects of each and all? Are they to be found everywhere, or, if not, where? And, harking back to Ariely's work itself, why don't they always apply?

The problem of context

In some ways, as Samuels, Stich and Bishop (2002) have suggested, the debate is in large part about *how* rational people are and *in what circumstances*. It is to do also, and relatedly, with what kind of knowledge needs to be brought to bear to answer these questions. The experiments devised by behavioural economists, unfortunately, are not well designed to answer the questions posed by the approach. It might even be that the experimental method isn't especially helpful when the topic is choice and reason. The experimental method may be good for other topics within psychology, but, for this, it might create as many confusions as it provides answers.

For example, there will be some rules of reasoning that people typically apply in certain contexts but not, perhaps, in others. Understanding what those rules might be, however, requires empirical investigation. Whether the experiment is a good way of undertaking relevant investigations into these empirical matters is not clear: context seems precisely the thing that the method seeks to avoid, not capture. The problem for behavioural economics is whether their experiments answer how people reason more generally and how one might determine where the sites are of this reasoning. Our discussion shows that, all too often, the experiments tell us very little about this – though of course, and justifiably or not, they can be read as implying much more.

There are more than the limits of evidence that come to mind here. There are also issues to do with what comes before experiments start. It is one thing to argue that human beings do not always behave in accordance with principles of utility maximisation, even when they have the requisite knowledge to make informed choices, and quite another to assert that these 'irrational' choices involve a systematic bias. In the first place, we should ask the question that Gigerenzer (1996) and others ask, which is why we should apply standards which have to do with the rules of logic or with the application of various statistical and probabilistic devices when we think of human reasoning. Why should we think of behaviours which do not 'fit' the principles of utility maximisation as 'systematic irrationality'? There are lots of good reasons to do things which don't abide by probabilistic criteria for judgement or the rules of logic, after all. As Sandis notes (2012), good reasons are very eclectic phenomena and can't be reduced to the analysis of economic rationality.

Be that as it may, typically, experiments in the behavioural economics tradition are designed to show how people cannot and do not follow the rules of logic in many of their operations and instead display various biases. The most famous example of this is the so-called Linda test, reported by Kahneman, Slovic and Tversky (1982). These researchers described the following scenario to subjects in their 'experiment':

> Linda is 31 years old, single, outspoken, and very bright. She majored in philosophy. As a student, she was deeply concerned with issues of discrimination and social justice, and also participated in anti-nuclear demonstrations.

They were then told that Linda was either:

(a) a bank teller, or
(b) a bank teller and is active in the feminist movement.

Subjects were then asked to judge which of the two statements is more probable. About 85 percent replied that the most probable statement is the second one. Linda is both a bank teller and active in the feminist movement.

The nature of the fictional Linda's commitments would not matter at all were it not for the fact that Kahneman, Slovic and Tversky (as well as Kahneman and Tversky somewhat later, 1996) argue that this kind of result is stable – it is found across many different tests. Why is it significant? Because the stable result shows that human reasoning is inconsistent with the so-called *conjunction rule*. The conjunction rule states a basic statistical proposition, that the probability of any single event (A) being true cannot be less than the probability of that event *and* of another (independent) event (B) being true. For example, if we took a room in which half of the people were male and half were female, but all had a banana in their pocket, and calculated the probability (A) that any one of these people would eat their banana before 12 p.m. as 50 per cent and the probability (B) of any individual being male or female as 50 per cent, then (assuming our gender has nothing to do with our propensity to eat bananas before 12 p.m.) we can calculate the probability of any single person as being both female *and* having eaten their banana before 12 p.m. as 25 per cent (50% × 50%). The probability of the single event (B) – male or female – cannot be less than 25 per cent. Indeed, as we know, it is 50 per cent. Going back to the example of Linda, it cannot possibly be the case that, logically speaking, it is more likely that Linda is both a bank teller and an active feminist than that she is a bank teller alone (or a feminist alone). Yet that is what people seem to believe. People are not 'logical', Kahneman et al. assert.

So what is happening when people break this conjunction rule (of which they have most likely never heard)? What Kahneman et al. show in the Linda experiments is that people use simple heuristics rather than make the calculations that some versions of rational choice would lead us to expect. They might, perhaps, use a representativeness heuristic as a case in point, meaning that, when they see descriptions of Linda as 'deeply concerned with issues of discrimination and social justice', they will assume such qualities also stand for pro-feminist attitudes.

Sturm, in his article 'The "rationality wars" in psychology' (2012), provides a nice summary of the conceptual and evidential arguments that are hidden in this reading of the Linda experiments. Other experiments, couched in different ways, show different results – they evidence something different. When the 'Linda' problem is represented in the following way – 'There are 100 people who fit the description above. How many of them are (a) bank tellers, (b) bank tellers and active feminists?' – the 85 per cent bias is reduced to about 20 per cent (see also Fiedler, 1988; Hertwig and Gigerenzer, 1999). On top of this, Charness, Karni and Levin (2009), following the same experimental protocol as Kahneman and Tversky, found that the conjunction fallacy was greatly reduced if incentives for getting it right were introduced or if subjects were allowed to consult with each other before giving an answer (particularly noticeable when the group consulting was three or more people). The way experiments are set up in the first place also has a powerful effect on behaviour.

This points towards the conceptual framing of the inquiry. Sturm:

> The crucial point here is that the language used in these tests is by no means innocent, and that the understanding of core terms

in the task questions can be influenced by prior information. In the 'Linda problem', Kahneman and Tversky presuppose that the terms 'probable' or 'more probable than' and 'and' are all that counts when we test reasoning abilities. Moreover, they assume that these terms have to be understood such that 'and' is the logical 'AND' (&), and that 'probable' conforms to principles of mathematical probability theory. However, ordinary subjects do not understand them in these ways, especially not within the context of the Linda problem. (2012: 74)

If subjects are applying rules at all, then, they may not be applying the rules that are being tested in the experiment. The language used in the experimental set-up presupposes a certain way of looking at the problem and leads subjects to interpret it in a specific way, to draw inferences from it. Subjects may, for instance, interpret the initial statement as implying something like, 'Even though Linda is a bank teller, she remains committed to principles of social justice and equality.' And this would lead them, quite naturally, to pick the second of the two options. As Camerer has argued, this tendency may be better explained by other linguistic assumptions:

> some apparent biases might occur because the specific words used, or linguistic convention subjects assume the experimenter is following, convey more information than the experimenter intends. In other words, subjects may read between the lines. The potential linguistic problem is this: in the statement 'Linda is a feminist bank teller,' subjects might think that this statement 'Linda is a bank teller' tacitly excludes feminists; they might think it actually means 'Linda is a bank teller (and not feminist).' If subjects interpret the wording this way none of the statements are conjunctions of others and no probability rankings are wrong. (Cited in Charness et al., 2009: 2)

Failures to reason properly of the kind that Kahneman and his colleagues uncover are then only such if one assumes that the reading of the tasks used to demonstrate this turn on the following maxim: that people abide by the notion that they 'must endeavour to apply the rules of formal logic to this problem, a problem which is unambiguously stated'. On both counts this should not be accepted.

Language, rationality, experiments

Kahneman provides other kinds of illustrations of how the mind 'thinks' that evidence his notion that there are systematicities to its irrationalities. He argues that 'Studies of priming have yielded discoveries that threaten our self-image as conscious and autonomous authors of our judgements and our choices' (2011: 55). Priming refers to the idea that certain kinds of word or activity act as stimuli for associated words and activities. Thus, if, as Kahneman puts it, 'the idea of EAT is currently on your mind . . . you will be quicker than usual to recognise the word SOUP when it is spoken in a whisper or presented in a blurry font' (ibid.: 52). Kahneman cites Bargh's experiment that purports to show this but does not note that it has seldom been replicated, or indeed that it has become very controversial (see Bargh et al., 1996; Bargh, 2006). Doyen et al. (2012), for instance, in changing some of the parameters, found no such effect.

Besides, there is an important and all too frequent distinction between biases and heuristics that is also neglected. Biases would be, one imagines, fairly robust and inviolate facts of the mind's working. But some evidence seems to suggest that these biases are very substantially reduced when a 'problem' is restated, or when other conditions are established that affect what is seen to be the logical task (see, e.g., Hertwig and Gigerenzer, 1999). Consider this example, cited by Banaji and Greenwald (2013: 11). Invited to choose between the likelihood of different causes of death in the USA, it seems that most people provide inaccurate answers. Thus, choice 1 is between murder and diabetes, and it seems that most of us get this right (the former). Choice 2 is between murder and suicide, and the majority of us get this wrong (it is the latter). Choice 3 is between car accidents and abdominal cancer and, again, most of us get it wrong (the latter). It is argued that this is evidence of the availability heuristic. One of the authors, looking casually at these choices, judged rightly with the first choice and then said to himself, 'Nope, don't know', about the other two. One wonders what experimental results would have been obtained if the 'don't know' option was clearly present for people.

In a similar vein, Gigerenzer (2014: 76) cites a Dutch experiment where children were asked to pick their greatest fears from a list and subsequently invited to state freely what their fears might be. Although there was some overlap (possibly an artefact of choosing from a list first and then being asked to free associate), spiders, snakes and darkness were among the most common fears cited in the second part of the experiment. None were on the list.

Although it is a truism to say that the design of an experiment can have significant effects on the outcomes of an experiment, that this is so seems all too often neglected in this area. And, given this, it is all the more surprising how very limited and small-scale research can end up becoming a vehicle for making large claims.[4] Not least, even if we accept, as a case in point, the idea that 'priming' works in some situations, why on earth should we accept that this implies some radical discovery about how people reason in the general? Just as with the question of, let us say, how lazy we might be when confronted with some choice, or, by way of contrast, how willingly effortful and logical in our efforts in other contexts, that we are so hardly sounds like something one might discover. As we noted before, that people's reasoning has these characteristics is already part of common-sense knowledge; it is in the vocabulary of how we account for decision-making, our own and that of others, as well as how we account for the different places – or circumstances – in which we need to reason.

There is little doubt that people are not necessarily good at formal logic. Even if they are, it may not be because the species has a natural talent for it, but because some of its members have been trained in logic. Rather than assuming that the human brain is a calculating engine, with either inbuilt logical capabilities or inbuilt and systematic biases, we might assume that we have to learn *the tools* of logical thinking, such as schemes of formal logic or statistical reasoning, and how to apply them, and that whatever biases we do or do not display might be the result of any number of social and cultural factors – good training, bad training, as well as special instances of, say, tiredness, distractedness or habitual behaviour.

Part of the issue here is that, by and large, our reasoning faculties don't have to deal with situations where the kinds of constrained thinking characteristic of 'logic' come to apply. When we are confronted with these unusual situations, that we don't easily come to deploy the appropriate mode of logic can be shown experimentally. For example, the poor quality of 'logical work' is demonstrated by the famed Wason Selection Task (Wason, 1966). Subjects are given four cards, each of which has letters on one side (let's say the letters are 'C' and 'E') and numbers on the other side (let's say the numbers are '3' and '4'). When shown two of the cards with the letter side up and two with the number side up, subjects are asked to turn over just as many cards as they need to in order to establish whether the following statement is true: 'If there is an E on the one side, then there is

---

[4] See http://blogs.discovermagazine.com/notrocketscience/2012/03/10/failed-replica tion-bargh-psychology-study-doyen/#.UtO5nLRBXWb for a discussion.

a 4 on the other side.' Most people turn over just the cards which are showing 'E' or the cards which are showing 'E' and '4'. The point is that they would have to turn over the card with '3' face up as well in order to be certain that there wasn't an 'E' on the other side. Wason described this as a *confirmation bias*, because we tend *not to look* for things which might confirm our beliefs rather than falsify them. Most of us get tests like this wrong, it seems (see, e.g., Casscells et al., 1978).

There are many such examples of people's apparent inability (or unwillingness) to follow the laws of formal logic for specific tasks when it is appropriate. It would be foolish to suggest otherwise. What is at stake, however, is whether this means that people are, in any useful sense, irrational in some grander way, beyond the measure of the odd or peculiar cases such as regards the playing cards example.

A way of thinking about this is to consider one of the so-called logician's jokes. The joke goes as follows:

Three logicians go into a bar.
The barman says, 'Would you three like a beer?'
The first logician says, 'I don't know.'
The second logician says, 'I don't know.'
The third logician says, 'In that case, we'll all have a beer.'

The logical principles entailed in this laborious joke are not that difficult to follow. The first logician cannot answer the question as it is framed ('you three') because she or he doesn't know what the other two want. She or he could answer 'no' if she or he didn't want a beer but instead says 'I don't know', indicating that the possibility remains open. The same conditions apply to the second logician. The third, however, realising that neither of the other two has said 'no', is now entitled to say that they would all like a beer. According to the likes of Kahneman, if you don't get the joke then you are suffering from some kind of failure, because you are not following the rules of logic. We would, in contrast, say that it would be reasonable to say that these logicians are being rather irrational insofar as any one of them could say 'I can't speak for the other two, but I'm dying for a beer' (the reader might well be dying for a beer as well after reading this). The rules we follow in such circumstances are the *rules of language*, not the *rules of logic*.

There are numerous situations in which the rules of logic are subordinate to the rules of language, and these include many of the experiments that behavioural economists devise. Instead of showing how people don't deploy logic, they show that they do deploy the logic of words. This doesn't mean that one cannot look at how people can struggle to analyse logically. One can construct experiments that show this. But such experiments need to be carefully devised and the lessons from them treated with circumspection. After all, people live first and foremost in a world of language, not in a world of logic, like Turing machines.

Beyond language?

We are back, at this point, to the main propositions of rational choice, which can be summed up as, 'given what they know, people act in accordance with principles of rational self-interest'. 'Given what they know' takes on a major importance here, since all the above experiments, even if we accept their methodological foundations, suggest that people do not always know how to apply the rules of logic but may be very adept at reasonable judgements involving the following of other, linguistic and cultural rules.

What is clear, in our view, is that many of the assertions made by behavioural economists are predicated on experiments involving relatively small numbers of people (typically a set of undergraduates). If the claim was merely that, depending on environmental conditions, people do not always behave in the wholly rational way predicted, we could have little complaint. Remember, it is not. The claim is that people are *systematically* irrational. In much the way that economists assume that preferences are ordered systematically, behavioural economists assume that our biases, or tendencies towards them, will be exhibited in ordered ways. The evidence to support such a claim remains contestable.

Now, we need to be very clear about what we are saying. It is entirely plausible to suggest, as Kahneman and others do, that, in situations where they are not called on to reflect carefully or perhaps have little time to reflect, people may well rely on immediately available information and sometimes draw the wrong conclusions from it. At the same time, we know of no experimental work which gives us a robust way of distinguishing between the circumstances in which people are likely to behave this way (heuristically) and those in which they are likely to reflect 'more logically' on matters – or more systematically, as it is put by Kahneman.

In any case, and just to deepen the muddles here, it is not clear whether these two types of reasoning are well characterised. As Gigerenzer argues, there is

a widespread misconception about the nature of heuristics. According to the heuristics-and-biases view (e.g., Kahneman

2011), our thinking can be explained by two systems, described by a list of opposing characteristics. System 1 is said to be unconscious, works by heuristics, and makes errors. In contrast, System 2 is conscious, works by logical and statistical rules, and does not seem to make errors. This picture does not fit the facts. First, every heuristic we have studied can be used both unconsciously and consciously . . . thus, heuristics do not stand in opposition to consciousness. Second, heuristics are not the general source of errors but can lead to more accurate inferences than logical or statistical methods . . . Heuristics and errors are therefore also not aligned. The two-system view has overlooked the distinction between risk and uncertainty: statistical methods are required when dealing with known risks, heuristics when dealing with uncertainty. Rather than spending our time knocking heuristics, we need to study their ecological rationality; that is, to find out when they work and when they don't. (2014: 240)

Gigerenzer is probably the most persistent critic of behavioural economics. He spends a considerable amount of time, for instance, disproving the notion that careful, conscious calculation will result in better investment decisions than some simple 'rules of thumb' (see Gigerenzer, 2014: chap. 5). Without seeking to adjudicate between Gigerenzer and the behavioural economists on this (and/or related questions of reason and logic more generally), what we do want to point out is the somewhat odd fact that all 'sides' in this debate are able to marshal evidence to support their opposing views without seeming to deal with evidence that *does not* coincide with their claims. So much so that one is left wondering whether there is any balanced perspective being taken in these debates.

There are many issues here. Are experimental results, often drawing on small populations, typically made up of undergraduate students, as we say reliable? Are the theories about the brain as a calculating engine really as robust as their proponents suppose, or are they merely assertions, starting places from which to inquire? As we have seen, this is what economics does – begins with a premise and doesn't claim that this offers a 'real' vision of the human animal. Is this what behavioural economists ought to admit to? But, if so, what is it they are looking at, if not motive and competence? Besides, how do we compare different views about the nature of motive and competence, into reasoning and its logics? Does it make sense to compare situational logics and in principle logics, for example? In any case, is confounding evidence properly dealt with by any of the views here? We would feel that, overall, the answer to these questions leans towards a 'no'.

Nudging choice

Of course, these are arguments which, on the face of it, concern only a relatively small number of academic commentators. However, things are, in reality, a little more consequential. If, as behavioural economics asserts, there is a systematic tendency towards irrational choices and if, as seems to be the case, it is believed that this leads to sub-optimal ('incorrect') decision-making, then surely we should draw on the expertise of those clear-headed, 'system 2' thinkers in order to help us make better decisions?

There is a view, which one could call liberal paternalism, that would say that this is so. As it happens, it is exemplified by a contemporary notion, 'nudge theory', that seeks to capitalise on some of the claims made by behavioural economics. It is to this we now turn, since this opens up a whole new vista on the question of who 'owns' reasons and who is competent to act on them, and thus returns us to the topic to which Ariely unwittingly led us: the question of what it means to be conscious and thus to make choices – choices that might be right or wrong, but are made by ourselves nevertheless. This in turn begs the question of what the experimental method is meant to do when it is used to offer evidence about such reasons. For, as we shall see, the power of experiments is used to nudge people into thinking differently about their own thinking.

Thaler and Sunstein's book *Nudge: Improving Decisions about Health, Wealth and Happiness* (2009) is, like Ariely's *The Upside of Rationality*, a book for the public domain. But if the latter volume evokes the inner workings of the mind, the consequences of Thaler and Sunstein's written words are political: they have to do with the management of society. Like behavioural economists, they are much concerned with the issue of choice, and, like them, they argue that such decisions are subject to influences that draw people into making bad choices. Like Kahneman, they argue that the human brain uses two 'systems', though they use slightly different terms – in their case the reflective and the automatic. But, like all, their key method to demonstrate their views is experimental.

Space precludes detailing all of their arguments. Be that as it may, what one comes back to after reading their work are the kinds of questions we have being posing as regards behavioural economics. One wants to ask, in what conditions do people reason reflectively and when automatically? Are the occasions for reflection always the same? On the other hand, when people are unreflective and inaccurate in their approach to reasoning, is this also systematic? Are there specific occasions when this happens, or are there other factors, the number of concerns to be taken into account, say? (For discussion, see Hochman and Yechiam, 2011; Yechiam and Telpaz, 2013; Gal, 2006.) What role does experiment have in the research? Are the experiments done well? Do they distinguish properly between the rules of language and logic?

When one looks at the methods and evidence presented by Thaler and Sunstein (and by other authors), and thus attempts to look at the question in a balanced way, one is left wondering whether there are sufficient scientific grounds for the arguments being made. There appear to be a mix of assertion, methods that seem to be used in a manner which can best be described as selective, and then extreme claims. And these claims are often full of contradiction.

Lest it be thought that we are taking sides in these disputes, let us clarify our position. It is not that we think that there is or is not such a thing as, in the case of Thaler and Sunstein, 'loss aversion' or, in the case of Kahneman, 'representative bias' – notions that we haven't explained – but we do not think the experiments these researchers undertake demonstrate these biases or aversions; in our judgement, they don't demonstrate very much at all.

We do not think we need now to say anything more on that point – this failure; errors on the Linda experiment are sufficient proof of this, we feel. What is important, however, is the way in which the experimental basis – the mode of the evidential nature of these claims – has become part and parcel of what one might say is the credit given to them, especially in the public domain. When we say this we are suggesting that the claims are not judged with sufficient reference to the quality of the data used; the data seems to be taken for granted, since it is the experimental method that creates it. We say this having noted that the data demonstrates appreciably less than is being claimed for it. Yet what one sees in the public domain is the opposite: a notion that this is good science. Awards are given to the research; politicians coin phrases about nudging the public to think differently; our hidden biases are treated as accounts of why we should allow 'experts' to choose for us. The claims made about choice, about how human reasoning is not well done, have become part of common currency.

Whether this is an accurate way of describing this cultural moment is a moot point, but what does seem of importance is that there is a longer-standing issue about the use – or misuse – of experiments to explore human conduct, and particularly human choice, over many years. Augustine Brannigan has, in our view, demonstrated quite persuasively that 'experiment' has been a very powerful tool in the armoury of rhetoric for those who have claimed to look at human choice throughout the latter part of the twentieth century. This rhetoric often verges on the disingenuous. In his book *The Rise and Fall of Social Psychology* (2004), Brannigan investigates some of the most famous social psychological experiments of the past fifty years. In these, the method has been evoked to justify claims about how people choose not just wrongly but in ways that lead to cruelty; how they choose in ways that are not truthful but are subordinate to what the crowd says; and how choice is easily controlled by the suggestions of others. Experiments prove all this.

Brannigan is very much in favour of good, traditional experimental science. Indeed, he writes *The Rise and Fall* in an attempt to reassert the essential components of such a science. He points out that the purpose of any experiment, social psychological or otherwise, is the doing of something that seeks to uncover an otherwise opaque truth; it is objectivity that it is after, not subjective perspective. Other considerations, like politics, morality, the subjective, should play no part. Experiment is also a label for what is methodic; it must be repeatable. Raw data is collected in order to test a clear hypothesis that others can replicate. Experiment should involve randomly selected data; variables should be clearly identified and controlled; there should be comparison groups (i.e., a control group); and so on.

Brannigan notes, balefully, that any examination of the history of social psychology will show that, in contrast, experiments in this discipline do not always abide by these rules. How they fail to live up to these standards echoes what we have just seen in the work of Kahneman and others. Brannigan says that, typically, experiments in social psychology are not experiments as in the natural sciences; they borrow heavily from common-sense knowledge; they often deal with issues that cannot actually be resolved by facts (i.e., the problems are conceptual, not factual); and they do not result in the accumulation of knowledge. In his view, they are more like demonstrations of 'moral facts', and they use the experimental method as a dramatic way of showing this. Science is thus transformed into theatre. And this is consequential. For the genius of theatre is of course that it demands that the audience takes the play in good faith, that it suspends disbelief and the critical faculty. What those who make science theatre do is precisely to stop those who look at the science being critical. If they were to be critical, they would see that it is bad science. Given that this is indeed science we are talking about, that so many social psychologists should make this move should abhor the serious minded; it certainly does Brannigan.

It is worth reporting some of the examples that Brannigan provides, since they highlight how 'experiment' can be altered from being an effective technique of science into a vehicle for making claims that can avoid examination. The very merit that experimentalism can claim in science can turn, his book shows, into the excuse for doing the opposite of what science stands for.

Solomon Asch's (1952) study, cited approvingly by Thaler and Sunstein, is one example of this inversion or negation of science. Asch's work concerned resistance and conformity to social pressure. He wanted to see under what conditions people would either accept or resist group pressure. A background assumption was that this might help us understand the effects that media propaganda has on public opinion. Subjects (in this case a group of young male undergraduates) were asked to assess the relative length of three lines against a 'stimulus line' drawn on a cardboard sheet. Apart from a single subject each time, everyone else in the room was a 'confederate' and was specifically instructed to choose incorrectly. Asch reports that subjects mimicked the majority opinion one-third of the time. Three-quarters of subjects went along with the majority view at least once. A third caved in at least half the time. Again, it may well be the case that peer groups can exert an influence on behaviour; one can hardly dispute that. Those of us who, in our youth, wore platform shoes and/or flared jeans have their history as proof. However, that is hardly the point. The issue is one of experimental validity as against common sense and, in particular, claims that seem beyond what common sense would allow. Asch says: 'there are times when one must choose between stark alternatives that have very much to do with the question of independence. Germans who lived near concentration camps could not escape the choice of breaking with their social order or of forcibly suppressing a range of facts' (1952: 496). Brannigan responds: 'I would again hazard an opinion that [the experiment] tells us nothing informative about the effects of propaganda in the 2nd world war. . . . It says nothing about genocide and the political use of scapegoats . . . it says nothing about national animosities' (2004: 49).

Brannigan points out that, in the real world, people engaged in assessing the merits of propaganda have a history to go on. Their opinions are based on their experience of this history. In Asch's experiment, people have no history to go on – quite the opposite – since the real purpose of the experiment is disguised. The experiment, then, possibly demonstrates that *some* people, *some* of the time, tend to conform to the opinions of others when they have nothing else to go on and – maybe – when there is *very little at stake*; but, beyond that, the experiment shows little else.

Further, and probably most importantly from our point of view, whether or not the results are robust seems to depend on both the historical era and the cultural milieu in which attempts to replicate took place. There have to be serious doubts about whether experiments of this kind are telling us anything about universal psychological features, or whether they justify the kinds of claim sometimes associated with them – like Asch's claim that they tell us about the reasoning of Germans between, say, 1941 and 1945.

To give an example of the problem of generalisability, or robustness, Perrin and Spencer (1980, 1981) attempted a precise replication of the Asch experiment in a British context, using male undergraduate science, maths and engineering students. They conducted 396 individual trials and found that a participant conformed with the incorrect majority exactly once.[5] LaLancette and Standing (1990) report very similar findings.

There is also the question of why people conform or what their conformity says about the subjects. In fact, Turner et al. (1987) have pointed out that, in post-test interviews of Asch-like experiments, some subjects point to their uncertainty over the correct answer in the tests. That is because the subjects imagine that the researchers knew the correct answer and this answer was especially opaque to the subjects – else why are they asked it in the experiment? In other words, conforming to social 'norms' might not be the explanation at all. It has been argued that there are, in fact, two quite different ways in which people can be induced to conform. It might be that 'normative conformity', as Asch claims, is likely in some circumstances while 'information conformity' is more likely in others, as Bond (2005) suggests.

In a particularly interesting re-examination of Asch's findings, Hodges and Geyer (2006) insist that, rather than demonstrating conformity, these demonstrate people's willingness to tell the truth in the face of peer pressure (after all, two-thirds of participants did not conform). They suggest that 'multiple values and multiple relations that properly constrain the actions of those in the Asch situation . . . participants work pragmatically to negotiate these conflicts in ways that acknowledge their interdependence with others and their joint obligations to values such as truth' (2006: 2–3). They go on to point out that the modal response to every critical trial was dissent, not conformity. While 28 per cent of participants conformed more than half the time, 26 per cent *never* conformed. The point here is that, even if we respect the validity of the findings, more than one explanation of them is possible. Hodges and Geyer go on to say, quite plausibly:

---

[5] It might be worth pointing out that in another study, involving figures of authority, they got results much more like Asch's, though still did not manage to replicate them.

we could think of it in the following way: How can participants speak the truth about their situation in a way that honours their personal integrity . . . and is sensitive to and respectful of the experimenter, the other participants, and the situation in which they all find themselves? . . . in such a complex ecology, people might do just what average participants in Asch's study actually did. They might mostly give their own view (a simple perceptual conviction), but occasionally go along with the majority just to let them know that they had paid attention to them. (Ibid.: 5–6)

In any event, what one can see is that Asch's work is so flawed that it is difficult to draw any conclusion from it. He wants to make very large claims but uses experimental data only in a loose way and does not provide proper control or test findings in other experiments. If we are to believe Brannigan, Asch doesn't want to use the method of experiment to do science, he wants to use it to convey his ideas. Methods are used rhetorically, Brannigan says, as a device to convey a point of view. They are not used to prove ideas or uncover evidence. Proof and evidence don't matter.

Of course it might be that Asch's work is a one-off. But Brannigan's lament for an experimental science shows that it is not. In reporting on Zimbardo's (1972) famous work on 'guards' and 'prisoners', he shows that this involved no clear hypothesis and also entailed inviting TV cameras in to record events before the experiment took place – hardly a picture of scientific objectivity. Generalised claims about the 'brutality' of guards and the 'passivity' of prisoners were made without justification.

Brannigan critiques Milgram's (1974) famous 'electric shock' experiment too. This was designed to test obedience to authority. Lest Brannigan be thought of as a maverick, others have subjected Milgram to the criticisms he makes, including the bizarre behaviour of the experimenter who, as Orne and Holland (1968) report, somewhat implausibly, sits by 'while the victim suffers, demanding that the experiment continue despite the victim's demands to be released' (1968: 287). The possibility that subjects proceeded on the simple basis that, in an experiment taking place on a university campus, 'nothing can go wrong' is simply ignored. In a later experiment, conducted away from Stanford University, participants were less willing to continue. Besides, in pre-tests, without any authority figure, subjects were just as likely to inflict the maximum voltage. In fact, the biggest decline in subjects' willingness to go on was when the 'victim' banged on the wall – some of those tested laughed when the 'victim' shrieked with pain, the strong implication being that they didn't believe any pain was being inflicted.

As Baumrind has put it, 'far from illuminating real life, as he claimed, Milgram in fact appeared to have constructed a set of conditions so internally inconsistent that they could not occur in real life. His application of his results to destructive obedience in military or German settings . . . is metaphorical rather than scientific' (1985: 187). In a questionnaire conducted after the experiments, only 56 per cent of subjects stated that they believed real pain was being inflicted (62 per cent of 'defiant' subjects did believe there was real pain), 40 per cent were 'unclear' about what was going on, and so on.

We are reporting specific accusations about the quality of the various experiments conducted under the name of behavioural economics and, as a precursor to the emergence of this approach, in experimental social psychology. We are suggesting that experiments can be used to distract attention away from the precise quality of evidence – from the requisites of science. The studies mentioned above have achieved canonical status; their findings are well known, taken as truths, as science. Their validity is simply assumed and the results obtained regarded as 'proven'. That this is so, we are suggesting, is not because science is evident in the studies or in their treatment. Something about how they were undertaken and something about how they were read thereafter has resulted in their being treated differently – as things that should be treated as matters that are not to be disputed or doubted – as incorrigibles. Brannigan thinks it is the use of the experimental method as a form of theatre that has achieved this.

It is vitally important we are clearly understood as not critiquing the experimental method – on the contrary. Rather, we are arguing two points: firstly, experiments need to be carefully done and claims made carefully matched to the evidence; and, secondly, the conceptual foundations of the resulting claims need equally careful examination.

One should add that achieving success in the experimental method is not easy. It is difficult not only in its broad shape but also in its details. Constant attention is given in the scientific literature, for example, to how attempts at science and at using the experimental technique fail. Take research that shows that statistics in such work is sometimes inept, if not downright dishonest. Goldacre, in his book *Bad Science* (2008), gives examples of both. Of particular interest, Goldacre later, in an article in *The Guardian*, cites the work of Nieuwenhuis et al. (2011) on error in significance tests. Roughly speaking, the error goes like this. We can do tests of two independent sets of conditions and may find significant results in one but not in the other. The basic problem lies in how big a difference there is between the significant result and the non-significant one. Clearly, in order to assert a causal relation, one would have to show that the 'difference between the differences' is significant. Astonishingly, Nieuwenhuis et al. identified 157 papers in the neuroscience literature where there was potential for this kind of error and discovered that it was made in half of them. Goldacre, commented: 'They broadened their search to 120 cellular and molecular articles in Nature Neuroscience, during 2009 and 2010: they found 25 studies committing this statistical fallacy, and not one single paper analysed differences in effect sizes correctly.'[6] As well as being methodologically flawed, results are not always replicated. This is the case, for instance, with Rosenthal and Jackson's (1968) work on teacher expectation; in experiments, results are often subject to more than one alternative explanation, and so on.

The quite widespread acceptance of the results of these studies would seem to be good evidence, ironically, for the occurrence of confirmation bias. Such bias can be understood without need for psychological theories about competence and motivation or experiments – people often believe what they prefer to hear, social psychologists included. But that is not the point we are making here. What we are noting is that the experimental method can be used to place a sheen on research about human choice that is simply undeserved. The experimental technique turns out not to be a mode of inquiry, but a step in an effort to stop the inquiries of those who want to learn about choice. The results of these studies imply that choice cannot be treated as rational, reasoned and sensible but somehow corrupt, false and irrational, something that experts could correct if they were allowed to do so. Thus we are back to nudge theory and of course the odd premise of behavioural economics. If economics assumes people are rational and doesn't have much evidence to show this, so behavioural economics (and many in social psychology) starts from the opposite premise. But it doesn't have much evidence to persuade one that a starting assumption should turn into an empirical assertion.

Governing through nudging

So, despite the obvious problems associated with so much of this experimental work, Thaler and Sunstein think it ought to be

---

[6] (www.badscience.net/2011/10/what-if-academics-were-as-dumb-as-quacks-with-sta tistics/#more-2405).

possible to use the insights they appear to generate to intervene consciously in the decision-making processes of others, and that of course is the main thrust of their book. When done by such institutions as local and central government agencies, these influences, or 'nudges', should make for better decision-making and behaviour. Certain people, in their words, can be 'choice architects'.

Choice architecture refers to the idea that, when confronted with an array of different choices, we may make our choice on the basis of some of the above heuristics; we may (because we don't have much time, for instance) ignore certain possibilities, and we may even, sometimes, sit down and make very conscious calculations. Nudge theory is predicated on the view that it is better if someone with a degree of expertise about this architecture encourages us to make the 'right' decision rather than leaving us to mess up in all the familiar ways. It brings up the intriguing idea that it is somehow better if others make choices on our behalf.

This management of the 'choice architecture' does not entail any force but, rather, involves subtle forms of (largely unconscious) encouragement. The conception is something we haven't looked at before, and that is the idea that we ought to avoid influencing people directly and should influence them indirectly, gently, through nudges.

One example Thaler and Sunstein provide ought to be of interest to many people working today who may or may not have an eye on their retirement. Much like the UK and many other countries, the USA ultimately will have to face up to the problem of its ageing population and how to provide for it. Thaler and Sunstein make two recommendations for 'solving' this difficulty. The first is an automatic 'opt-in' for pensions schemes, something the UK government – in one of its more paternalistic moods – has, in fact, done. Such 'nudges', however, evidently trade on relative indifference. What we call the 'how much is at stake' clause here basically means that people in the UK are not, for the most part, being asked to sacrifice a large part of their current income in order to save for the future. They can be 'nudged' into that kind of saving because the amounts are not felt to be dramatic. One might say that it seems a quite natural way of reasoning, since it allows that the future might hold out the promise that incomes will be higher than otherwise, at relatively little cost. We are not wanting to ask whether this is rational or not, however. It certainly 'makes sense'.

The corollary of paying out relatively small sums, however, is that people's reward in terms of pension income will be relatively small. Exactly how this will lead to the solving of the coming crisis in support for the elderly in the UK, at least, is unclear. As an article in the *Financial Times* (20 January 2013) argued:

It is clearly not sufficient that workers save at the 8 per cent minimum contribution rate over the long term. This will have to rise considerably if these new savers are going to build up a meaningful retirement pot. There is a danger in the current UK auto-enrolment framework that too many workers will not wake up to this fact in time. So how can we move things on beyond just a nudge?

The details of this example aside, nudge theory is based on claims and assertions, not evidence that one would happily accept as scientific. These assertions and claims are not very profound either, though that doesn't mean one would dispute them at a common-sense level. Thaler and Sunstein's work asserts that people can be influenced (unconsciously or otherwise). They assert, too, quite rightly, that, in any policy-related domain, *something* has to be done – whether good science or any science at all is involved isn't necessarily salient. Some choice has to be made.

We can have no objection to the rough idea that some subtle 'nudges' may indeed produce desired effects. What is really at stake is whether the 'scientific' foundations for claims about the need for nudges, the mechanics of motive and competence implied, and so on, are as robust as is assumed. Selective use of cases and evidence does not give strength to Thaler and Sunstein's view; it makes it seem duplicitous, since it implies that, in all cases, the great and the good make better decisions than plain ordinary folk.

If nothing else, and leaving aside questions about science, there is the issue of who does the nudging. 'Good government' would seem to be Thaler and Sunstien's answer. But, as Waldron (2014) points out, not only do governments make mistakes, they also sometimes set out deliberately to deceive us. Moreover, why should we presume that the best way to change behaviour is to provide nudges rather than an education for people that might lead them to make better, more informed choices themselves? This would be nudging them to the right answer, but nudging them to think. The irony of this, given the assumptions of behavioural economics, hardly needs stating.

Does economics need psychology?

In sum, a great deal of popular, influential and reputedly scientific work draws on one kind of assumption or another, often astonishingly uncritically, and this leads the researchers to make some very broad and general claims about human decision-making. Behavioural economists and those in experimental psychology who undertake related studies are not alone in this, as we shall see. To return to our main theme, it is perhaps worth noting that the need to incorporate psychology into economic thinking is not universally accepted.

Gul and Pesendorfer (2005), for instance, argue that economics doesn't need psychology. They refer to 'neuroeconomics' as any position that seeks to merge the psychological with the economic, and, as this happens, thus they also assume that physiological matters come into play too. They want to distinguish 'true utility', based on psychological states which might include, for instance, 'happiness', from an economic notion, 'choice utility'. For Gul and Pesendorfer,

> In the standard approach [of economics], the term utility maximization and choice are synonymous. A utility function is always an ordinal index that describes how the individual ranks various outcomes and how he behaves (chooses) given his constraints (available options). The relevant data are *revealed preference data*; that is, consumption choices given the individual's constraints. These data are used to calibrate the model (i.e., to identify the particular parameters) and the resulting calibrated models are used to predict future choices and perhaps equilibrium variables such as prices. Hence, standard (positive) theory identifies choice parameters from past behavior and relates these parameters to future behavior and equilibrium variables. (2005: 6; emphasis added)

In this view, economics comes to focus on revealed preference because economic data comes in this form – as revealed preferences. Economic data can – at best – reveal what the agent wants (or has chosen) in a particular situation. Such data does not enable the economist to distinguish between what the agent *intended* to choose and what he *ended up* choosing, what he chose and what he *ought* to have chosen.

It is important to emphasise that Gul and Pesendorfer accept that studying how people make decisions is part of the business of psychology. They agree that neuroscientific studies of 'how the mind works' offer the possibility that they will reveal the way in which the mind *does* work. This may be very different from what economists suppose. Putting economics on a secure scientific footing if that were the case would, therefore, involve very significant changes in its central ideas, its conception of 'how the mind works'.

As mentioned, however, many of the supposedly front-line issues in the human and social sciences frequently involve divisions over issues that have been under discussion for many years, even centuries, and the sides being taken are often little more than rehashes of quite long-lasting lines of thought. Understanding 'how the mind works', in one sense, is not a matter of exploring inner operations occurring in a mental realm but a matter of describing the organised patterns of activity which are manifest in people's behaviour. This is what *de facto* the vast bulk of human and social sciences *actually* do. For, as we have seen, economists do not necessarily need to know why people make the choices they do, and economic data gives us no information about their reasons. They only need to know that they make these choices consistently and accord with some hierarchy of preference. Consequently, no amount of 'neuroeconomics' can refute economic models because they are based on different kinds of concept and are trying to explain different kinds of thing. Where behavioural psychology seeks to rectify the errors made by economics, treated as a kind of primitive brain science, Gul and Pesendorfer argue that such a perspective misunderstands what economics is trying to do, for it is not a primitive brain science at all and is perfectly capable of dealing with inconsistent preferences, mistakes and biases within its own terms.

Gul and Pesendorfer are defending a particular conception of economics, one in which – as we have said – the model does not have to correspond closely to reality. As they say:

[according to Kahneman] ... subjective states and hedonic utility are 'legitimate topics of study'. This may be true, but such states and utilities are not useful for calibrating and testing standard economic models. Discussions of hedonic experiences play no role in standard economic analysis because economics makes no predictions about them and has no data to test such prediction. Economists also lack the means for integrating measurement of hedonic utility with standard economic data. Therefore, they have found it useful to confine themselves to the analysis of the latter ... economists, even when dealing with questions related to those studied in psychology, have different objectives and address different empirical evidence. (2005: 2)

Psychologists and economists, in this view, have different purposes. They study different kinds of behaviour, and the evidence for one makes little difference at all to theories which derive from evidence of the other. The core of the difference is that Gul and Pesendorfer are defending models – particular conceptual constructs that relate to each other in defined ways – and models to boot which are concerned only with economic choices. Data, in their view, is not about the brain or the mind but only about revealed preferences. This data doesn't correspond to any kind of individual behaviour. Nor does it provide a basis for any assessment of motivations, reasons or justifications. As they put it:

> economics and psychology do not offer competing, all-purpose models of human nature. Nor do they offer all-purpose tools. Rather, each discipline uses specialized abstractions that have proven useful for that discipline. Not only is the word trust much less likely to come up in an economics exam than in a psychology exam, but when it does appear in an economics exam, it means something different and is associated with a different question, not just a different answer. (2005: 9)

Wood for the trees

There are some very important issues here. Our assessments of different approaches to the problem of choice depend on three distinct but related things: on evidence and the way it is collected, on the kinds of concept we deploy in support of our perspectives, and on the purposes we have in advocating the perspectives we have.

Be that as it may, neuroeconomics would represent a very important step forward in our understanding of human choice if one could substantiate the propositions upon which it is founded and identify robust experimental conclusions to support it. It might provide exactly the basis for guiding choice through the form of paternalism that is suggested in the 'nudge' literature. After all, if neuroeconomics can demonstrate that human satisfactions can be maximised in certain ways, as evidenced by changes in brain state, we are well on the way to Utopia. Regardless, what is at stake here is the possibility that economics has relevant statements to make about normativity – the moral foundations of social life. We should not, however, underestimate the controversy. Gintis, in an Amazon review of Caplin and Shotter's 2008 collection, says:

> My personal experience is that when a new research area is born, many of the smartest and scientifically committed people fail to understand simple issues, and make assertions that are completely indefensible. In the short-run, in the face of a group of hopeful innovators, there is a 'circling of the wagons,' in which groups of researchers with opposing viewpoints utter statements that are both incorrect and exhibit a high degree of hostility, contempt, and anger.

As we explained above, one view is that the kind of microeconomics which underpins standard versions of the rational choice hypothesis has little or nothing to do with the interests of neuroeconomics. Others clearly see it as providing a new and powerful foundation for understanding behaviour. Zak (2008) lays out the foundations of the neuroscience programme when he states that 'economic decisions are made in the brain' and that 'the brain is an economic system'. What does this kind of microeconomics need to do in order to substantiate this ambitious claim?

In effect, argues Camerer (2008), it needs to demonstrate the validity of certain assumptions. These include the following: the idea that the brain is the organ that makes choices; that neuroeconomics can use technological advances in understanding the choice-making organ – such as brain imaging and the like; that, through this, rational choice theory can be enriched; and that this in turn can allow behavioural economics and neuroeconomics to find ways of improving welfare economics.

Now, these make up nothing more than a promissory note. They are not statements about what has been achieved. Camerer, along with other neuroeconomists, believes that these propositions will be proved correct by the further development of brain science. He thinks that understanding brain states helps us decide between competing theories about choice and its mechanics because those theories should be understood as resting on suppositions – if not direct claims – about what is going on in the brain, so evidence about what *is* going on in the brain can only support one (if any) of them. Suppositions will turn into proofs.

This sounds straightforward albeit rather simply expressed. But one would need to decide whether the proposition that the brain is the organ that makes choices is even a logical statement let alone one which can be subjected to empirical testing. The fact that changes in brain state can be observed via new technology in and of itself tells us nothing at all about whether brains make choices. After all, we suspect that most people would accept the simple statement that 'people make choices'. If both these sentences are true, then 'people' and 'brains' are synonymous. Either that, or we mean quite different things by 'choice' in each of these two sentences. That is, exactly what is meant by the notion that we 'make choices' at all is not entirely clear. The standard model in economics relies on a picture of a limited number of alternatives from which a selection can be made on the basis of maximum utility, given adequate information. 'Revealed preference' describes only the outcome of some putative selection.

Saying that Camerer's remarks are promissory suggests the

need to be sceptical about what current brain science can actually show. Imaging techniques have enabled the display of the levels and patterns of electro-chemical activity that go on in the brain at particular times, but it should not be assumed that researchers have a sound understanding of what 'mental' activities those electro-chemical ones evidence. As we will shortly illustrate, there can be serious misunderstandings/misrepresentations of both the relationship between the machine displays and the activities they purportedly capture, as well as in the statistical analyses applied to the data being displayed.

Levy (2013) describes fMRI, a common method of imaging the brain, as working in the following way. It is based on the fact that active neurons consume more oxygen than inactive ones, which in turn produces an increase in blood supply to that area of the brain. The haemoglobin that is linked to oxygen is 'paramagnetic', meaning that its concentration corresponds to an electromagnetic signal, so we can measure active areas of the brain. fMRI can sample the results in a matter of a second or two, meaning that over the time taken to complete a task it can sample changes many times. Levy asserts too that there are a number of such experiments in relation to choice parameters which purport to show, for instance, variations in the right orbitofrontal cortex among people who have varying responses to ambiguity.

One of the best known of such experiments is that of Hsu et al. (2005), who set up an experiment to study decision-making in ambiguous circumstances. Briefly, subjects choose between receiving a certain amount of money or betting to win a higher amount, based on the colour of cards drawn from a pack. In one experimental condition the risk is known, in the sense that subjects are told how many cards of each colour there are, while under different conditions they are not. The point here is that different areas of the brain are seen to 'light up' in the two experiments.

It would be foolish to argue that there is no relation between brain states and behaviour, and we are not trying to do so. What is at stake is the robustness and reliability of such results, and here there are reasons to be careful. Indeed, Hsu and Zhu acknowledge, in drawing inferences about decision-making under uncertainty, 'our hypothesis is necessarily crude given the limited state of our knowledge [it raises a number of possible empirical tests]' (2013: 158). We should not exaggerate what we know about brain states, even if we accept they have some causal relationship with real-world choice behaviour (itself not established). As Ross has pointed out, many of the inferences drawn from the branch of neuroscience that concerns itself with why evolution has failed to produce rational decision- makers 'do not yet seem to have produced the results that justify the excitement that typically accompanies popular reports of the research' (2010: 21).

Let us look, then, at the nature of these experiments with a care for behaviours, actions, demonstrables, and the claims that can be said to derive from them – from observables. An extreme example of the problem of being sure that what the technology displays is correctly understood is given by Bennett and his colleagues (2010), who famously showed with their 'dead salmon' experiment that what appears to be a very precise way of measuring brain activity is potentially subject to many sources of error. Bennett took an Atlantic salmon and placed it in an fMRI scanner. He and his colleagues then showed the (dead) salmon a series of pictures relating to certain kinds of social situation, and this generated images. When they analysed the volumetric pixels (or 'voxels'), it seemed that they had data that demonstrated the salmon was thinking about these social situations.

Bennett and his colleagues won the Ignobel award (given for making people laugh, then making them think) for this piece of research, because what it actually demonstrates is how easily error can occur. The problem has to do with the relationship between signal and noise. Signals are, by definition, meaningful; they convey useful information. Noise is all the other stuff. The relationship of 'signal' to 'noise' depends on the sensitivity of the machine. Set too high, the risk of false positives is high; set too low, the risk of obtaining no significant results at all is high. Decisions about such matters fall into the category of 'art' rather than science. If, as with fMRI, any single scan can produce 130,000 'voxels' (or data points), one has to be very, very sure that there are no false positives. As for the statistical analysis of the supposed evidence, Vul and his colleagues (2009) have noted that results from fMRI studies have reported levels of correlation that are so high as to be rated mathematically impossible. In 'Puzzlingly high correlations in fMRI studies of emotion, personality, and social cognition', they say:

> To sum up, then, we are led to conclude that a disturbingly large and quite prominent segment of fMRI research on emotion, personality, and social cognition is using seriously defective research methods and producing a profusion of numbers that should not be believed ... we suspect that the questionable analysis methods discussed here are widespread in other fields that use fMRI to study individual differences, such as cognitive neuroscience. (2009: 285)

Other, and even more technical, sources of error are described by Joseph and Atlas (2009). Other researchers show how the chain of argument from magnetic pulse to gross behavioural data contains a series of 'risky' estimates and sources of error (see Ross, 2010). Aue, Lavelle and Cacioppo (2009) describe some of the problems of inference involved in this kind of research. The focus of these criticisms is less on data points as sources of error than on alternative explanations for any given set of data.

Besides, it has been argued that the results of such inquiries are often based on interpretations which simply assume the validity of pre-existing psychological theories. Kihlstrom, for instance, has argued that such findings never seem to lead to changes in theorising: 'To the contrary, it appears that precisely the reverse is true: psychological theory constrains the interpretation of neuropsychological and neuroscientific data' (2006: 16, cited in Aue et al. 2009). Coltheart (2006), also cited by Aue et al., has made similar observations. Kanaan and McGuire (2011) have made much the same points about the specific problems associated with using fMRI data in relation to psychiatric disorders.

Words, descriptions, explanations

Those who are ambitious to be scientists often suppose that what successful scientists do is explain phenomena and, quite naturally, then preoccupy themselves with the question of what form explanations should take. The fact that the relevance and effectiveness of an explanation depends entirely upon the correct identification of the phenomena that are to be subsumed by it is often treated as a relatively trivial matter, one which is handled fairly carelessly, with the result that many proposed explanations are questionable just because they don't appear to identify the phenomenon soundly. Identifying the phenomenon is very much a matter of describing it, and describing is done very largely by means of language. It is, therefore, quite a common complaint across many disciplines that what are presented as findings are often no more than artefacts of the language being used to describe them. Our discussions of the 'Linda' experiments showed this very clearly.

This kind of problem can originate in the fact that different disciplines use different vocabularies, vocabularies which differ not only in words, for they often use many of the same words, but, more importantly, in *the ways in which* the same words are used. When it comes to discussing relations between different approaches, the fact that one may be dealing with two or more different vocabularies is often neglected, and it is wrongly assumed that what seems to be the same word does not continuously carry the same meaning in that context.

As a case in point, in the argument about standard economics and neuroscience, the notion of 'optimum satisfaction' can be used in – at least – three different ways. It can be used as part of the vocabularies of the two kinds of science and also as part of the ordinary language that we speak independently of affiliation to any technical pursuit and its associated vocabulary. Because we all use those words, it can easily and wrongly be assumed that, when we use them, we are all of us, standard economists, neuroeconomists, and those of us who are bystanders to their disagreements, interested in understanding the *same thing*. We've already warned, at least partly, of the idea that, when we are talking about people's choices, we are all talking – albeit more or less directly – about the brain. To neuroeconomists it would seem unreasonable to suppose that we would not all benefit from a better understanding of the brain from exploration of how it works as an electro-chemical structure. After all, laypersons can't have any awareness of what kind of electro-chemical transactions are going on in the brains of other people, or even in their own brain. The neuroeconomist is right in this: we as ordinary punters know absolutely nothing about what, in neurological terms, goes on in the brain, and so we have no means whatsoever of making informed guesses about what might be going on there when someone decides to buy a new car, say – that is, makes a choice of some kind.

Consider a contrast here, which shows that we might imply the brain in our discourse about choice: in many particular instances it isn't the brain that matters. Saying that someone chose a new car over a used one because of the protection insurance doesn't depend on any assumption about the brain at all – we are talking about a person and their circumstances, and not their brain. The argument provoked by Gul and Pesendorfer's polemic has been characterised as an argument over the relations between 'positive' and 'normative' economics, essentially between economics' purely reportorial function, its portrayal of how economic relations work, and the contribution that it can make to improving welfare. That the standard economic model has contributed relatively little to our understanding of the large complexities of real-world interactions is, we think, broadly true. Suggesting that it could and should do more, however, is akin to a complaint that one's football team is rubbish and could be a great deal better if only we could find ways of making it a great deal better. Unless we find robust and reliable methods for doing so, and have clear agreements about what it means to say 'better' in the first place, nothing much is achieved in the statement. Though it seems unkind to say so, that, we suggest, is the current state of play with neuroeconomics. No one would doubt it could be done better, but how and to what ends is not clear.

Conclusion

We are not the first to note that what are supposedly experimental results are often as much artefacts of the language used to report them as anything to do with physiological processes captured by the experiments – processes in the 'brain', say. Experiments about 'decision-making' can, for instance, be based on a linguistic usage that presupposes what a decision looks like and perhaps have relatively little to do with the actual processes by which people go about conducting their lives. Rubinstein (2000) was possibly the first to make note of the way in which economic theories are predicated on the use of particular terms, but, more importantly for our purposes, Ferraro, Pfeffer and Sutton (2005) draw attention to the way in which 'theories can become self-fulfilling because they provide a language for comprehending the world. Language affects what people see, how they see it and the social categories and descriptors they use to interpret their reality. It shapes what people notice and ignore and what they believe is and is not important' (2005: 9).

Now, the observation that knowledge is socially constructed is, in and of itself, a fairly trivial one unless one subscribes to the view that this somehow problematizes notions of 'truth'. *How* it is so constructed is less trivial. The observation that theoretical choices strongly influence choice of topic, methodology, concept formation, and so on, is certainly more consequential. Here, there is the strong possibility that the interpretation of experimental data (and indeed any other kind of data) can be significantly influenced by the theoretical choices already made, and these theories are articulated in language, in words.

This is not saying quite the same thing as the somewhat trite observation that data is always 'theory laden', for in our view the degree to which it might be so rather depends on what kind of data and what kind of theory one is talking about. The point is more specific – that any given set of findings can be described in more than one way, and the data which is used to support any perspective on choice (or behavioural psychological data in general) comes already laden with views about what 'choice', 'utility', 'rationality', and so on, might be. As a case in point, and as Dean points out: 'While neuroeconomic models aim to describe the process by which choices are made, in practice most retain the as if flavour familiar to economists that characterise many economic models . . . This is because most neuroeconomic models are couched in terms of variables that are latent, or unobservable – such as rewards, beliefs, utilities, and so on' (2013: 164–5).

Not all choices are to be understood as related to beliefs, nor all to rewards; the concept of utility is even more otiose. What is certain is that not all the choices people make can sensibly be said to occur in the brain. To be sure, the brain functions as people make choices. But some of the choices they make are essentially behaviours, to be understood by what the behaviours in question show. One's choice for a car is the car one chooses, not some brain state. Such choices are visible to others, in other words, and are not invisible, being inside the head – the home, so to speak, of the brain. One cannot find a car there, just as much as one cannot find a choice.

In that respect, neuroeconomics runs up against but does not resolve the very problem that led economists to attempt to expunge 'subjective' categories from their theoretical vocabulary in the first place, namely, that one can't identify people's beliefs, aspirations and the like independently of their behaviour but can only attribute these on the basis of that behaviour – what they do. The relationship between belief and action is presumed; it is not proven. As any good economist will admit, in many of their research inquiries, there aren't sufficient empirical bases for saying that people have this belief or find that satisfying, only to say that they are acting *as if they do*. For economists this is OK; for those claiming interest in motive and competence this is worrying. Given that some of the perspectives we are concerned with argue that their views can support policy-making about human happiness, this is even more worrying – since it isn't just the quality of science that is at issue. Neuroeconomists propose that they can do a better job than, say, welfare economists in deciding policies to maximise well-being – this has encouraged arguments which condemn the use of measures of economic prosperity, such as the total size of and rate of growth in gross domestic product, as indices of well-being. Neuroeconomics recommend the identification of better measures, ones identifying levels of happiness. If so, then we really need to be sure that the data upon which measures of 'hedonic' utility are based is accurate. We are some way off being sure of that, to say the least.

In any case, and to return to the previous chapter, economics is often said to involve 'methodological individualism', which entails supposing that all complex socio-economic patterns are the fairly direct product of aggregating individuals' actions. Descriptions of the features of markets are always, then, descriptions of what some connected assortment of individuals is doing. The methodological individualist doctrine insists that 'rational explanation' is quite distinct from 'psychological explanation', since it says little to nothing about psychological processing of individuals but operates by focusing on the relations of means-to-ends when viewed as an aggregate.

There is a basic principle about rationality here, but it is little more than assuming that persons respond appropriately to their situation (in the light of what the person wants to do). If one wants to buy something in a market that uses only cash, then one had better have money to hand over in order to pay for it. Given the forms in which situations are in effect socially defined, there is no need for an exploration of the individual's psychology. This provides one of the reasons why the standard economist's model of the 'economic agent' says so very little about that agent's motives and competence beyond the obvious – that they have motives and that they can be competent in achieving them.

A famous contribution to debates about economics' methods was written by Milton Friedman (1953). Though he gained notoriety in the public domain for recommending monetarist models to policy-makers, he also vehemently insisted that it didn't matter if economists' models were 'unrealistic' about how people make economic choices. In his view, all that matters is that economists' models enable them to make effective predictions about what the data shows. He certainly didn't suppose that the economist wrongly transfers properties attributed in the model to the people being modelled, but insisted that the economist's operation was really an 'instrumentalist' one (though there is controversy as to what kind of an instrumentalist Friedman actually was). In this view, the measure of models is their use as tools for generating effective predictions, ones which were applied in an *as if* way, treating people *as if they were* perfectly rational.

We don't say that Friedman's argument, though very influential, settled the matter. Methodologists still debate the ways in which their models are unrealistic, whether or not it is legitimate to use unrealistic models for the purpose of a science, and whether the kinds of unrealistic assumptions which are used are justifiable, or are at least harmless. It ought, also, to be clear that, where unrealistic assumptions are in play, it is not mandatory that they be applied. It is very often clear in the setting up of a model just how, in key respects, it is unrealistic. As we noted in the previous chapter, one version of perfect rationality involves the consumer being modelled, for instance, as having complete market information. Of course real people don't have that kind of knowledge, but the initial point of giving everyone perfect knowledge is a way of eliminating the need to try to deal, within the model, with a fact which is often plainly involved in markets – which is that information isn't evenly spread. *In the model* it is being assumed that differences in information make no difference to the transactions being modelled, the assumption being necessary because modellers are aware that, in real markets, it does make a difference.

Borges's fantasy (1998) of the map that achieved ultimate accuracy by being made the same size as the country being mapped could be understood as a satire on the idea that models should be thoroughly realistic – whereas their whole point is to make it easier to reason abstractly and generally about their elected phenomena. This reasoning is articulated in the ways models can be seen and altered and shaped. The phenomena in such models are not all and everything, from the brain to the pocket, from psychology to economics, but things focused on for a reason – such as addressing the ins and outs of the imagined object, the economy. They are focused on in a particular way that allows certain sorts of investigative operations. This ambition is in service of thinking analytically about the organisation of those phenomena. The ambition does not seek a kind of composite portrait of instances of those phenomena. As Don Ross (2002) argued, there is no compelling reason to assume that the stock model of the economic agent need be a model of a human individual at all. Ross objects that the neuroeconomists are preserving, not challenging, the fundamental supposition of standard economics. Neuroscientists, according to Ross, are generally, though not inevitably, supposing that the economic agent is identical with, and not just sometimes instantiated by, the individual human being, but this supposition is in fact at odds with the modelling practice of economics. Ross provocatively proposes that, if we treat people, animals, countries and institutions as equivalent examples of simple goal-directed and feedback-governed systems, then such problems disappear, but we end up with Borges's vision. Models that try to encompass everything come at a price. For their comprehensiveness will force them to strip important distinguishing properties from the entities thus captured. People and institutions and animals will become the same, since all they would be are shapes on a map; and all that the researcher could do is play with the shapes, wondering what the world would look like if the pieces were put together in a different way. This would be science fiction, not science. We are back to Brannigan's complaint, that there is too much theatre in the science of choice.

4

CHOICE IN CONTEXT

In the preceding two chapters we traced the gradual move from a 'classic' economic position to one which is predicated on some amalgam of economics and psychology, and a version of experimentalism in particular. We have seen similar assumptions about the animal in the foliage of disciplinary views, though we have (argumentatively) said that the animal itself may be better thought of as a construct of disciplinary perspectives than a creature constructed with evidence. We noted that the perspectives themselves have sought to address this lacuna by seeking improvements in their starting assumptions and in their data-gathering techniques; they have all wanted a more realistic animal in their sights, though each has different ways of achieving this. Even so, we saw that all of the perspectives continue to treat the creature as a unit, singular, autonomous, and hence the choices of the creature as individualised. Choice is not, in this view, a social matter. We saw, also, that understanding how 'context' might relate to decision-making is not a part of the remit of the perspectives we have looked at.

Nevertheless, and particularly in the psychological view, we have found perspectives which suggest that the various biases and heuristics constitutive of how the human mind works are defined, in part, by the sites through which the human travels. Place or context has some connection to the mind's work, to how reasoning unfolds. Various objections have been raised to this apparently commonsense notion – that one fits how one thinks to the circumstances at hand. One of these objections is that allowing context to affect choice is inconsistent with the notion that the individual decision-maker is autonomous. For it implies that understanding choice is not only about how the human chooses, since the agency of that choice is subject (somehow) to the constraints of place. One feels like saying that the seemingly reasonable assertion that place matters has thus quite profound implications for the perspectives we have been dealing with. For them, choice is always something that occurs in the head, in the brain. This is disregarding what that choice is about – choosing the sex of a child, choosing whether to eat fried locusts, or dog, for tea, and so on. But if choice is subject to place (context), then somehow that process of choosing escapes from where these disciplines have insisted choice occurs: in the human brain. Somehow choice moves to the world outside or, rather, combines the inner and the outer. This is an odd formulation of course; it seems peculiar to say that choice moves its dwelling place. But this is what some have begun to argue, even if it seems to contradict certain elemental and basic assumptions in economics, in psychology and in the marriage of the two, in behavioural economics. The case for 'distributed cognition' is to be found in this move – the notion that the mind is within the head and yet, somehow, outside.[1]

We won't consider this move here, since we are not interested in investigating where the mind might be – assuming that is a sensible question, which many would doubt. We are interested in the relationship between the mind's rational work and the norms that might govern or affect that reasoning. These norms are social in various respects. They can affect choice in diverse ways regardless of place, though sometimes place helps focus them in particular ways. We are also interested in the different ways in which confronting norms and place can be treated. One approach is to stick with the notion that the human is the autonomous reasoning agent, and to assume that each individual has to work their way *through* norms and context in ways that treat these as matters of 'uncertainty', where they are factors beyond the comprehension of the individual but which nevertheless have to be processed, factored in, by the autonomous mind. Another is to abandon the centrality of the individual and make the external factors, the social ones, the ultimate arbiter of choice. In this view, choice has well and truly left the head.

Our task in this chapter is to consider how various perspectives deal with these often intertwined and at times startling concerns. The perspectives we will consider include the classic economic one, with its notion of the decision-making human being optimising choice, as well as various types of sociology that build on the rational actor premise but which come to emphasise the social actor more. What we will see is that attempts to mediate between the mind as a rationality engine and the mind as constrained by circumstances and/or society end up pointing towards conclusions that can be somewhat contradictory. One such contradiction is the

---

[1] For a good summary of this view, see Clark (2003).

suggestion that rational goals get replaced by social goals, when these social goals are somehow defined as not being part of the mental machinery. Another muddle, following on from this, has to do with the starting assumption that the human acts rationally. That rationality must be redefined if what the individual reasons about is only partly what guides their actions. Other external facts do so as well. Does that mean that human reasoning is limited? Why call it rational then? Or is reason just fallible when confronted with social matters? Certainly we saw that behavioural economists like to assume that the mind is poor at its processing, but they came to that idea through comparing the mind's work with some variants of logic. Here we will see that it is social matters that make a 'rational fool' of the individual.

Limits of rationality

An initial way into the problem of context and the related notion of normativity is through the 'bounded rationality' hypothesis. We mentioned Gigerenzer (2007) in this regard, but the term is most often associated with Herbert Simon (1967, 1990). In this view, we should not treat rationality as a universal human capacity, one in which the 'laws' of reason are invariant, but instead see that principles of rationality vary according to the context or environment of choice. The rationality of the market place may not be at all the same as the rationality of, say, sexual behaviour. The norms governing what is a 'good decision' in one context are hardly the same as those in the other; they are bounded. Reason, in this view, is normative in the sense that it can be assessed as being done well or badly, but only with regard to circumstances to where it is done.

Psychological processes are implied in the bounded rationality view. The election of an optimum course of action might involve very complex calculations. Herbert Simon thought that the idea that ordinary people could make complex calculations in organising their daily affairs unrealistic. The human mind is not capable of processing complexities it occasionally confronts, he thought, and individuals don't possess sufficiently sound assumptions or evidence bases to navigate their way through these when they have to. More often they work with very uncertain knowledge about the circumstances at hand. They have to do this with their limited processing functions. Simon argued that, instead of 'optimising', people typically 'satisfice' (i.e., settle for, or are satisfied with, a sub-optimal solution).

Simon is thus continuing with the received notion of optimisation to which we alluded in chapter 2, but is treating it as motivational rather than as a default required to ground model-making. He is arguing that, for example, in contrast to the idea that business managers make decisions relative to the objective of relentlessly maximising profit, they do in fact have other priorities, other motives. As we remarked, they commonly aim for a good deal less than maximum possible profit, seeking only profit levels which are 'good enough' (e.g., will keep shareholders happy). In this way they 'satisfice' the desire for profit. 'Satisficing' means that decision-makers do not first identify all alternatives and then rank them; they review one possibility at a time until they find one that yields a return greater than some 'threshold' they have set themselves, and adopt that one. Theirs is a 'good enough' or heuristic strategy. The latter also implies that, along with these notions, the bounded rationality view introduces the idea that decision-making itself is an activity subject to its own cost–benefit calculations (i.e., measures of its self).

Now Simon had a somewhat cognitivist view of what 'context' might mean here and uses terms such as 'task environment'. Context is not a socially constructed or emergent phenomenon, say, nor one subject to rules of interpretation. It is, rather, determinable as if it were a representation in the mind. Simon only implies this; it is unclear whether this is precisely what this psychology implies. It is one thing to argue for a relationship between context and rationality and quite another to specify what that relationship consists of in terms of mental activities – models of reasoning, and so on. Sturm (2012) points out that such a relationship might have a number of different forms and that each has various implications. One such view holds that bounded rationality indicates a psychologically 'realistic' mental process, when realistic means not that some good representation of the external wold is created inside the mind but that the mind has tools for dealing with the world that are practical, capable of letting the brain process the world effectively. This is what is meant when, for example, Gigerenzer and others, following in Simon's footsteps, speak about 'fast and frugal heuristics' (cited ibid.). These heuristics look like statements about mental processes.

If it is these sorts of things that are implied in the psychology of bounded rationality perspective, then along with this goes the need for methods or techniques to understand what these heuristics and 'principles' are and how they function in different types of context. For Sturm, as for others, the role of psychological method in the determination of such questions is obvious – in their view, laboratory techniques and experiments provide access to that evidence. Note, however, that 'sound' judgement is at stake in such inquiries – not the sound judgement of the experimenter but that of the subjects studied. The notion of bounded rationality does not merely describe what kinds of rule might be in place when decisions are made in a certain context; it also implies that these rules, once identified, constitute the best way forward – that what people do is right. Judging this from the techniques of psychology is not at all an easy thing to do; some might even say that the experimental are not adroit at this at all. As we saw in the previous chapter, it really is very difficult and at times insensible to learn from the specifics of a test as regards the properties of the world at large. For one thing, there are problems of language which make the interpretation of experimental results very hard. As we saw, the logic of words has no 'time out', and so, when people are given instructions for experimental activities that are coached in words – and one would want to ask how else they might be given? – they listen to those words in real-world ways where the logic is subtle and most particularly intertwined with assumptions and consequences. They do not listen as if they were Turing machines treating the words as logical systems that have no reference to the world. Thus the problem is not that the experiment cannot be seen to be applicable to the real world, but that the real world stops the experiments being successful as experiments.

Proof of reasons

It should be clear, then, that the problem of defining rationality is, for bounded rationality theorists, at least in part an empirical matter. There is a need to investigate and describe how people go about their decision-making activities, observing how they reason about their circumstances. One wonders whether any psychology is required for this approach – certainly not the methods of that discipline if those methods are confined to the experimental. But, as we say, most advocates of this view tend to use psychological concepts to label context – task environment mentioned above being one. As they do so, they carry along the baggage of this view too. They retain the idea that one can contrast some perfect reasoning pattern with some practical and lesser form. Gigerenzer and Sturm, however, think that the utility thesis is useful: 'one can infer from empirical research what norms of rationality are best, as well as how human reasoning can be improved' (2012: 2).

One wants to ask where this ideal comes from. Besides, exactly why should it be assumed that rationality is the efficient selection of means towards given ends if those means–ends relationships differ from context to context? Surely there will be various rational-efficient approaches, not only one? It is never really explained in the bounded rationality literature why the acceptance of context doesn't bring into doubt the idea of a perfect rationality that transcends context. Forms of rationality that vary from context to context are all glossed as essentially the same (only situated). This way of thinking about rationality allows the incorporation of cultural values, emotions and other 'non-rational things' as affecting motivation while preserving a sense of rationality as somehow universal, above and beyond the specificities of the cultural here and now.

One might ask whether we have any evidence that this is so – that reasoning has universal forms, presumably echoing some psychological make-up that is fitted to context. Even if we did, Ross (forthcoming) points out that this might not matter from the view of, for example, economics. Though he agrees that economics should be 'decidable by empirical facts', he observes, in a way similar to Gul and Pesendorfer's argument in 'The case for mindless economics' (2005), that most economists are interested in markets rather than in individual decision-making as such. Where markets are bounded, he suggests, this is for reasons that have to do with institutions and not with psychological dispositions. If this is so, what is relevant empirical evidence for economics would not be psychological (or even neurological). Empirical studies of the psychology of bounded rationality would, in Ross's opinion, have only limited power to affect conventional economics, whatever benefits they might have for psychology.

The question then is who is the audience for bounded rationality theorists? Simon himself turned to the topic of management and business decision-making and hence a discipline that slips in between economics, psychology and sociology – namely, management science. This certainly seems to be the readership of Simon's *Administrative Behaviour* (1947) and March and Simon's *Organisations* (1958). But perhaps a more interesting possibility is alluded to in the title of a book he wrote much latter, *The Sciences of the Artificial* (1969). We shall explore this later on.

Types of reasons: commitment

This doesn't mean that economists other than Ross have failed to think about the question of context and, more generally, how reasoning might have shapes other than reflecting utility optimisation calculations. Many have sought to broaden what constitutes the basis of rationality. If Gary Becker attempts to expand the basic economic view of means–ends rationality to cover non-economic matters, as we can see in our discussion of *Accounting for Tastes* (1996), then Amartya Sen has sought, in *Choice, Welfare and Measurement* (1982), to bring into economic models of reasoning matters that do not just reflect the pursuit of self-interest. His solution to this, if solutions they are since they are much contested, also begs questions as to what proof of their existence and operational consequence might be.

Sen's criticism of rational choice is basically that explaining the kinds of choice we can and do make in practice, in everyday life, needs to rely on a great deal more than the motives of individuals. It may be that these can be understood from the rational choice view, but this is not enough, Sen argues; matters other than personal motives need to be factored in. In his view, the basic economic conception of welfare, as a case in point, is derived from assuming that people are essentially, even solely, motivated by self-interest. This neglects, Sen says, the extent to which individual choices involve and might be governed by other, less self-interested considerations. In a nutshell, he argues that people do (and, if they do not, then they ought to) incorporate information about the interests and needs of *others* in their choice-making deliberations. That they do so means that the basis of choice is thus to some degree social. The social includes the opportunities, freedoms, rights, duties and responsibilities of others and their intertwining of those considerations with one's own. The narrower version of rationality excludes such social matters and thereby, so Sen argues, makes 'rational fools' of us. In fact, 'fools' is a bit kind – as he sees it, the narrow view in effect tells us that we are subject to economic determinations of what to calculate as best and nothing else. In Sen's view, this is hardly to reason at all in a human way but to act merely like a calculating machine.

To illustrate: if our concern is – for the sake of argument – poverty, then we need to take into account many more factors than simply income and capital to define and explain it. According to Sen, we need to factor in such elements as gender, health, age, location and social capital, as well as inequalities of information. Being poor is not simply a matter of money (or a lack of it) in the pocket. Rather, one needs to understand how social factors as well as monetary ones are oriented and come to be relevant to those in situations of poverty. Only thus can we explain poverty. There is a need to understand, especially, the 'capabilities' of human beings. These cannot be understood entirely at an individual level or in relation to the processing of utility maximisation; capabilities are more than this – at once something to do both with people themselves and with their relations with others – the corporate body, if you like.

In essence, Sen argues that there are (at least) three types of motivation encapsulated in people's capabilities: their narrow self-interest, their capacity for sympathy, and their commitment to others. The first might be thought of as the 'pure' type of rational choice; the second as encompassing some relationship between personal well-being and that of others; the third to do with relations – though it is not very clear or precise what is meant. As Peter and Schmid put it, commitment

> refers to a kind of behavior which is motivationally unrelated to the agent's [own] welfare, however broadly conceived. The clearest case of action from commitment is when one feels compelled to intervene in a certain matter, even if doing so leaves one worse off. In other cases of committed action, there might not be a negative impact on one's welfare. What matters, however, is that increasing one's welfare is not the central motive. (2007b: 4)

Commitment and the welfare of others are then somewhat muddled – the meaning of the word 'commitment' being too loose perhaps. We shall come back to say more about this later. In particular, the issue we will pick on is how, and even if, 'commitment' can become a 'reason' for action while being something other than 'rational'. For Sen seems to want to treat commitments as of another order, bound to when one seeks to describe social action from the outside, as it were, from a theoretical point of view and not, so to speak, from the actor's point of view. His is a perspective that emphasises social values, even if those values might contradict the achievement of an individual's utility maximisation.

In the meantime, it is hardly surprising that Sen believes that the pursuit of self-interest by each individual may not be the best way to improve individual or aggregate well-being. His is an argument for employing collective resources to pursue individual welfare independently of individual self-interest. If we think of human welfare as individuals being in the best condition they could be, then individuals are not necessarily the best judges of what that state might be, and in any case individual pursuit of self-interest will not deliver that best state, since individuals are not necessarily aware of what the best state could be. Hence, rather than measure individual welfare against what the chooser thinks would be most satisfying, we might measure it against the capabilities that individuals have, what is possible for those individuals – i.e., what they are capable of as human beings. This would entail, also, an interest in what they are capable of as social entities, as things that can create collective goods.

This is one of the reasons why Sen's view is sometimes called the capabilities approach. What someone is capable of being doesn't depend just on their personal preferences, because individuals are capable of being things other than what they happen to be. What they could be instead can perhaps be determined by comparison with what other people in different circumstances are, since in some respects what they are shows something that other people can also be. It might also illuminate the conditions that enable them to be something else; what they could be might also be related to what combinations of people can do. A poor and uneducated farmer may pursue his self-interests as he sees them as effectively as it is possible to do, but in the end he will remain a poor farmer. Nevertheless, a poor farmer has the capability of becoming a much more prosperous farmer if, for example, supplied by other farmers and producers with fertilisers and the skills required to use them – when others' capacities guide his own.

Whether people's welfare is optimised in terms of their individual self-interests, in other words, doesn't answer the question of whether they are capable of achieving a higher level of welfare if the conditions under which they make their choices are changed to be more social. Thus, Sen has argued against the idea that famines are the fault of those who are subject to them but are a result of the conditions which affect the distribution of farming support and food internationally.

A sociology of rational action

There is considerable similarity between 'capability', as Sen develops it, and the idea of 'social capital' that has become fashionable in sociology (see Lollo, 2011, 2012). Indeed, it is not unreasonable to say that Sen's arguments constitute a sociological 'turn' in economics which leads us naturally into a consideration of various apparently similar views in sociology, and it is to those we now address ourselves. The 'turn' has to do with the recurrent objections to classical economic ideas from within sociology itself, though the nuances of these complaints are quite particular. For these emphasise what is seen as the excessively individualistic nature of the economic view. The focus on the decision-making capacities of particular individuals doesn't sit well with sociologists, who feel that this individualism can't take sufficient or systematic account of the extent to which social life is a collective affair. This isn't quite the same as Sen's notion of capability, which is still essentially to do with the individual – it is the individual's capabilities that are at issue in Sen's view, even if these capabilities are social in nature.

Even though there is this fundamental divide between the sociological and the economic vision, there have been repeated attempts to recast sociology by following the example of economics in building something like rational choice modelling into the discipline. As we shall see, these attempts find themselves in difficulties, as they discover that the compromises they end up making lead to ambiguity about the basic notion of rational action and the centrality of the individual as a rational choice-making machine. This hasn't stopped sociologists offering insights on the topic of choice, but it does mean that this discipline, like the others we have been looking at, has to work hard to define what it thinks choice is and what is particular – and valuable – about the view it offers on the subject. What one finds is that these efforts, particularly from the orthodox position in sociology, form an echo of Sen's notion of commitment, though for them the label is social capital. This is some kind of stuff that demonstrably affects individual actions through linking those actions to the corporate body of society, of others with whom individuals necessarily and naturally co-exist. Social capital is the logical outcome of the sociological view that people are essentially collaborative, or at least cultivated to be so. But this outcome sits uneasily with the basic starting place of the rational choice model. A concern with social capital can end up with some sociological perspectives taking the individual out of the situation altogether, making the actors in the view hardly decision-makers at all, merely servants of social process. To this extent the applicability of the rational choice theory is reduced, if not lost altogether, and changed into something else. Social action is hardly rational action in this view; it's society's rational needs that dictate what people do, and thus this kind of rationality makes fools or dupes of people themselves, since their reasons don't matter. They are of no consequence.

Reasons in action

One of the key dimensions of differences in the social sciences, we have been arguing, concerns what form reasons might have and, relatedly, the premises that follow on from taking these forms as starting places. We have said that much of these arguments have to do, often unwittingly, with the language of the disciplines. These differences don't really entail describing different reasons, that is to say, but start from differences about what kind of reasons count in analysis and how these are described. And reasons are always described – told and evoked in words which have both their everyday usage and their disciplinary baggage. One of the difficulties here is that these words are sometimes treated as merely vehicles for the evidence and not as part of the evidence all along. When one uses the word 'irrational', one is defining it as opposite; when one describes the bounds of reason, one implies there is some other kind of reason – pure, unsullied by context. But how this is so is related to the contrast that the disciplines themselves make: to be irrational in economics is to miscalculate utility optimisation; in psychology, a person is irrational because of limitations in their mental apparatus; and so on. There is another important aspect of language, too. Our language articulates the concepts we live by, what we think is the measure of things – what is good and bad, what looks like a 'capability' that is 'human' rather than 'merely' economic. We shall keep coming back to this topic later on in the book. For now, we want to note that there has always been an especial tension between economics and sociology in terms of language and the things that are labelled as evidence.

Emile Durkheim famously argued, in *The Rules of Sociological Method* ([1895] 1982), that sociology needed to be a separate discipline from psychology and economics. Whereas we have seen how psychologists have sought to make the psychological the premise of all choice-making decisions, Durkheim argued that no society is possible without a normative order, a set of shared moral conceptions – in the jargon, *social facts*. These are quite different from psychological phenomena (and even economic ones), and consequently what gets treated as reasons for choice, even what choice consists in, is different in sociological, psychological and economic views.

Along with Marx, Durkheim felt that the study of 'society' had to be more than the study of individuals; it had to look at the social fabric between these individuals. Sociology has tended towards this view ever since. It is not individual's notions of the choices they face that have been central to sociology, but something else: facts produced through their interaction with others, say, facts that aren't processed individually but are confronted by the social body itself. Durkheim's *The Rules of Sociological Method* was all about what these sorts of phenomena might be. In the effort to demarcate social facts, the individual was to some extent left out of the equation. Somehow individual choice became subsumed in institutional ones. No wonder, then, that some thought the implication of Durkheim's later book *The Elementary Forms of the Religious Life* ([1912] 2001) is that society worships itself. There was no role for the individual in this view; their autonomy as creatures who could rationally govern their affairs is sacrificed on the altar of the greater good – society itself.

Not all sociologists took such an anti-individualist view. Indeed, some others have been especially interested in seeking ways of solving the riddle of combining individual and social reasons. Max Weber, in particular, wanted to place the individual, and individual reasoning about social facts, at the heart of inquiries, just as much as he wanted to include social facts – though in his case he coined phrases such as 'institutional facts' to label whatever these might be.

In Weber's view, there are various forms of 'rationality' underpinning individual behaviour. While he is sometimes described as a 'methodological individualist', more importantly for our discussions, some (see, e.g., Coleman, 1986; Kiser and Hechter, 1998; Norkus, 2000) have suggested that he adopted at least one version of rational choice theory in his answer to what and how people choose: they weigh up their means–ends goals and choose accordingly. But he is quite distinct insofar as he treated the concept of rationality as an intrinsic tool to the analytical task: in his view, not only does one seek evidence of rationality in people's actions, but the analyst uses their own measures of what is rational to see what form the observed rationality really has. Weber's (1922) definition of sociology thus combines the use of a notion of rationality as a tool to describe social action and a tool for allowing understanding of that action.

We mentioned at the outset of the book that rational action is typically transparent to our everyday understanding – a rational connection is a logical one, one that it would make sense to perform. Accordingly, such actions are rational from the point of view of the observer. It is actions which depart from the rational course that aren't transparent to understanding and therefore can call out for explanation. As Weber saw it, building a rational model of some course of action could provide a yardstick that could be compared to – more interestingly, contrasted with – reality (i.e., observed behaviour). The behaviours in question are both those that make sense and, more interestingly, those that require analysis – ones where the reasons behind that action need to be 'uncovered'. Rationality here is a construct, in Weber's view; it is an 'ideal type' which can be compared to actual, identifiable social contexts and thus be a tool in explication and analysis.

Hence, if a military strategy can be identified as the most rational one to follow in a battle, then it is plain why someone would choose it – it would be the way of winning the battle. This is easy to understand. However, what is less easy to comprehend is why military leaders do not always follow the rational course and why as a result they end up, sometimes, losing battles – it being irrational to do so. In Weber's view, having an idea of what that rational course might be enables the researcher to focus on identifying those aspects of the battle that might obstruct a leader's capacity to recognise the optimally effective course or prevent him following it through. Seeing what is ideal can help one see what constraints on reasoning are in play, to put it in behavioural economics terms.

Weber and rational action theory

When put thus, Weber's view does sound remarkably like the rational actor view used commonly in economics, albeit applied in expressly social contexts and with the added component of rationality being a tool of understanding. Weber's emphasis on reason and means–ends decision-making is quite consistent with economic models. There are distinctions, however, not least in the degree to which rationality can be thought of as a universal principle. Weber thought that people's capacity to act in a rational fashion depended on social conditions, on there being the means for effective means–end reasoning available in the culture, and that this would have particular forms. In some sense this implies a kind of relativism, though it would be better to say that Weber assumed that objective measures of what is right reason are always and inextricably tied to social conditions. It makes no sense to say that people in, for example, medieval England were less rational than people in that country today; the real question is how rational people were, given what was known about what was rational then.

This can be illustrated by Weber's thinking about bureaucracy. Weber thought of bureaucracy as a decision machine, an apparatus that concentrated administrative experience and expertise in an effective and efficiently arranged structure. The question for him was how to come up with a technique to understand how well this machine worked and to help specify its properties. He proposed an 'ideal type' (a model) of bureaucracy as a methodological tool for the investigation of real administrations. This was not a means to define perfection that the real world ought to seek. It was a tool for the researcher trying to uncover real reasoning in administrative contexts. Building an ideal type of bureaucracy requires a researcher to work out what would be the optimum – logically consistent – way of ensuring that concentrated expertise could be most effectively applied to that type of institution's main task – undertaking administrative decisions.

Through his ideal-type construct, Weber was able to come up with what he thought were key features necessary for such an organisation to make good its work. Staff within it would need to be specialists, for example, and, hence, appointment to the bureaucracy would need to be on the basis of qualification. Staff would also need to be paid for, and solely employed by, the bureaucracy. In this way they would not be open to suborning (and hence corrupting) by others for income. Bureaucrats made good decisions because they were expert and independent, in other words. A by-product of this would be that people at large could depend upon and learn from the output of bureaucratic decision-making for their own decision-making. Thus the social context in which bureaucracies developed would affect the character of individual reasoning, even in matters not to do with administration.

Weber did not imagine that all bureaucracies, all bureaucrats or all societies in which bureaucracies operated resembled his fully worked-out picture, because this is not the case – it is too ideal. Nor did he think all reasoning by all people in societies in which bureaucracies flourished would be infused by bureaucratic rationalities. His view is that the model's primary role is to organise a researcher's thoughts, to let them focus on the question as to why some actual bureaucracy didn't or couldn't take measures to secure the independence of its employees from external dependence, for example, and how this form of corruption might infect the quality of reasoning elsewhere in society. Weber was not concerned simply with reasons in the abstract, then. He wanted to capture and understand the reasons that were abided by, avowed if you like, both by bureaucrats, say, and by others outside such organisational structures, and he offered a technique – the ideal-type method – to get to that understanding.

Superficially, then, Weber and the rational actor economics we have been dealing with have something in common: some notion of efficient thought. But there is an important difference, and there are two aspects to this. The first we have explained already, but it is worth restating. If we have seen how behavioural economists think of human reasoning as somehow an impoverished form of logical thought, and if some economists like Sen think that reasoning is a combination of a desire for optimising personal need with some kind of social needs (manifesting also some 'capacities' that merge and reflect the individual and the social), Weber treated reasons as causes of action, *whatever those reasons were*. The technical problem for sociology was to understand both what they were and how they were interpreted by those who acted according to them. Studying the reasons people had, in the way Weber described (through tools that allowed reasoning forms to be understood), could be the basis for a particular science: 'a science concerning itself with the interpretive understanding of social action and thereby with a causal explanation of its course and consequences' (Weber, 1922: 4).[2]

These reasons are quite unlike those of concern to the economic rational choice approach. The key difference, it seems to us, is Weber's concern for the reasons that people themselves have. As Norkus puts it, 'The interpretive understanding of a social action can be identified with the reconstruction of a subjective definition of the situation' (2000: 261). Weber's view does not rely on revealed preferences. He does not seek to define what goes on inside people's heads simply by looking at what they do and imputing what goes on. He seeks to define that internal reality as it is – as if it were not hidden because it is subjective. This is quite a different claim from any of the other approaches we have looked at before – not just the economics one but the psychological one too.

The French sociologist Raymond Boudon explains why. In *The Logic of Social Action* (1981) he shows that we can only define subjective rationality ostensively (i.e., that when we say 'X had good reasons for doing Y, because . . .') if we have adequately provided some description of the beliefs and motivations in question. Boudon argues that we cannot expect realistically rational individuals to have adequate (or perfect) knowledge of social situations in the real

---

[2] There is one further caveat, and this points towards a delicate problem that Weber elided in his work. For though he sought causal accounts of human action, and though the causes he sought were reasons – not psychological mechanisms, say, or the outcomes of the market – he still accepted that individuals have to choose the reasons they act on. Having chosen, they are then caused to act in accordance with those reasons. Is choice then caused? Weber answered the question only by gently coaxing out ways of avoiding it. His most famous study, *The Protestant Ethic and the Spirit of Capitalism* (1904–5), argued that there was a connection between variants of Protestantism and the moral codes of capitalistic enterprise. He explained that certain individuals came to see that saving and investing capital could be a means to demonstrate their status in God's eyes, in particular as ones who were predestined for salvation. But this connection was not causal in the first place; there was an affinity that was identified by certain individuals who elected to make the connection. Weber claimed that his empirical research showed that these individuals had a predisposition for this connection, that they were sensible to the possibility of it. Because of this they made the choice they did. But this is not exactly a causal connection – hence the centrality of the phrase 'elective affinity' in the book. His analysis showed the affinity, but it could not assert the election. The first act of choice, if you like, was to see the affinity between the world of God and the world of the market. The choice itself was to elect to bring them together, to make God's work through industry, but that was a human choice, an individual choice, what they elected to do.

world, and so their 'rational' behaviour can only be understood in terms of 'good reasons' – as if their reasons were a form of bounded rationality. But Boudon's point is not to suggest this – that reasoning is constrained. It is rather that the capacity to provide ostensive accounts of others' reasoning is not a reflection of, say, logical calculation of situated reasoning (namely the behavioural economists) or some other notion of psychological machinery (and one thinks here of the social psychological experiments we considered in the previous chapter); it is the much more profound assertion that this presupposes a *degree of intersubjectivity* – that one person's reasons are available to another. This is quite a different perspective than any we have dealt with so far and alludes to our suggestion that language articulates the everyday concepts within which we live. We mentioned this earlier, and it will become important later on in the book.

Types of reasons in contemporary sociology

For now, we are noting some subtleties and unique aspects to Weber's view while also recognising that his concern for 'reasons' has allowed some of the basic notions of rational action theory to enter into sociological thinking. While Weber might have been keen to assert the distinctiveness of the sociological view, as did his great French rival Durkheim, the topics on which he focused have allowed this distinction to blur. Rational action-type accounts have been a component of sociology for a long time and have often invoked Weber – even when one would think the distance between Weber and such accounts is too great.[3]

Perhaps the best-known contemporary sociologist who adopts a fully blown rational action perspective is James Coleman. The most important statement of his approach is to be found in his *Foundations of Social Theory* (1990). In this, Coleman tries to link many, if not all, of sociology's traditional interests in 'social facts' to rational choice. He is convinced that rational choice theory can solve many sociological questions, though that does not mean questions about individual choice. Coleman has no interest in the individual. His primary field of empirical research is education, and he uses his rational choice notions to account for why school funding makes little difference to educational achievement. In his view, general social background does, as does the 'quality' of schools and teachers.

---

[3] Rational choice theory has been incorporated into Marxism as well, for example. See Elster (1985, 2000). See also Wright (1985).

Coleman has been influential in more than this respect – not only for bringing economic forms of reasoning into sociology. As it happens, he was also a pioneer of mathematical modelling and one of the first sociologists to use the term 'social capital' – something that we have seen has also been important in economics, even if economists don't use the term. But there is an important distinction between Coleman and Weber we ought to note. Coleman abandons altogether one of Weber's basic premises – a concern with the subjective experience, and, as we say, the connection between fields of understanding and the reasons that cause actions. What particular teachers or students elect to choose is somewhat orthogonal to his analysis of educational achievement, for example.

For the set of phenomena to be explained by the perspective is the behaviour of social systems (large and small) and not the behaviour of individuals (see also Coleman and Fararo, 1992). Though the behaviour of actors in the system is required, all that this involves is a theory of transitions between the levels of the social system behaviour and the level of behaviour of individuals. This is mostly treated as a macro–micro connection. Some psychological theory is required too, to account for the wellsprings of individual action, but little attention is given to this by Coleman. In these respects, the difference from Weber's view is made all the clearer: in Coleman's view, individuals are effectively constrained.

Whatever its premises, some commentators view the approach of Coleman and Fararo as far from mature. Some view it as effectively a form of empiricism – large data-sets are used, but few or no elaborate causal models seem to exist or are being developed through the data; it ends up being merely an approach to finding statistical regularity: 'Coleman uses simple empirical methods to tell simple causal stories and does not develop elaborate causal empirical models' (Heckman and Neal, 1996: 107). Of course, the use of large data-sets requires a sophisticated application of statistics. We remarked in the previous chapter that this sophistication is absent more than it should be. Smith (1972), for a further example pertinent to Coleman's topics, pointed out that some simple coding errors led to an exaggeration of peer effects on educational attainment in Coleman's work.[4]

Large data-sets have also been a central concern for another major advocate of sociological rational choice, John Goldthorpe

---

[4] This might be true, but, regardless, variants of sociological rational choice, and especially Coleman's work, have been used extensively for policy-related research in the UK and elsewhere. One such area which has a resonance with contemporary work around the Web is research into 'collective behaviour'. See Zablocki (1996).

(Goldthorpe, 1996a, 1996b,1998), who points to several different kinds of rational choice notions that we covered in previous
chapters – strong, weak or situational. Goldthorpe wants to defend
a 'weak' rather than a 'strong' version and isn't too interested in
the situational. Strong rational choice theory would suggest that
people typically make choices based on self-interest, but there are
complexities here that are not always well understood, he argues.
Not least, Goldthorpe insists, people can only act 'rationally' if they
have good knowledge of the conditions in which their decisions are
made. In real life, this is far from the case. This means that it is actually very difficult to provide any measurements as to whether people
are actually behaving 'rationally' or not; what one can say is that
they act rationally given the circumstances.

Even so, and distinctions between the types notwithstanding,
Goldthorpe is a defender of 'rational choice theory', since he is
convinced the perspective fits quantitative data perfectly. Large
scale data-sets 'need it' as explanation, in his view. It provides the
theoretical means to move from correlation to cause. It works, he
argues, better than 'value-based' approaches to social life because
it is evidence based and so identifies 'real causes', while value-based
approaches are not always evidential (this has been challenged,
for instance, by Edling, 2000). Partly because of these claims,
Goldthorpe's work has proved quite influential. It has arguably
reinvigorated statistical, large data-set methods in sociology and
generated considerable research in many areas.[5]

Goldthorpe is convinced that combining rational choice (or
action theory, his preferred term) and large-scale data-sets enables
a move from correlation to cause and thus also allows some knowledge of the reasons that people themselves abide by, the reasons
that result in their behaviours. This seems implausible, however.
Certainly, the economic view of rational choice, which as we have
seen is predicated on 'revealed preference', has nothing to say about
the 'subjective interpretation of action', of the individual's point of
view. It does not seek to do so because it does not need to. Its explanation is not about that phenomenon – the reasons people have are
out of bounds. It is about reason when seen from the outside, as it
were, when society is the object of the disciplinary imagination, not
an individual person's point of view or the reasons that guide their

---

[5] These include social mobility (Breen, 1999; Jonsson, 1999; Morgan, 2002), educational inequality (see, e.g., Breen and Goldthorpe, 1997), the sociology of religion
(see, e.g., Finke and Stark, 1992; Stark and Finke, 2000) and even criminology (see,
e.g., Becker, 1968; Clarke and Felson, 1993; Chainey and Ratcliffe, 2005; Cohen and
Felson, 1979).

action. We think that the same holds true for Goldthorpe, even though he wants to claim otherwise.

Disciplining reasons

There are some interesting questions here. We certainly agree that both Coleman and Goldthorpe are very ambitious, seeking to answer questions that seem enormously large – such as why collective action happens. The 'economic version' of rational choice theory seems to label a confined set of topics and by dint of that would appear to exclude some other topics – and yet both proponents of the view in sociology we have mentioned claim it can answer almost all questions. We saw in chapter 2 that economists are very keen to discipline their inquiries, to make it clear what they can and cannot answer, to exclude some matters from inquiry that their techniques need to take as assumptions – such as how or why individuals reason. But what one sees in sociological takes on rational choice is something of the reverse: a lack of discipline.

This somewhat 'greedy' theorizing may be why another rational choice theorist in sociology, Jon Elster, has moved further and further away from rational choice over his career, although he has done much work in spelling out and applying the logic of rational choice for sociological topics. In his earlier work, he tried to show how 'preference formation' underpinned our rational choices. Marxist accounts were, he argued, made plausible by the rational choice view. Class formations identified in this view have rationalities, he claims, and the different attitudes of different classes relate to their different types of knowledge. This is a weak version of rationality which holds that different classes have different ideologies – or, rather, different relations to ideas. The dominant class can prevent the subordinate class from acquiring knowledge about the true form of class relations, for example. The rational choices of each class are thus constrained, their rationality being weak; but the overall outcome of the interplay of these rationalities is a society ordered and understandable through rational actor theory – where the actors in question end up being social classes with various degrees of knowledge.

That may be so, but Elster creates a problem for himself. For he thinks that 'pure' economic or psychologically founded rational choice thinking does not encompass the 'felt circumstances' of everyday life. Part of his research has entailed trying to understand subjective rationality in ways that will allow him to incorporate that rationality into his larger models, models that focus on group rationalities, or the rationalities of the interplay between groups – classes, in other words. To achieve this, Elster has to weaken the notion of rational choice that underscores his view. He does so by allowing the concept to be multiple things at once:

> The statement that people behave rationally is partly constitutive, partly methodological, partly substantive. It is constitutive in the sense that human beings are characterized by the desire to behave rationally. It is methodological in the sense that we have to assume that other people are by and large rational if we are to make sense of what they say and do. And it is substantive in the sense that on any given occasion, the assumption of rationality is open to empirical confirmation or disconfirmation. (Elster, 2000: 24–5)

One will recall that economists don't worry too much about whether some individual behaves rationally or not. Indeed, though they start their inquiries from the premise of rational choice, they are actually interested in how rationality is manifest in behavioural outcomes, in revealed preferences. Whether those revealed preferences tell us the real reasons why people act doesn't really matter to them. The felt life, what people themselves think and reason about, is of no matter. Similarly with psychology, the subjective experiences of individuals, what they think are the reasons for their actions, are to be replaced by what the scientific method uncovers as the real reasons. And yet Elster wants to incorporate the 'felt' life. This seems to be missing the point, which is that the rational choice allows the analyst to create a perspective that bypasses the need to concern itself with what people think – this is not a problem, then, but can be seen as a virtue. It allows the construction of an analytic point of view.

In sociology, this is not new at all. For example, long before Elster, Goldthorpe or Coleman wrote, there was a flourishing sociology that had very little interest in the felt life but which sought focus on the rational properties of action.

George Homans, in *Social Behavior* (1961), suggested that human behaviour could more or less always be understood as rational but required a particular understanding of goals and means for sociology. Homans subscribed to a deductivist position – human behaviour could be logically derived from the general principles governing all animal behaviour. These were basically the principles from Skinner's behaviourist psychology, which treated behaviour as learned patterns induced by rewards and punishments. In Homans's view, these could build up into general macro-level statements about social groups and institutions – and, as this happened, a move from the psychology of Skinner to a true sociological view could appear.

Humans are motivated by a much wider range of goals than most animals, Homans argued. They seek approval and money, whereas pigeons are interested only in food. Rewards and punishments may be different from species to species, but the mechanisms involved (of repeating those patterns of behaviour which have been rewarded in the past) are the same. Homans connected this individualistic psychology to the social by extending the range of 'rewards' beyond the material ones (such as food) which would suffice for rats and pigeons and held that the approval of others is a fundamental human reward. Approval is a 'generalised reinforcer' that can bolster the repeat performance of a wide variety of specific activities. Because of its generalised character, Homans saw approval as directly parallel to money. Both money and approval are general means of exchange in social interaction, with money playing this role in economic relations and approval in social ones. Thus, social relations can be conceived as analogous to economic relations in being exchanges (of approval in response to performances), with the achievement of some gain in approval (a kind of 'profit') being the driver of action and interaction.

Another sociologist, Peter Blau, saw an opportunity to dispense with Homans's behaviourism altogether and elaborated a view of social action modelled more closely on economic exchange – and hence elaborating a version of rational action that was even more sociological in bent. In his *Exchange and Power in Social Life* (1964), he argued that reciprocity was the key to human interaction. Evidently, the motive for any social act – i.e., an act addressed to another person – if one subscribes to a view of rational self-interest, can only be that one expects a return response at least equal to the cost of the initial act. Regardless of whether Blau is as reductionist as Homans (see Fine, 2000: 68–70), the resulting perspective, *exchange theory*, is largely predicated on the view that human networks/communities are aggregates of the dyad – behaviours between pairs of individuals. In this respect there is divergence between the starting premises of economic rational action models and this sociological view. Where rational choice implicates choices in a market, exchange theory relates it to interactions with other individuals. The point here is that whatever goals one has can only be achieved through interaction with other people, and thus achieving those goals will depend largely on what other people do. This is the basis, for instance, of Thibaut and Kelley's (1959) notion of 'behavioural sequences'.

Stretching the scope of reasons

The logic of using the rational choice perspective in sociology is then to come to a view where the reasons for actions are derived in large part from social considerations; it is social or cultural capital, whatever that might be, that frames or causes the choices that people make. As a concern for this develops, so a concern for and even a sensitivity to the reasons that people themselves avow abates – the reasons they state may not be the same as the reasons ascertained by analysis of social capital, for example. For rational choice-minded sociologists, then, the central problem is how their starting premise, that action is rational, can be compatible with what they take to be the phenomenon central to their own field: namely, the extent to which social life is a matter of collective behaviour and where this implies the possibility that the individual might conflict with the social and where the individual may not be aware of all aspects of social considerations anyway – or even any of them.

Various attempts to navigate through this apparent impasse have been proposed. Pierre Bourdieu, especially in his 'Forms of capital' (1986), argued that social capital is to be understood not only as contributory to individual betterment but also as a means by which successful individuals can maintain their advantages. In this view, social capital is also divisive capital insofar as individuals and their classes appropriate it for their own ends. The development (or creation) of social capital is seen as something that is (mainly) intentional or strategic.

Thus, Sabel (1994) argues that social capital is a result of actors committing themselves to ongoing negotiations based on shared understanding of common goals. Hechter (1987) similarly sees group solidarity as being a function of various stages, which include the devising of rules and procedures, which get institutionalised over time, internalising rules and procedures, adjustment to the expectations of others, and so on. Members moderate their behaviour so that these correspond to the expectations others have. There is a clear bias towards seeing these collectivities as being involved in a quite conscious process of defining and pursuing goals and means. Albee and Boyd (1997), for instance, characterise this in terms of community development. This brings to mind Bourdieu again: 'the aggregate of the actual or potential resources which are linked to possession of a durable network of more or less institutionalized relationships of mutual acquaintance or recognition' (Bourdieu 1986: 248; 1980).

The long and short of it is that the notion of social capital, though of recent provenance in sociology, in fact has its echoes in the ideas of normative cohesion to be found in the starting moments of the discipline, above all in Durkheim and his *Elementary Forms of the Religious Life* ([1912] 2001). In this view, sociology does not privilege reason and rationality but emphasises social reasoning, whatever that might be – even if that reasoning is to be understood as a function of social systems, of mechanisms of economic exchange, say, or in the management of power through affiliation and obligation. The trouble with this view is how to fit these concerns with the felt life of individuals – to reconcile, if you like, an interest in reasons that people don't have but which society does, and seeing how they fit together. The solution is to say that social reasons are individual reasons, that individual reasons are also social. This is not such an easy stance to preserve, however, and doing so can come at the cost of letting the social view alone be the explanatory vehicle. When this view is unsullied by considerations of the subjective, it is clear that doing so does not produce a model that can explain all the reasons that can be said to account for human choice, but it does produce views that can characterise some of them, especially those that are seen from afar, when society itself is the imagined object, not the inner workings of the human mind. Hence the value of the exchange theory model, hence the value of various forms of class theory, hence the value even of analyses that show what might be the reasons that educational impact is not what it might be.

Social capital and economics

The aetiology of sociology aside, the development of the concept of social capital has allowed it to become a phenomenon that might be treated as if it were an economic good. According to Coleman, for example: 'We make a mistake both in society and sociology. The mistake is simple and correctable: we fail to recognize that the social capital on which primordial social organization depends is vanishing; we fail to recognize that societies of the future will be constructed, and that we should direct our attention to designing those social structures' (Coleman, cited in Fine, 2001: 75). This is also the rub of Putnam's famous book *Bowling Alone* (2000). Once social capital is viewed in this way, it can be seen just as much as an object of economic inquiry as of sociological inquiry (indeed, who was first rather depends on whether one sees the likes of Coleman as an economic sociologist or as an economist with an interest in the social). And it has proliferated as an explanatory vehicle. World Bank economists Narayan-Parker and Pritchett (1997), for instance, evoke social capital in their analysis of the economic life of Tanzania. In their view, it works in five distinct ways: in improving society's capacity to monitor government; by increasing capacity for problem-solving; through facilitating innovation diffusion; in reducing information imperfection; and in increasing informal safety nets.

In other words, social capital is a term that points towards matters that economists from Sen onwards have themselves recognised as important. The move has been to make self-interest seem less naked, so that which is sought entirely independently by one individual, and wholly at the expense of other individuals, can now be thought of instead as something which involves some acknowledgement of commitments to others. This is allowing us to return to one of the lacunae in Sen's work – just what is a commitment? It is some form of social capital, presumably, but what exactly and what consequences does it have for the basic model of decision-making in economics?

In our view, questions such as this expose the relationship between the empirical and the conceptual. Referring to Fine's position on Putnam (2001: 83–96), at least in respect of his critique of rational choice theory and the notion of social capital, one cannot begin an empirical examination of the relationship between social capital and any feature of social life before one has carefully interrogated the foundations of the concepts one wishes to examine; these are built in the language of the disciplines themselves just as much as they are intertwined with everyday concepts. We saw in earlier chapters that attempts to use rational choice theory and to develop variants that exploited experimental techniques and psychological emphasis were all bound up with notions of science and objectivity, for example. A feature of Sen's thoughts worth recalling here lies in the tension between economics as a 'science', one which broadly accepts positivistic notions of objectivity, and the notion of normativity or 'value'.

Mainstream economics has distanced itself from any consideration of normative issues and has, at most, trod very gingerly into the 'cultural' arena where normativity of some kind would be central. The tension is evident. If human beings are self-interested utility maximisers, then values and sentiment are not important to our understanding of their behaviour except insofar as they are presupposed in the ways in which options are identified and characterised. Waking up in the night and wanting to snack can be characterised as having a preference for protein, and one of the options available to the snacker is to go down to the kitchen. To proceed to the baby's bedroom would be another option; babies are a perfectly good source of protein, after all. This isn't really an option, though, since for most of us it is unthinkable to save on the price of a packet of crisps by eating our offspring – the same argument applies to the guest room, by the way. If, in the case of the baby, one takes into account the savings on all those things required specifically for the baby's use and in the short run at that, the proposition begins to seem more attractive. Sen argues that there is an almost complete absence of interest in ethics in economics despite any empirical justification for doing so (i.e., ignoring this topic). It is not that ethics are merely guides to how people might act; they are evidently embedded in acts of all kinds.

There have been attempts to reconcile this indifference with this fact – that moralities of various kinds are constitutive of action, rational action included. One is to argue (in the manner of John Rawls in his magnum opus *A Theory of Justice*, 1971) that morality leads to mutual benefit. Everyone gains. A second way to avoid the apparent absence and redefine the notion of 'goal' is to include values. This, for instance, is the strategy adopted by economists such as Kenneth Arrow (1951).

A more recent attempt, and one which has a direct relationship to the online world, as we shall see, is to extend goal orientation into new aspects of normativity. These basically include notions of trust and reputation (see Cabral, 2005). Leaving aside the definitional problems associated with concepts of this kind, there is no doubt that studies of the 'virtual' have come to take a substantial interest in reputation, largely predicated on game-theoretic assumptions (see Lui et al., 2002). We return to this in chapter 7.

Tying the social to the rational: the case of commitment

Before we can do so, the key problem in Sen's work is, as we say, what the implied relationship is between commitment and rationality. Sen's concern, it will be recalled, was whether the economic view of rationality provided an adequate picture of normativity. It is one thing to have emotions or sympathies, in his view, and another to reason rationally about these; economic concerns, about how to spend and invest, can fit in with this regime too. But in his view it is another thing to have commitments. Commitments have the effect of modifying or displacing goals, he says. It is

> not only important for characterizing the demands of rationality, but also for explaining behavioral variations between different societies and over time. The admission of committed behavior within a theory of rationality, not only enriches our conceptual understanding of rationality, but also helps us to

understand actual behavior better, through taking note of the varying role of commitment in different social circumstances. (Cited in Morris, 2010)

Sen's approach is hugely controversial. How can one's goals, which exist, one presumes, in a causal relationship to action, be displaced and yet one still have action that is rational? Pettit (2005; see also Pettit, 2002), for instance, argues:

> The goal represents the success condition of the action and will be discernible in how the agent is disposed to adjust the behaviour as circumstances change and as different interventions are clearly needed for the realization of the condition [i.e., that goal]. To imagine an action that is not controlled by a goal of the agent, by the lights of this approach, will be like trying to imagine the grin on the Cheshire cat in the absence of the cat itself. . . . When Sen alleges that goal-displacing commitment takes the agent beyond the control of his or her goals, then he is setting himself against [the basic notion] about action. What rational choice theory asserts on the minimal interpretation is that rational agents act out of a concern for maximizing the expected realization of their goals. And that is precisely to argue, that rational agents aim at satisfying or fulfilling their desires, according to their beliefs. (Pettit, 2005, cited in Morris, 2010: 49)

So where are commitments if they are not beliefs?

Some of the controversy over Sen relates to basic issues which we tried to dispose of in our chapters on economic views. We pointed out that, although modellers can treat preferences as self-interested in that they exclude all concern for others, there is no need for them to do so. It is at least as viable to attribute other-regarding preferences – one can prefer to do something that makes another person happy over doing something that makes them miserable (or vice versa). Sen's is effectively a campaign to include a wide range of other-regarding preferences in the model. His notion of personal goal-displacement – though obscure and perverse-sounding – is no more than the idea that people can adjust what they want to do in the light of its effects on others. In his view, one can give up pursuing some of one's own objectives in order to (help) fulfil someone else's objectives. In that sense, and only in that sense, does one make their goals one's own.

What Sen is perhaps best understood as trying to show is that the 'what's in it for me?' question isn't really relative to (some) other-regarding preferences and social norms – that the rational choice isn't to be contrasted with other-regarding choices that somehow impose on the individual. The seeming difficulty of doing this results only from the way the problem is set up by Sen himself. He sets up the self-interest conception and so encourages us to think that people choose to do one thing rather than another on the basis of the answer they get to the question 'What's in it for me if I do A or if I do B?', and only this. They don't ask what is in it for others. Sen wants to say there are cases which just don't fit the former and which do sometimes include the latter. What he seems to be doing is extending the topic of what is a factor in choosing.

To illustrate: Wes wants to buy his grandson Lewis a surprise present for his birthday but realises Lewis is convinced he will be given the video game *Garden Plants versus Zombies*. Recognising that Lewis will be very disappointed if he doesn't get that game – and knowing how disappointed Lewis can get – Wes gives up on his idea of a surprise and buys that game. There is nothing in this for Wes, over and above the fact that Lewis has a happy birthday. The same goes for many ethical and moral matters. What is in it for the Good Samaritan other than the fact that the right thing has been done, help has been given to someone in need of aid? Both Wes and the Samaritan have done what (in a broad sense) they want to do, but it would surely be wrong to describe their actions as self-interested. So Sen's essential point is that, if you think of preferences as self-interested, in the sense that deeds will only be done if they are in some materialistic sense 'profitable' to the doer, then there are doings that evidently cannot be subsumed under that conception.

Sen's proposal that there are considerations other than preferences that figure in human behaviour, and that these should include such things as 'sympathy' (fellow-feeling) and 'commitment' (as just discussed), turns out then to entail allowing more factors to be assessed in choice. While distinguishing commitments from other kinds of motivational forces, Sen is differentiating only different kinds of preferences. As Hausman notes, 'like most economists and philosophers', Sen 'offers no explicit definition of preference' but does 'consistently emphasize that economists have used the word "preference" to refer to many different things' (2005: 50). Despite these diverse uses, Hausman nonetheless is confident that there is a 'central notion of preference in economics and decision theory' and that he has put his finger on it – 'Preferences thus imply all-things-considered-rankings' (ibid.: 53), which consist of the chooser's 'overall evaluation of the objects over which preferences are defined. This implies a ranking of those objects with respect to everything that matters to the agent: desirability, social norms, moral principles, habits – everything relevant to the evaluations' (ibid.).

If Hausman is right, then Sen's notion of 'commitment' is not adding anything to economics because economists already recognise (though, Hausman complains, they do not explicitly and consistently do so) that the maximisation of value includes not only self-interest but other things such as values, obligations, and so on. In his view, they can be – and already are – constituent of preferences as understood by economists, so Sen is really only singling out one kind of preference from among the range that economists already recognise. Sen emphasises those in which considerations of an ethical kind are predominant, as opposed to those which are motivated by considerations of personal advantage – crude economic advantage, say.

In our view, his reasons for doing so are not really related to the nature of rational choice but are an aversion to a notion of science that gets appended to that perspective. This notion of science would seem to preclude concerns for moralities and norms. The problem of language then turns out to do with what is implied as associated with a method or a starting place: in Sen's view, rational action is handicapped by what is excluded by the science of it. Science doesn't look at norms, and hence rational choice approaches don't either. But as it happens, and as Hausman notes, this isn't necessary for rational choice theory. It is only the case when this view is joined with another view, a view about science as not being concerned with value. Sen's critique of the rational turns out to be a critique of something else.

Conclusion

We said at the beginning that our purpose in this chapter was to consider how various perspectives deal with the question of the 'mind' in choice scenarios, such as the question of mental capacity and how people reason, together with the question of context and how that affects thought and choice. We have focused on variants of economics and sociology that address these issues and, in between these, some psychologies that have been interested in context, on what bounds reason in particular places, and how those bounds are intermingled with mental tools – heuristics and such like. Issues to do with 'methodological individualism' – the idea that society is nothing more than its individuals, as against a notion of social facts, which somehow exist independently from the individual, have been central to our considerations also, though there is some variation in how all these issues spill out in particular arguments and points of view.

We have seen that economists continue to want to treat everything from the starting point of the individual acting like an economic agent; social capital in this view is merely another measure of what will optimise utility for *homo economicus*. Though Sen would like to claim that his view shifts the notion of rational man in economics, close examination suggests that the shift might be quite marginal, consisting really of a complaint that the economic sciences are morally bereft. We have seen that some sociologists are averse to allowing the individual to be the starting place of their inquiries, even if they agree to the notion that action is rational. We have seen too that they are not particularly interested in what is called the mind, certainly not in its mechanisms. What they are interested in is defining what kind of reasons the mind deals in – social capital is one of the sources of these reasons, or perhaps one of its kinds. Oddly, in their efforts to define 'social' reasons, we have seen that some sociologists tend to take the individual out of their topics altogether and make all reasoning an output of (or caused by) the social in some broad sense. In doing so, they subtly remove the actor and the actor's reasoning from the scope of their inquiries. Reasons are social, not individual; the mind's work is not a person's, it is, in effect, society's.

Some sociologists admit this freely – it being a kind of social functionalism – while others skirt around the claim, trying to hide this consequence of their argument. Perhaps they are still worrying about Weber. We saw that he wanted to preserve the mind of the individual in sociological inquiry. We took particular interest in Weber since it could be said that it was his interest in 'reasons' and 'rationality' that led to the use of various rational choice notions in sociology. We noted that, while he was interested in the subjective point of view, this interest is, in fact, a concern for the intersubjective. This might be a route to allowing social considerations to be naturally individual ones too, though this is barely taken up by the sociologists we considered. Whatever, this is certainly something to which we shall return, especially when we talk about Harold Garfinkel's work in sociology.

In any case, and in sum, both the economic and the sociological views we have sketched have sought to extend what they allow into their descriptions, but both views end up with disciplinary perspectives that seem to be rather constrained by what they treat as choice: in one, the individual is merely an economic machine that includes some social considerations in its calculations; in the other, he or she is an automaton of social mores where the reasons of the self are obscured from view.

This doesn't mean that the interplay of these two disciplines around the idea of rationality, on the topic of why and how people choose, has not been productive, but it does suggest that the productivity is often tied to disciplinary dispositions. As commentators try to navigate their way through these dispositions, they often look outside of the thresholds of the disciplines, treading on what might otherwise be thought of as rival disciplines – competitors in the scientific business, one might say. Sociologists are loath to accept an economic perspective as much as economists are to accept sociological ones. Oddly, psychological matters are often treated as the common ground on which these squabbles occur. This apparent common ground is full, we would suggest, of potential fissures and traps for the unwary.

Sometimes, however, moves across and within disciplines point towards quite new perspectives and solutions. We mentioned in our discussion of the bounded rationality viewpoint the publication by Simon of *The Sciences of the Artificial* (1967). This was suggestive, we remarked, of new ways of treating the topic of reason and rationality, of choice and its features. Key to this is having a view on how to understand and identify notions such as beliefs, desires and goals, and how all these concerns might be 'calculated' in ways that reflect what Simon adjudged to be the powers of the mind. In Simon's work, and indeed in that of most bounded theorists, such calculation points towards the psychological and in particular the limits of the brain, of how the mind works – brain and mind being proxies for each other in these arguments. The important point here is that, in this view, the psychological is not a matter of subjective reasoning in the manner of Weber; it is, rather, a matter of cognitive functioning, an empirical matter of a particular kind where the starting assumption is that the brain has to filter input down to its level, its limited capacities. Definitions of how this might occur point towards new notions and new sciences – as in the title of Simon's book.

There are various reasons why the particular interpretation of what the psychological might be have come to have the form it does – a form that emphasises how the world 'out there' has to be rendered as the world 'in there', in the head. One was the influence of the American philosopher Quine, who was writing at about the time that Simon was producing his books. Quine argued, in *Two Dogmas of Empiricism* (1951) and *Word and Object* (1960), that epistemological questions about things such as 'reasons' were effectively psychological questions about 'processes' and that these processes are representational – i.e., things 'in the head'. As Goldman puts it in *Epistemology and Cognition* (1986), in this view, and roughly speaking, human beings are information-processing machines that produce 'mental structures' (in their brains) which represent the external world in various degrees of accuracy. There will be various structures for the various components to be processed – beliefs and such like. Given that there are multiple such structures and that each will be variously good, the brain treats them as resources for a heuristic process that aggregates across these mental structures – these representations.

> We have a large set of common beliefs about the actual world: general beliefs about the sorts of objects, events, and changes that occur in it. We have beliefs about the kinds of things that, realistically, do and can happen. Our beliefs on this score generate what I shall call the set of normal worlds. These are worlds consistent with our general beliefs about the actual world. . . . Our concept of justification is constructed against the backdrop of such a set of normal worlds. My proposal [i.e., Goldman's] is that, according to our ordinary conception of justifiedness, a rule system is right in any world W just in case it has a sufficiently high truth ratio in normal worlds. (Goldman, 1986: 107)

Something like this is found in *The Sciences of the Artificial*. Much artificial intelligence and, latterly, machine-learning systems research continues to be based on this basic approach. As Sent puts it:

> The concepts Simon developed in bounded rationality served as a springboard to his interpretation of artificial intelligence. Simon's bounded rationality program . . . offered an open window into the workings of the human mind. The same ideas of 'heuristic' or 'rule-bound' search, 'satisficing' behaviour, and 'goal, sub-goal' strategy that shaped Simon's theory of bounded rationality also became key concepts in his problem-space approach to reproducing human-style reasoning . . . Simon's bounded rationality program embodied ideas for programming a computer how to think. An understanding of the 'real' processes at work behind human decision-making allowed Simon to build computers that replicated these processes and to serve his interest in finding out how people made decisions. (1997: 334)

This is not the only outcome of the interplay of the disciplines and their various attempts to articulate rational choice. Another, though closely related, is the turn to *game theory*. We will deal with this in a later chapter, but this approach is thought by some to offer a way of understanding how reasoning unfolds in different contexts: the rules of the game are, as it were, defined situationally. Different situations impose different rule constraints and different outcomes (forms of winning). But games are always played by creatures who desire to seek optimisation; players are always rational, in this view.

In later chapters we will address various forms of artificial intelligence, game theory and much else besides. As should be clear, just what is meant by these concerns is at once methodological and empirical, a reflection of conceptual starting places and analytical topics. As we have seen, debates about rational choice theory, its evolution and reshaping in different disciplines, have not produced, and probably never will produce, a solution and a corrective, a perfect definition of the reasons people can have, of the treatment those reasons are given, or of the link between those privately held but intersubjectively demonstrated reasons and those elaborated by the techniques of the social sciences – the ones deduced as social capital, say, the capabilities of humans, the commitments of social groups, the habitus of culture. As we said at the beginning, there are various avenues between which one can choose when looking at choice.

5

EVOLUTIONARY CHOICE

The difference between what people say and what they do has pointed towards and offered proof that, for some at least, why they do things is unfathomable. Certainly, if an individual were to confine themselves to the reasons that people avow, these evidently wouldn't always correspond to what those people do. In this regard, and as we have noted, there is a major fault line in arguments about why choices get made. Some theorists are interested in how individuals reason their way to a decision (how they reason given some information or context, say) while others are interested in the causal factors involved in decision-making, and here their focus is not on how an individual chooses but on the levers that affect that choice. It is not so much a matter of investigating information, of how people reason given some facts, but of how reasoning itself is constrained. We have discussed these constraints or 'levers' and how they appear from the point of view of sociology and behavioural psychology: the former are social levers, the latter, cognitive. But we have not yet mentioned one further input, that of *evolutionary psychology*. Here, views from biology, evolutionary biology particularly, as well as from philosophy are combined. The work of Edward Wilson, Daniel Dennett and, latterly, Steven Pinker are representative of a whole raft of ways of explaining what makes people act that evokes Darwin's notion of evolution. Each, however, takes a slightly different view on what this entails, on the phenomena they seek to examine, and thus how they explain what choice might be (if they explain it at all).

We begin this chapter with a view that combines Darwin and the idea of evolution with the notion that humans are essentially social, and how this is 'naturally' reflected in their decision-making, in human choices. This has come to be known as 'sociobiology'. This perspective takes us further away from an orthodox picture of individual 'rational' decision-making towards choice-making as somehow corporate, and sees the preferences manifest in these socially driven decisions as in part, and somehow, inherited through biology. Decisions in this view reflect the corporate good of the species (or at least the gene).

Of course, the issue is in the somehow, in how decisions come to reflect that greater good, and much of this chapter will ask not whether there is some connection between the essential biology of the human species, but how this shows itself in measurable, demonstrable and relevant ways to the question of human choice. And, for this to be practical and sensible, one would need to know precisely what the ecological view is proposing as its starting premises. As we shall see, saying that our genes made us do it doesn't really count either as an explanation or as a starting premise. It's either fatuous, being at such a high level of generality that it offers nothing we could not agree to, or a way of excusing our behaviour, distracting attention from our real motives.

There are then two problems for the evolutionary view on choice: the first is to clarify just what is meant by how evolution manifests itself in human action, and the second is to offer insights that can be evidenced given the starting definition. What we will see is that different proponents of this view offer different characterisations of what the view is and then turn to different kinds of evidence; this itself doesn't always echo or resonate with the other views, sometimes even the particular view. Consistency about what the evolutionary view entails is then an issue. And, besides, evidence often seems weak. The result of our review in this chapter will not, however, be to say that the evolutionary view has little to offer our topic but that, at the current time, it is far from clear what this view entails. Whether in the future something more will be made of it is an open question.

Sociobiology

If human beings are rational in the universalistic and optimising way proposed by rational choice perspectives, then it seems reasonable to say that we need some explanation of the goals they seek to optimise. As we have seen, economics tends either to ignore the problem of goals or to opt for simplified preference models. Sociology, meanwhile, provides cultural explanations; here 'culture' is evoked to explain whatever is left over when rational choice accounts have finished saying what they can about individual choice. We also saw that some attempt at explaining how motivations might underpin behaviour is made in neuroeconomics – and here the turn is emphatically towards the biological and away from the cultural. Arguably, none of the views we have considered are entirely satisfactory. Sociobiology (and, more generally, other variants of views deriving from evolutionary psychology) purports to give us another kind of answer and, not entirely coincidentally, to do a job that the disciplines we have been looking at (economics, sociology) have seemed incapable of doing themselves: offering a view that somehow combines the historical shaping of the human, how the physiology of the brain as well as the senses has evolved, with the self-evident variation of cultural systems. Whether the views we now address are successful in this remains to be seen.

Sociobiology came to prominence with the publication in 1975 of a book of the same name written by Edward Wilson. Wilson was an expert on ants and was interested in the way that some animals and insects are social, as, for example, ants and bees are in being divided into different specialised and cooperating kinds (drones, queens, etc.) He came to wonder how social scientists could possibly think that human life is an exception to the all-encompassing framework of post-Darwinian biology – the fact that some insect species had a social nature that was unproblematically accepted as a fit subject for biological (evolutionary) explanation led him to the question of why the natural sociality of human beings should not be explained by evolutionary biology as well.

If we remember that, for as long as there has been a sociology, it has been a fundamental assumption of the discipline that human society is in some way unique,[1] it is not surprising that the proposals Wilson puts forward turn out to be extraordinarily provocative. Starting from the more or less uncontested position that evolution explains much of the physical nature of species (ignoring the outré views of the intelligent design community) through natural selection, Wilson extends this principle into arguments concerning the

---

[1] See, for instance, the symbolic interactionists and their fundamental tenet regarding the symbolic nature of human thinking in comparison to the stimulus–response nature of animal behaviour. G. H. Mead (1932), symbolic interaction's founder, had sought to explain the origins of the human mind in the evolution of biological characteristics such as the brain and the vocal cords but had also argued against stimulus–response behaviourism as the general basis for understanding life. In his view, the behaviour of individual humans was freed from the determination of environmental stimulus because of their acquisition of symbolising capacities. This meant that human beings respond to their environment through interpretive processes rather than causal ones. It was this – the fact that human responses are not environmentally determined – that featured strongly in interactionist thought after Mead and that led to resolute and comprehensive rejection of biological determinism as an explanation of human conduct, and it was this that made symbolic interactionism a progenitor of what became 'social constructionism'.

organisation of human social life in the general. He does so in order to explain the reasons for human behaviour (including the choices humans make) in terms of evolutionary advantage:

> The social sciences and humanities have been blinkered by a steadfastly nondimensional and nontheoretical view of mankind. They focus on one point, the human species, without reference to [other species] ... Immersed in minute details of local culture, the typical sociologist fills the role of the local naturalist among the social scientists. He is not much concerned with the limit and ultimate meaning of human behaviour. (Wilson 1996: 100)

And, by this, he means its evolutionary trajectory, how evolution shapes what humans are (and hence do – including their choice-making).

Wilson draws attention to the ways in which ants can be considered social, including that they have a division of labour and that they cooperate. They can, in short, behave altruistically (though altruistic is not a motivational term in this context, referring only to those activities in which the costs of a doing to its doer are greater than the benefits it confers on another). Wilson argues that ant social life is hugely complex, very 'expensive' in terms of maintenance, and cannot be explained by learning. If ant social life is not culturally transmitted, then it must be genetically inherited, he says. It would follow that human behaviour can be understood in this way too. Just as with ants, human cooperation of whatever kind comes about because there is a 'best fit' with evolution.

Choosing sociobiologically

This account of choice draws on some notion of a cost–benefit calculation manifest in choice behaviours. Perhaps the best-known illustration of such calculation is the so-called group or kin selection hypothesis, whereby it is argued that there must be some biological mechanism by which individual ants 'sacrifice' themselves for the group good – a mechanism that is a calculation of some sort. This was first suggested long before the publication of *Sociobiology*. Hamilton put it forward in the 1960s, for example (see Hamilton 1963, 1964). This view holds that the proportion of genes inherited explains why some females in social insect groups are the workers and exist to help another female, their mother, the queen, to reproduce. This is because they cannot themselves reproduce – their genes don't allow it, and so, as it were, they calculate to support the queen. In contrast, cuckoos, brought up in nests by birds with which they share no genetic features, with 'siblings' to whom they are also unrelated, will push those siblings out of the nest to die. But, again, it is the genes that can be said, in this view, to result in these behaviours; these are calculated acts.

Lest we get too far away from our primary interest – human rationality – we need to understand that this view entails arguing that a cost–benefit calculation in terms of perpetuating the same genetic material 'fits' the variable pattern of 'sacrifice' in social species – and determines what the sacrifice is in each case. So, in this line of thought, human actions will be equally constrained or determined or explained by genetic dispositions. Hence, and to paraphrase, because those who are closest to us, such as our brothers and sisters, share a larger proportion of our genes than others, our behaviour towards them will be calculatedly different from the behaviour we manifest to those further away from our genes – strangers and the like, distant relatives if relatives at all. The 'cost–benefit' calculation is in terms of the benefit to our common genetic material that arises if we engage in preferential behaviour with those 'close' to us.

This is, of course, an 'as if' version of organisms, since it is not being said that the species in question – ants, cuckoos or even humans – engage in actual calculations or in any realistic sense make choices that evoke their genetic basis. Nor is it clear how the genes would recognise the near and far, those related and those not. Even so, it is clear that humans do have the capacity to make choices, and so, to avoid further confusion here, it is perhaps wise to add that the theory is meant to identify a biological basis for the pattern of preferential treatment for closer kin that humans *tend to exhibit* rather than to give a motivational account that points to real choices. In other words, this view of the relationship between a species' evolutionary inheritance and actual behaviour is one that talks about tendencies, not reasons for choices.

At this point, and given a potential confusion here about choice and tendency, we should cite Fararo, who suggests a direct correspondence between rational choice theory and this take on the importance of evolutionary biology:

Rational choice theory is an umbrella theory for social science in a sense somewhat analogous to Darwinian theory for the life sciences. In both cases theorists begin any analysis by trying to comprehend the phenomenon to be explained in terms of the principle of the umbrella framework. Of special interest are phenomena that seem to be outright contradictions of the principle. For the life sciences, the existence of altruistic behaviour among animals is such a problem. How could a species exist if its genetically determined behavioural repertoire includes giving an alarm signal to others? By doing so, the animal makes itself especially observable to a predator. This means an increase in its chance of being killed and hence a decrease in the chance that its genes will be propagated to the next generation. Over evolutionary time such a behaviour should disappear. Thus we find theoretical model building about altruism exciting theoreticians in the life sciences, with new ideas such as inclusive fitness being invented to bring the phenomenon within the explanatory scope of the umbrella theory, in this case Darwin's theory. . . . Corresponding to fitness functions in evolutionary theory, we have utility functions in rational choice theory. Theorists attempt to comprehend any and all social phenomena under the umbrella of rational choice. But this ambition runs into phenomena that appear to contradict the fundamental framework-defining principle. As in biology, we find great interest in trying to bring these phenomena within the explanatory scope of the umbrella theory. These are explanatory problems of general-theoretic interest and not merely of historical or empirical interest. (1996: 303–4)

In other words, the idea that animals may exhibit behavioural preferences which seem to limit their prospects of survival is akin to the idea of 'irrationality', which might be troublesome for rational choice theory. Such things need to be explained. As we shall see in later chapters, one solution is an extended game theory which attempts to deal with ('solve') exactly this kind of problem from the rational actor point of view. But, for now, the point of raising this is to note how Fararo provides an example of a more general consequence of particular theoretical stances that can arise – that a general, or 'umbrella' theory can determine what kind of questions are interesting. The distinction between 'selfish' and 'altruistic' kinds of behaviour is an instance of this. If the theory predicts that the selfish kind of behaviour is somehow more 'basic' than 'altruistic', then the existence of the latter has to be treated as a puzzle and in need of special explanation. Altruism would be irrational, selfish behaviour rational. Of course, one can foresee the shape of answers to such conundrums: that humans are genetically wired for certain sorts of altruistic actions, for example, or that the outcome of joint endeavours might be for the general good, even though individual actions are selfish – as in the case of game theory.

This evidently takes us into a new territory and away from rational actor theory. But if we return to genes and sociobiology, rather than seeing rationality purely in terms of individual self-interest, it posits biological reasons for preferences which involve the social group. On the face of it, therefore, it seems to provide some grounding for a biological underpinning to ethics, or 'altruism' as it is conventionally called in literatures of this kind. The argument from sociobiology is roughly that altruism is an investment. By behaving altruistically, we build trustworthiness that later pays dividends in the reciprocal behaviour of others.

Note here that there seems to be an explanation of normativity because moral sentiments and the emotions that accompany them are assumed to help enable people to cooperate and to punish those who don't. Ridley asks in his book *The Origins of Virtue* (1997) (see his later two books as well: 2003, 2004) why, for example, is there so much cooperation about if life is a competitive struggle? Why, in particular, are humans such eager cooperators? He traces the evolution of cooperative arrangements for mutual benefit back to the origins of cellular life (in other words, he sees cooperation at the level of the cell).

Reciprocal altruism and group selection are offered as biological explanatory mechanisms, and the role of moralistic punishment in controlling free-riders links psychological, moral and economic dimensions of cooperation. Human physiological and cultural capabilities for inventing and exploiting social exchanges – a willingness to cooperate and to punish those who don't, reputational mechanisms for increasing trust, moral sentiments that act as a kind of social glue – are key to the success of our species, in Ridley's view. A more sophisticated version of this perspective can be found in Sober and Sloan Wilson's *Unto Others* (1998). They argue that there may well be more than one kind of altruism. Firstly, there may be a biological altruism, one which is genetically determined, along the lines we have already discussed; and, secondly, there may be what they call psychological altruism. Of course, how one might, in practice, tell one from the other is not something that is easy to resolve.

From species to minds

It should be clear that sociobiology is likely to have many limitations and many critics. It is not certain, to begin with, whether Wilson, for instance, is simply wanting to say that evolution must have some role or wanting to specify what that role might be – the examples that he and others in his wake bring to bear are either too vague or depend upon comparison between species – humans and ants, for example – that are easily mocked. Some researchers who nevertheless favour an evolutionary approach, but who recognise that Wilson's sociobiology or Ridley's altruism arguments are unsatisfactory, have modified the basic premises of the approach and placed greater emphasis on the evolution of the human mind. With this take, they think evolution can be said to have spawned the psychological structures characteristic of human thought. This new perspective is nonetheless still competitive with many social scientists' views, since it bears upon sociological and anthropological conceptions of 'culture', especially insofar as this encourages the view that psychological characteristics are acquired and reproduced through learning rather than genetic transmission alone; in this view, thought is a cultural apparatus but its form is genetically structured.

In a classic paper, Tooby and Cosmides (1992) go straight to the point. They argue that 'culture', as sociologists and anthropologists understand it, is deeply problematic, since it does not explain where culture comes from or provide any psychological basis for how cultures come to be one way rather than another. This is where a view informed by evolutionary psychology claims a significant improvement, Tooby and Cosmides claim. The brain, like all other organs, is a product of evolution, and 'meaning' is therefore a function of brain activity. The brain has a clear and standard structure which has evolved according to the same principles as other organs. Included in this structure will be all the things that make thinking – and hence conscious choice – possible. In this view, cognitive processes of one kind or another, including representations and categories and resulting choices, are naturally *computed* by inbuilt systems of rules (or by pattern matching), and these rules and patterns constitute the 'mind'. These rules are subject to, and indeed caused by, evolutionary forces, and so, just as the body is a product of our genetic inheritance, so too is our reasoning. It follows from this that our choice behaviour is thus, in principle, explicable by the natural teleology of adaptive 'advantage'.

What this picture provides is an explanation of why we tend to make the choices that we do, because our brains have been biologically programmed to elect those options which confer greater likelihood on the continuity of the replicators into future generations. It is the rule-based processing work that the brain does which enables us to make choices in the first place.

Now, in one reading, this is undeniable: our cultures depend on our thinking; our thinking depends on our minds, which relate to our brains, which are made up of neurons, and so on. This is a long way, however, from proving a causal link between all these topics, as we shall see. If taken too literally, this view produces arguments such as, for example, that we think in a certain way today because this manner of thought helped maximise some kinds of behaviours in the Pleistocene era. The trouble with such a claim is either that this is meant at such a high level that no evidence is necessary (it being little more than a truism, given the premise: that we have evolved), or it begs the question of what the behaviours that are linked would be. It seems obvious that how or why humans might have chosen sex in the Pleistocene era would be on the basis of different considerations from how or why someone might choose sex today – they are both indulgencies, they both consume time, they both produce outputs, but surely they are understood differently. And surely it seems obvious too that differences are contained in the cultural measure – the thing that the evolutionary view is wanting to claim it can capture.

The point we are making has to do with the question of what evidence could be adduced to show linkages between behaviours then and behaviours now. As we say, sex isn't all in the mechanics; it's also about interpretation and form. These aren't merely empirical problems, then, but also conceptual ones; it is not clear how the evolutionary view can determine what the relevant evidence might be. The problem with even revised versions of evolutionary psychology is that, when these views attempt to address plausible instances of decision-making, choices that, on other evidence, entail choice, the resulting claims seem very weak or at least unclear. The problem is not that one should therefore doubt the possibility that the starting premise (that we have evolved and that this affects our motivations for making choices) is wrong, but methodologically it seems difficult to know how to judge where and when this evidence is to be applied.

We should not assume that adaptive arguments are necessarily wrong, then, though very many of those from evolutionary psychology are highly speculative. However, some questions can legitimately be asked, and these are not simply the easily made contrasts between types of behaviour and the implied choices made with regard to them, as we have just posed. They are as much conceptual as empirical, methodological as much as analytic. Such matters are not merely questions of clarity; they are very often quite profound and point towards deep issues to do with evidence and how it is identified and assessed, as well as what evidence a starting premise points towards as constituting the kind of evidence it is interested in.

Reasons and sex

Take, for example, how some within the evolutionary psychology perspective try to explain culture and its dynamism with reference to sex. Typically, evolutionary theory casts its view over millennia, but it seems evident that human affairs alter quite a bit quicker than that, so, to be helpful in explaining how human choice creates that dynamism, a perspective informed by evolutionary theory needs a view on this. One example of such a view, and one that at least offers some evidential explanation (leaving aside for the moment whether this is good or bad) can be found in an argument put forward by Miller (2001). He proposes that something about how and why we choose our sexual mates has consequences for the speed of cultural change. To put it briefly, Miller argues that large brains evolved as a result of sexual selection:

> Ever since the Darwinian revolution, this survivalist view has seemed the only scientifically respectable possibility. Yet it remains unsatisfying. It leaves too many riddles unexplained. Human language evolved to be much more elaborate than necessary for basic survival functions. From a pragmatic, biological viewpoint, art and music seem like pointless wastes of energy. Human morality and humour seem irrelevant to the business of finding food and avoiding predators. Moreover, if human intelligence and creativity were so useful, it is puzzling that other apes did not evolve them. (2001: 2)

This then leads to his central argument: 'I . . . argue that the most distinctive aspects of our minds evolved, largely through the sexual choices our ancestors made' (ibid.: 3). In this view sexual selection produces traits that are quite different from natural selection, because sexual selection, unlike natural selection, is based on human choices. Miller suggests:

> one of the main reasons why mate choice evolves is to help animals choose sexual partners who carry good genes. By comparison, natural selection is a rank amateur. The evolutionary pressures that result from mate choice can therefore be much more consistent, accurate, efficient and creative than natural selection pressures . . . As a result of these incentives for sexual choice, many animals are sexually discriminating. They accept some suitors and reject others. They apply their faculties of perception, cognition, memory, and judgment to pick the best sexual partners they can. In particular, they go for any

features of potential mates that signal their fitness and fertility.
(Ibid.: 9)

The core of Miller's argument is that our brains – which, he wants
to argue, in keeping with evolutionary perspective, determine the
structure of our thinking – evolved not because of natural selection,
but because intelligence is a fitness indicator to the opposite sex; and
it is this that leads to sexual choices, and this in turn produces the
brain forms we currently have. Hence, Miller proposes that sexual
selection is the 'thinking person's' natural selection. All the elements
of nature formed the basic building blocks of ancestral past, but it
was the 'explosive' use of the 'thinking cap' that has made human
beings so unique: 'sexual selection seems to have shifted its primary
target from body to mind' (2001: 10).

Miller's case is, as we say, an attempt to solve an apparent
problem for evolutionary psychology – that is, to explain the link
between natural selection and matters that one would imagine
Darwin himself might have avoided considering, namely cultural
ones. Culture changes occur much more rapidly than the other
phenomena that the evolutionary perspective looks at – body size
and functioning, and so on. One set of phenomena take millennia
to 'evolve', the other only decades. But Miller says cultural change
can be explained by sexual selection. Sexual selection, in his view,
acts fast, much faster than *natural selection*. Human culture is, then,
a by-product of the large brains produced by sexual selection. Most
of our culture is not necessary for our survival but is a function of
the kinds of display we associate with fitness indicators. The human
mind's most impressive abilities are 'courtship tools, evolved to
attract and entertain sexual partners' (Miller 2001: 4). Miller makes
the case that 'sexual selection is unusually fast, powerful, intelligent,
and unpredictable. This makes it a good candidate for explaining any adaptation that is highly developed in one species but not
in other closely related species that share a similar environment'
(ibid.: 8).

The fabric of an argument: explanation and evidence

Miller proposes that fitness indicators have all sorts of forms.
Artistic expression in general, like vocabulary creation and display,
has its origins, for Miller, in its role in our early history as a fitness
indicator, for example. Art and sex are thus bound, in this view.

Now, we needn't take such generalisations of this kind too seriously, but we should at least recognise that such arguments are

attempts to provide some synthesis of genetics and culture. They need to be brought together if they are to explain such things as our evolutionary path as manifest in cultural behaviours. Whether they are at all successful, of course, is a very different matter.

As with other perspectives in this field, this variant of the evolutionary view seems to lose some of the care required in its positioning. Initial claims are justified with acceptable but quite modest proofs and are then suddenly extended to implied claims without much justification. It seems reasonable to say that sexual choice is affected by culture. It seems reasonable also to say that sexual choice might affect the speed of change in a species that is at odds with the more traditional view about evolution. But it is altogether another thing to say that a large brain is, in fact, a fitness indicator that drives sexual choice for the very simple reason that evidence that this might be so seems to be rather thin on the ground. Is one to suppose that artists have a more lively sex life because their art is a fitness indicator – that they have, in other words, Bigger Brains? Is it really the case that artists have more sex than others with smaller fitness indicators? Is it also the case that the sex they have is more likely to lead to progeny than sex between, say, those who don't have such 'fitness'? After all, it is only if this were the case that the artist's genes would come to dominate the gene pool and so displace those with smaller brains. And, as a further consequence of this, it is only thus, one assumes, that society can come to be replete with 'good art' and with people who have big brains that in turn produce all the other measures of cultural diversity – the phenomena that this take on the evolutionary perspective wants to explain or account for.

Doubtless there are things one can say about sexual lives in modern society, but doubtless too there will be many theories that compete on this front, and many more may even seem to fit the same evidence. Thus, to accept Miller's view, one would at least hope that he would dispose of alternatives first. And, as he would do so, one would hope as well that he would address evidence that suggests that the relationship between, say, desire and human choice is not always related to 'size' (even when the 'fit' object may be varied – not just a brain, say, but shoulders, height, genitalia). Remember, what we are saying here is not that, in principle, evolution has no role in explaining human choice. The problem is what features of choice it might explain, what might be the evidence for this, and how might one judge whether the evidence fits any particular claim.

We have made similar observations about behavioural economics/ psychology – one finds muddles, strange or inflated claims, and evidence used in unjustified ways. Likewise here. What we find in this approach, exemplified in Miller's work, is one of the main

problems with evolutionary psychology. Those who adopt its view
see the hand of natural selection everywhere. They take apparent
facts – the 'fact' that men have more sexual partners than women;
the 'fact' that women are better at noticing details than men; the
fact that men have better spatial awareness; and so on – to suggest
a nice fit with evolutionary psychology's account of historical
adaptations over millennia and current, comparatively short-term
(mostly cultural) adaptions. They argue, not very convincingly,
that evolutionary 'facts' manifest in culture can be discovered
independently of culture – as if what counts as fitness was not itself
culturally coded and can simply be defined as evidence and proof.
There is little regard for well-known sociological and anthropological matters such as the difficulty of what 'counts' as an example of
something from one culture to another, or the existence of incon-
venient evidence such as the 'fact' that women in Sweden tend
to have more sexual partners than men. Much more problemati-
cally, not only are there immense problems with what is treated as
'creativity', 'art', but also with categories such as 'intelligence' and
fitness. Debates about such matters ought to be predicated on
agreed definitions, but unsurprisingly they are not. Without clarity
about these it is hard to know whether one can properly evidence
what might be criteria for mate selection. Do people look at the
cultural artefact and then always treat that as implying brain size?
Do all cultural artefacts measure brain size? What is the measure
here? When is the measure applied – at first looking? What pre-
dominates here is, above all, conceptual vagueness, which in turn
creates immense difficulties in terms of identifying what counts as
evidence. There are then great difficulties entailed in the notion
of evidence in these debates. One odd by-product of this way of
explaining cultural practices via evolution and sexual practices
is to make the cultural practices seem something other than they
are.
    It is hardly surprising, then, that objections to the evolutionary
psychological perspective on why we behave the way we do are
legion – it really isn't at all clear what is being claimed or what
evidence might be brought to bear on those claims. It doesn't help
when the likes of Wilson throw incendiaries on the debates with
claims such as this:

> In hunter gatherer societies, men hunt and women stay at
> home. This strong bias persists in most agricultural and indus-
> trial societies and, on that basis alone, appears to have a genetic
> origin ... Substantial evidence exists that boys show persis-
> tently more mathematical and less verbal ability than girls on

average and are more aggressive from the first hours of social play at age two to manhood. (Wilson, 1996: 92)

The commotion is even greater when we look at explanations of rape from the evolutionary perspective (see Thornhill and Palmer, 2000; Travis, 2003; Dupre, 2001; Lloyd, 2003). We do not propose to discuss such matters further, except to point out that the controversies are not only about matters of empirical fact but also, as we say, conceptual.

This does not mean that there cannot be a biological element to our dispositions or preferences. The problem is finding methods for identifying which they are. One constant complaint about 'evidence' in these arguments is that it takes many different forms: culture is one thing, prehistoric behaviour another. It is very difficult to see how evidence about each can be placed alongside the other like two kinds of stuff. This isn't even apples and pears or chalk and cheese; this is footprints and bones, paintings and books; this is to compare what one can never hear, the sound of ancient voices, with the cacophony of the age of YouTube. This is to juxtapose the imagined sexual practices of long-dead cave dwellers with the known sexual practices of contemporary undergraduates (the latter being the normal source of data in psychology of course). Chalk and cheese are easy in comparison to all this. According to Allen Orr, 'evolutionary psychology suffers a methodological problem: it is at times surprisingly unrigorous. Too often, data are skimpy, alternative hypotheses are neglected, and the entire enterprise threatens to slip into undisciplined story-telling . . . ask a molecular biologist who's sceptical of Darwinian psychology. You won't hear that the slate is blank; you'll hear about 'soft science' (2003: 18).

From evolution to computation

The evidence we have been seeking thus far has been demonstrably behavioural – to do with sex, for example. But this is not the only type of evidence marshalled to aid the evolutionary perspective. Other approaches place different nuances on the starting premises and, as they do so, go in search of different proofs.

In the next part of the chapter, we look at advocates of the evolutionary view who claim that the manifestation of evolution on human affairs is different from that proposed by either Miller or Wilson. In the case of the first we shall address, Steven Pinker, his evidence is experimental and illustrates, so he claims, the relationship between the use of words and apparent 'brain response'.

Evolution shows itself through (or in) the secret codes of language. In the case of the second, Daniel Dennett, language is at once the topic and yet the problem for the evolutionary perspective: in his view, the reasons people have for the choices they make are not based on scientifically observable truths but are the result of the evolutionary production of metaphorical techniques. The language of reasons offers a false representation of what really drives choice. A different language of real reasons needs to be devised, Dennett claims. The third is Richard Dawkins; his connecting of language to evolutionary psychology is most clear and well known. He has a notion that cultural phenomena, like language, evolve in much the same way as do genes. In particular, 'memes', a feature of language he claims to have identified, mutate and evolve and thus shape how people think and reason in ways that can be seen as evolutionary, as a linguistic manifestation of Darwin's hidden hand.

More particularly, Pinker's view starts with the premise that the mind is 'computational' – the nature of this computation being an output of evolution. The notion of the mind-as-computer is quite commonly held. As we noted in the introduction to the book, this is the view of John Duncan, for example, as outlined in his *How Intelligence Happens* (2010). In this view, rationality is a function of brain structure, and the brain is a calculating and computational engine which applies a set of determinate rules in order to make its decisions; all this machinery tumbles out of evolution. In this view, cultural variations can be linked ultimately to explanations which show how human beings are generally motivated to do what they do by being subject to and agents of computation. All one has to do is accept that the brain is a computational engine and that the rules it applies are determinate; one then needs to find proofs of this computation.

The trick that Pinker brings to bear on this common argument is to link this somewhat bare notion of computation – bare in the sense that one doesn't learn a lot about what this computation might look like except at a high level – with the idea that language, our everyday languages in particular, manifest the 'hidden rules' of that computation or, rather, display a mix of rules and systematicities that variously reflect the heterogeneous pace of evolutionary shaping and its manifestation in reasoning.

More specifically, Pinker argues, in *The Blank Slate* (2003) and *How the Mind Words* (2003b) (as well as in many other books and articles), that the mind is a modular construction, consisting of various components which interrelate functionally so as to process information. The mind is like a 'real' computer in that it has a structure which distributes different functions across its different parts. In the way that silicon computers have memory and processing functions designed in, so too does the biological computer – the mind – have perception, memory and other functions built into different parts of the entity. Also like a computer, the mind has information inputs from the outside – the environment – that are processed through structures already present within the mind's computational system. The computer analogy leads, furthermore, to the idea that the information the brain processes takes the form of 'representations', things which are meant to reproduce the character of its inputs as some kind of symbolic form. It is these that are subject to programmatic transformation. It is these programming processes that generate 'output' – an individual's response to their environment manifest in their behaviour. In the case of the mind, Pinker argues, in the manner of Chomsky (see, e.g., Chomsky, 2006), that the main representational forms used are those of language – in which case, language cannot be a *cultural phenomenon* but must be a biological one. A capacity for language must already be built into the brain if the mind is to be able to learn a native tongue. In other words, language must be innate.

For Pinker, this position needs the 'language of thought' hypothesis (also derived from Chomsky and further developed by Fodor, 1975). Since this language of thought isn't identical with any natural language, it needs to be identified by a special name. Pinker goes along with Fodor's 'mentalese'. In any case, representations form a critical link in the causal chain between inputs, processing and outputs – the thing, as it were, that articulates the mind as computer and that is the crux of the evolutionary claim in Pinker's narrative.

Pinker notes that this view of the mind does not 'fully' explain social behaviour. That is because the mind has evolved in particular historical and, in various ways, diverse environments, and as a result it has developed differentiated representational capacities. Some of these capacities (or computational modes) fit today's circumstances better than others. Some are adaptational dead ends, by-products in the sense that they do not themselves fulfil any functional needs (what Stephen Gould called 'spandrels'). Pinker suggests:

[My] claim is that reverse-engineering, the attempt to discover the functions of organs (which I am arguing should be done to the human mind), is a system of the disease 'adaptationism'. Apparently if you believe that any aspect of an organism has a function, you must absolutely believe that every aspect has a function, that monkeys are brown to hide among the coconuts. (1997: 165)

He does not believe this, suggesting instead that some but not all of the 'functions' and 'capacities' of the human mind are applicable to current circumstances. Besides, it is a methodological error to assume that all functions are right or needed; some are simply failures, red herrings, dead ends – 'spandrels'.

More important at this point is the status of 'meaning' in Pinker's work. He identifies it as one of a number of problems, including 'consciousness', the 'self', 'free will', 'knowledge' and 'morality', '[which] continue to baffle the modern mind' (1997: 558–9). This seems an odd thing to say: do people not know what they mean? What Pinker is arguing is that the things which people think are the meanings they operate around turn out to not to be as they appear. We act for meaningful reasons, but people do not necessarily or even often know the actual meaning – the thing that causes our behaviour.

Among the many examples Pinker uses to show this are experimental studies of how brain responses to particular words indicate a profound link between word types and neurological (and physiological) reactions of the brain. These types are, in a crude sense, like the 'types' that are defined in computer programming, and which are the entities upon which the computer operates and hence transforms in Turing's sense.[2] These are cases of mentalese, the representational forms that the mind subjects to a programme – that it computes.

So, for example, when a person reads an offensive word, the traces of their brain behaviour show a different response to when they read a commonplace, non-offensive word. Pinker suggests that the meaning of the word is not in its literal reference, that it alludes to a sexual act or other body function, say, but in how it is a *code* that prompts the body to react in a certain way. Offensive words cause the mind to shift its register to the emotional. This shift in and linking of certain words to behavioural reaction is a legacy of evolution, so Pinker claims. As it happens, the need for emotion is reducing in the modern world, he argues. This capacity to evoke it is a legacy of a now less important evolutionary characteristic.

The trouble with such claims, however, is that it is not at all clear that this is the right reading of the evidence or even whether the manner of gathering evidence is salient to the question being posed. After all, it would be odd from any perspective to treat a swear word as like any other. It is the nature of everyday vocabulary that some words are used purposefully and consciously as devices to elicit certain sorts of responses. Swear words are a case in point; they can

---

[2] Turing, A. (1936) 'On computable numbers, with an application to the Entscheindungsproblem', *Proceedings of the London Mathematical Society*, 42 (1936–7).

be used to convey one's own anger, or deliberately to cause offence, or merely as a form of punctuation. If, however, they are used for a range of purposes, why would we assume from traces of brain activity that our responses to them are always the same?

Besides, the manner of experiment elides important considerations that seem fundamental here. If it is the case, as we have just noted, that swear words create reactions, and that this is so results in their being consciously selected in the first place, one should not use a technique designed to bypass conscious aspects of an act to uncover the features and consequences of that conscious act. To use experiments to look at the interactional deployment of swear words is, then, to take out the phenomenon in question.

This doesn't mean that one cannot find evidence about the changing shape of language and its powers; it does suggest that perhaps one should look outside the laboratory. After all, Mary Douglas made much of the same topic in her anthropological study *Purity and Danger: An Analysis of Concepts of Pollution and Taboo* (1966). The argument there was emphatically one based on the idea that explorations to do with the moral landscape related to how people (as against animals) create meaningful systems that distinguish the species from other species and one group from another within the species. However, she argues that the phenomena of swearing and taboo more generally are not to do with genes or evolution; they have to do with intention and culture and how these 'evolve' (without recourse to mentalistic or cognitive argument).

What Douglas is saying, long before Pinker came onto the scene, is that, if the topic has to do with the cultural shaping of ideas, it is not examinations of brain function that pertain or have relevance but interactions between people. And that is why she asserts anthropological techniques (though one could propose others too, from sociology and history, say). This is not to say that what happens in culture has nothing at all to do with what happens inside a brain, but it does mean that, for the purposes of inquiry, this is not the salient topic. Cultural forms are. It is not what happens in the brain that matters but what cultural forms people produce. And cultural forms demand their own methodological tools.

Pinker seems entirely unaware of Douglas's work, reflecting in our view an utterly impoverished notion of what anthropologists and others mean when they talk about culture in the first place. This is despite the fact that he seems to admit that, for his arguments about words carrying a cargo of evolutionary functioning, and for there to be a provable link between the abstract patterns one finds in words and the often too real consequences of emotion (such as interpersonal violence), one would need evidence about cultural history.

This cannot be derived from the laboratory. His book on the history of violence seems to attest to this. *The Better Angels of our Nature* (2011) is meant to show that violence is in fact declining in culture; Pinker claims it confirms his notion that this decline is an evolutionary step reflecting the development of language as a computational tool governing human action and choice. The role of swear words as conveyors of a programmable type is diminishing in importance, according to this view. Unfortunately, in venturing outside the lab, Pinker seems to lose his empirical grasp. *Better Angels* was derided for its treatment of the historical evidence – one doesn't need to be a historian to know that the last century was the most murderous of all in history. Just how Pinker could propose otherwise has startled and shocked reviewers and readers alike. One is reminded of Brannigan's (2004) observations about the use of experiment when related to explaining cultural practices – the method isn't really used to provide evidence, it is used to hide the inadequacies of the evidence and allows those who invoke experimental data to make comments about cultural matters they believe for other reasons. Perhaps that applies here too; Pinker would like to believe that a move away from violence in human affairs is a measure of evolution. We choose diplomacy today whereas in the past we turned to the club. It would be nice to believe that Darwin's 'hidden hand' did indeed show these consequences. But truth suggests otherwise.

The language of misunderstanding choice: Dennett

Dennett's defence of evolutionary psychology in *Darwin's Dangerous Idea* (1995) is different from Pinker's, though it too places language at its centre. Indeed, what is so interesting about putting the two side by side in this discussion is how they alter, to some extent, crucial premises in each other's interpretation of what evolutionary accounts offer. If Pinker thinks meaning is unclear, Dennett thinks meaning should be the centre of investigation – when meaning is the 'thing' that people apply to their own and other creatures' actions to make sense of them. He asserts:

> One of the striking features of cultural evolution is the ease, reliability, and confidence with which we can identify commonalities in spite of the vast differences in underlying media. . . . What is in common, of course, is not a syntactic property . . . but a semantic property. . . . So it is only at the level of the intentional stance that we can describe these common properties. (1995: 356)

In a nutshell, cultural similarities exist at the level of 'meaning'. For Dennett, the intentional stance determines our attitude to 'meaning'. It is defined as 'the strategy of interpreting the behaviour of an entity (person, animal, artefact, whatever) by treating it *as if* it were a rational agent who governed its "choice" of action by a "consideration" of its "beliefs" and "desires" (Dennett, 1996: 27).

There is an important clause here, and that is *as if*. Dennett argues that ordinary human beings are not required to believe that 'agents' (i.e., themselves and other persons) have choices, beliefs and desires that in themselves have material reality; beliefs as such are not real in *that* sense. They are not truly part of the causal structure of organisms, the scientific cause of things. Rather, people need only to treat the reasons they adduce as, effectively, purely hypothetical entities. With them at hand, however, they can construct a basis upon which they can act. These entities are not tools for the analyst, then (as are Weber's ideal types); these entities (notions about intentions and reasons, and so on) are, if you like, theories for practical use, to be deployed by people to interpret their own and others' behaviour. With such conjectures, people can treat the activity of the apparently sentient organisms around them – or even machines if they pass the Turing test – as if that behaviour were caused by these conjectured mental qualities.

In effect, Dennett denies any intrinsic worth to the mental landscape that human beings evidently construct. In so doing, he seeks to avoid the problems of philosophy of mind that suggest that one cannot sensibly separate the language of everyday reasons from other forms of account without sacrificing important empirical ties. Dennett wants to insist that there is a distinction, an absolute distinction, between 'scientific' understanding of the brain and our everyday 'folk psychological' construal of each other's behaviour. He holds that a scientific understanding of behaviour must be thoroughly based on empirical matters, on material evidence (and hence he gets called a 'materialist'), but that our everyday ways of thinking effectively 'interpret' the patterns of our physical behaviour, allowing us to predict and adjust to the behaviour of others on an 'as if' interpretative basis. Or, to put this another way, people get along effectively enough for their everyday purposes without knowing anything (much) about the true nature of human organism and how it works, especially with respect to the brain. None of the interpretative tools actually make up identifiable parts of the human organism, so Dennett claims.[3]

---

[3] It is worth noting here that Dennett places his arguments with regard to the philosophy of mind. Although he is advocating what he proposes is an evolutionary

This view denies 'folk psychology' any role in the 'science of the mind' (or the brain). Instead, one should use evolutionary theory to directly explain the mind, and hence this will have to include culture – and all that entails – cultural variation and dynamism, the production of meaningful systems and cultural codes. According to Dennett, 'There is no denying that there is cultural evolution, in the Darwin-neutral sense that cultures change over time' (1996: 345). But this begs the question of what 'evolution' actually means in 'cultural evolution'. For Dennett, cultural evolution is 'not just a process that can be metaphorically described in these evolutionary idioms, but a phenomenon that obeys the laws of natural selection quite precisely' (ibid.: 345).

Like Pinker, Dennett's manner of thinking is a 'must be' type approach. Given this 'must be' starting place, his approach is one that seeks to corroborate this truth and treats evidence that doesn't do that as something to be ignored; it must be wrong. Since he can find no evidence of evolution in the reasons that people themselves have to account for their own and others' behaviour, then those reasons must be disregarded. Some other form of evidence is required. Among the answers he finds that he does approve of are those in the concept of 'meme', which Dennett gets from Dawkins. Dawkins, known for arguing that human behaviour is best explained by *The Selfish Gene* (1989), suggested a *meme* as a cultural equivalent of the biological gene, a linguistic unit that is a 'unit of cultural transmission'.

It seems a commonplace to observe that information can be easily shared through the process of imitation, or copying, so on the face of it such a view should be uncontroversial. Of course, when we are talking about information, we might only mean stuff that exists externally to us, perhaps on a piece of paper or a computer screen. What Dawkins means, however, is that information, analogous to the way in which it is handled in computers, can be viewed, processed and stored in the brain and then exchanged with other brains. For him, thoughts, attitudes, values, preferences, etc., are nothing more than units of information and thus can be combined and re-created in new forms within the head and in interaction between people. Words in a text can be separated from their narrative location and recomposed in newly minted narratives; the combinations of words making narrative elements can be reconstituted in new stories; what people say to each other can be – is – transformed according to the rules of evolution.

---

psychology view, the fabric of arguments come from philosophy, not from, say, the experimental cognitive sciences that flesh out Pinker's work.

The important point for us is that choice, in this view, is also treated as an output of information processing. Choice, then, is not the making of logical connections; it is more like the mixing of elements that give the (false) impression of logic, of being 'reasoned'. The real logic is the logic of statistical distributions of random possibility – choice in this view is little more than a powerful contagion – a chance outcome of randomness that implies, in human terms, reason and purpose. Indeed, Aunger (2002), following Dennett, uses words such as 'infection', 'contamination' and 'culturally caught' to describe cultural acquisition through memes – the stuff, as it were, upon which and through which people make and explain their choices.

In and of itself, this is tautological. For 'meme' we might substitute 'idea' and say that, yes, we sometimes share ideas. Indeed, if language – at least its constituent parts – is included under the heading 'meme', then there is an obvious sense in which we commonly share ideas and so 'infect' each other. Since the brain is structured to produce linguistic and other representations, then, if one wants to go along with the argument as to whether any of these will 'catch on' and propagate widely enough to make shared elements of a culture (to infect enough persons to make some idea change society) will be determined not merely by chance but by the thing that Darwin identified as the key: by their *fitness for survival*. In terms of human choices, the 'meme' is an explanation for why we choose to believe what we do – because it aids our continuity.

If all species evolve through the change and survival of genes, in the case of the human species there is a difference, then; for genes are supplemented by the evolution of memes. There is a parallelism between the two, according to Dennett: 'The primary difference between our species and all others is our reliance on cultural transmission of information, and hence on cultural evolution' (1995: 331). Cultural evolution is the primary explanation for recent changes in human morphology, and the argument can be applied to language as much as to any other cultural phenomenon, and indeed more so, since 'for culture we need language' (ibid.: 341). And language, like all phenomena, cannot be said to 'time out' from adaptation. Language, along with the biological machine that handles it, the mind, is inescapably subject to adaptive pressures, though ones that are representational in nature. Memes, in this view, can and do mutate and must be 'selected' on some basis. Memes must, in other words, 'fit' through adaptation.

Reasons for choices

Part of the popular attraction of notions like evolutionary psychology is that they suggest something uncanny: that the choices people make are not really their choices; that somehow people are leading out lives governed by forces that are beyond their comprehension. Given the everyday, common-sense commitment to the idea that people are responsible for what they do and, indeed, the evidence that they do in practice hold themselves and others accountable for what they do, for what they decide, this suggests something furtive is happening, that something is going on behind the backs of people and controlling them despite their sense of self-responsibility. It is as if they are fools in imagining they choose.

This appeals to those disciplines which desire such a view, a view that would allow them to claim to discover the truth of what people do and why. Constant disciplinary effort is put into finding causes (of various different kinds) which might explain why people do things; these reasons will conflict with the reasons people give each other. As it happens, the concept of meme gives a slightly altered view of this contrast, since it claims that the ideas people use to fabricate their reasons for actions are actually ideas that are using people as their bearers, and where the formation, change and spread is not the product of anyone's reasons in themselves but is better thought of as analogous to a disease epidemic. One doesn't own reasons, one carries them.

The trouble with this view, as with those we have already considered in this chapter, is what precisely is meant by meme and thus, more generally, the relation between this account and the reasons people avow. The substantial basis for the claim that they exist is only the acknowledged fact that language is independent of individuals, that it is shared and exchanged, and that it changes in ways that are beyond the individual. These changes seem somehow inexplicable, as if the sharing and shaping of ideas in language had some logic of their own that is, as it were, outside the reference of cultural matters and hence normal human understanding. It is thus ineffable and therefore needs some explanation. It is thus that Darwin's 'hidden hand' might be seen to come into play.

A demand for an answer, though, wherever it comes from, doesn't necessarily produce an answer. Dawkins himself admits: 'we do not know what memes are made of or where they reside ... Where genes are to be found in precise locations on chromosomes, memes presumably exist in brains' (introduction to Blackmore, 1999: xii). In reality, of course, and without the necessary scare quotes around 'evolution', 'whether such evolution is weakly or strongly analo-

gous to, or parallel to, genetic evolution . . . is an open question'
(Dennett, 1995: 345).

The fascination for notions like memes, echoing this greater
fascination for things that control people in hidden ways, is true in
the media world too, though in this setting the weight placed on the
concepts is somewhat playful and less scientific. However, perhaps
these concepts are worth looking at for what they tell us about any
scientific credit such views might have.

Godwin's law, presented in *Wired* magazine, is a tongue-in-cheek
expression of meme theory.

A 'meme,' of course, is an idea that functions in a mind the
same way a gene or virus functions in the body. And an infec-
tious idea (call it a 'viral meme') may leap from mind to mind,
much as viruses leap from body to body. By 1990, I had noticed,
something . . . had happened to the Nazi-comparison meme.
Sure, there are obvious topics in which the comparison recurs.
In discussions about guns and the Second Amendment, for
example, gun-control advocates are periodically reminded that
Hitler banned personal weapons. And birth-control debates
are frequently marked by pro-lifers' insistence that abortionists
are engaging in mass murder, worse than that of Nazi death
camps. And in any newsgroup in which censorship is discussed,
someone inevitably raises the spectre of Nazi book-burning.

But the Nazi-comparison meme popped up elsewhere as
well – in general discussions of law in misc.legal, for example,
or in the EFF conference on the Well. Stone libertarians were
ready to label any government regulation as incipient Nazism.
And, invariably, the comparisons trivialized the horror of the
Holocaust and the social pathology of the Nazis. It was a trivi-
alization I found both illogical (Michael Dukakis as a Nazi?
Please!) and offensive (the millions of concentration-camp
victims did not die to give some net.blowhard a handy trope).
So, I set out to conduct an experiment – to build a counter-
meme designed to make discussion participants see how they
are acting as vectors to a particularly silly and offensive meme
. . . and perhaps to curtail the glib Nazi comparisons. I developed Godwin's Law of Nazi Analogies: As an online discussion
grows longer, the probability of a comparison involving Nazis
or Hitler approaches one. I seeded Godwin's Law in any newsgroup or topic where I saw a gratuitous Nazi reference. Soon,
to my surprise, other people were citing it – the counter-meme
was reproducing on its own! And it mutated like a meme, generating corollaries. (Godwin, 1994)

We need not take this especially seriously, but it does show how certain kinds of vague question seem to prompt meme theory, notably – especially in the context of the Internet – how it can be that certain ideas spread so fast. Of course, a more sensible and nuanced version would have it that this has much to do with the population of people most likely to spend their time visiting sites engaged in the spread of ideas and images – YouTube; Flickr, etc. It might also have something to do with the cultural frameworks in which these groups exist, and this in turn evokes Douglas's anthropological methods and premises, not evolutionary psychology's interest in hidden matters uncovered in the laboratory.

It might not be so surprising, therefore, to discover that some sociologists (though not many) are sympathetic to meme theory. Runciman (1998, 2009), for instance, relies heavily on the concepts of the meme and 'practice':

the heritable variation and competitive selection of information which affects behaviour in the phenotype is a process which operates also at both the cultural level, where the information is encoded in memes – that is, items or packages of information transmitted from mind to mind by imitation or learning – and the social level, where it is encoded in rule governed practices which define mutually interacting institutional roles. (Runciman, 2009: 3)

Note here the acceptance of an information-theoretic viewpoint. Cultural transmission consists in 'packages of information'; culture and society can be thought of as 'evolving'.

Runciman argues that it makes sense to use the term 'meme' because it is a convenient way of linking the way such discrete packages of information constitute 'messages' transmitted from mind to mind to cultural change. He also believes, without showing much evidence, that this view on what we shall shortly call the classic sociological problem has 'displaced its competitors' (i.e., other accounts of cultural change) (2009: 54). Quite what this might mean is unclear. Perhaps the term 'meme transmission' is now generally preferred to such equivalent terms as 'learning' within sociology, though this seems unlikely. In any case, what Runciman is doing is rehearsing the classical sociological debates about institutions and their relationship to attitudes, values and beliefs – that is, the conundrum having to do with how the stable features of society interact with human agency. What is new in his account, if that is the word, is the introduction into this discourse of 'imitation' through the meme. As we saw in earlier chapters, there are all sorts of ways that one can solve the riddle of the sociological perspective: the relationship between structure and agency is one; this is another.

The important point is that Runciman's efforts should remind us that what he is trying to do is bring a view from outside his discipline under an umbrella perspective of his own discipline. As we saw with Fararo, starting views dictate not just evidence but the kind of questions that need answering; these starting explanations can be very powerful and difficult to shift within a discipline. What Runciman seems to fail to realise is that he takes the psychology and the evolution out of his claims and substitutes standard sociological tropes and methods. Ideas evolve, institutions constrain, individuals create change through myriad individual choices. This sounds like basic sociology, not some new view about human nature. It is no wonder, then, that his view would appear unedifying to his colleagues and even less interesting to those within mainstream evolutionary psychology.

Conclusion

What we have been wanting to show throughout the book is that no account can sensibly explain every aspect of human behaviour or choices made. What each and every account does – and can only do – is set out a starting premise and see how far that premise can take us. As should be clear, a feature of any inquiry is that it can dictate the kinds of evidence it needs as well as the methods apposite for the empirical work the approach implies. These methods and the evidence they gather also imply the kinds of question that are to be posed. We have seen that the evolutionary perspective sets up a problem of why culture changes so rapidly when it is evident that in other respects evolutionary change is very slow. This problem is manifest in its starting premises. From other views, the change of culture might be seen differently; indeed, for many in the field of sociology, as a case in point, the speed of cultural change is viewed as so slow as to require explanation: this is why theories of false ideology and such were devised.

We have sketched the views of various protagonists of the evolutionary psychology perspective and have shown that just what counts as evidence in their views is diverse, and this suggests not thoroughness but, to some extent, an anxiousness with starting premises and doubts about evidence. Claiming that sex drives cultural change is one thing; showing how this is so is another. Claiming that there are tendencies in the choices people make as regards mates or as regards their altruistic behaviour is a far cry from showing cases of behaviour that prove the starting assumption in either case is true.

Another problem, and still related to evidence, is conceptual and how concepts categorise or bundle different phenomena and questions accordingly. We saw, in the case of Pinker, for example, that he believes the mind has a modular structure – it is made up of different components that perform different functions. Now there is evidence that different functions are performed by different parts of the brain. This is not the same thing as saying the *mind* has modular functions. If one confuses the two, one is led to the wrong questions, the wrong methods and the wrong evidence.

Let us illustrate: it is one thing to say that the brain seems to store 'memories' in one area; it is quite another to say that a person uses their recollections mindfully. There is no location for 'the memory' in the latter, whereas there is for the former. The word 'memory' is doing *different things* in each case. In one, labelling a space, in the other, labelling an ability that is subject to judgement – good, bad, well done, and so forth. Pinker would want us to assume that there can be a blurring of two logically distinct categories – mind and brain and the use of related categories, such as memory – and he assumes too that the empirical referents of each are the same. What he wants, in other words, is to say that the brain's inner functioning maps onto cultural performances.

Yet, and as should be clear, it often makes little sense to marry the places of the brain with the acts of the mind. When one seeks to do so, one needs to show adroitness – care, to be blunt. As Coulter and Sharrock show in *Brain, Mind and Human Behavior in Contemporary Cognitive Science* (2007), many in the evolutionary psychology camp – and indeed more generally in cognitive science – are like Pinker, in that they run rough-shod over such important distinctions. Sometimes memory in the brain can be treated as connected to memory as an adjunct of mindful behaviour, but not always. This muddling can make sorting out the merits in the claims made from simple falsehoods very difficult.

As we saw with Pinker's investigation of swearing, effective investigation of that requires a focus on cultural acts and not on brain responses; indeed, to look at brain responses as if they tell one about that kind of mindful behaviour leads one to make the mistake of taking crucial aspects of the phenomenon in question out of view. To swear is a deliberate act; it is purposeful, one for which persons are accountable. To be sure, what is meant here as purposeful and accountable requires and deserves careful investigation, as Douglas shows in her book, but to remove that aspect from the phenomenon – its accountability in interaction for want of a phrase – is to remove the meat from the sandwich.[4]

All this points to something that is perhaps even more profound for our purposes. For what we have learned is that the diverse starting premises of evolutionary psychology, their conceptual problems and evidential limits notwithstanding, produce quite distinct characterisation of what choice 'is', whereas we saw in chapter 4, where we considered Sen and rational actor theory, that most economists end up taking a fairly common view about the mechanics and explanatory power of their perspective. This entails starting with a fairly contained and restricted notion of what the human chooser is and leads them eventually to settle on the idea that what people think they choose, or what they say they choose, does not matter to economics. It is what they buy that matters. And what they buy, for most economists, is assessed in terms of aggregates, and not in any instance. Economists are interested in the choices of the market, not the choices of the individual.

In evolutionary psychology, in contrast, no such agreement can be found. There is debate about how to define what choice is and hence how to measure it, just as there is debate about the relationship between types of choice. There is discord too about the relationship between the reasons people think they have and the reasons that evolution somehow (and in various ways) comes to impose on them. Some advocates of the evolutionary view argue that choice is a hidden cost–benefit calculation; but this can be linked to genes or to cells, or combined with other factors such as a desire for collaboration and altruism. It is not clear how one would see these calculations in action except in the aggregate. In any case, and unfortunately for this perspective, it is not clear what aggregates would be good for counting such matters. The range of sexual selection or the size of the brain? Cultural manifestations or births? Aggregates about what, and leading to what result?

Others from the evolutionary view consider some of these matters as irrelevant. They think evolution is manifest in the outcomes of language change. They are not too concerned with sex, with genes, with altruism and its markers. But, again, it is not at all clear what

---

[4] As it happens, Pinker's desire to transform cultural entities into physiological phenomena says quite a bit about the intellectual landscape of psychology. As Danziger notes in his *Marking the Mind* (2008), the object of inquiry in the sciences of the brain turn out more often to be to do with concepts that have been constructed through arguments that are essentially social and cultural and not evidentially produced. After all, the mind and the brain should not be treated as one and the same – one is emphatically a cultural artefact if ever there was one, the other a body system.

evidence might be brought to bear on language as a measure of evolution. Would it be changes in the instructions hidden in language, in the computational codes that affect the mind's outputs, in Pinker's take of Fodor's mentalese? Or is it to be found in the random behaviours of cultural transmission through words, in Dennett's interpretation of memes? These and many other differences are perhaps suggestive of the state of play in this field. It is also a reminder of one of the key lessons of this book: to understand what evidence one seeks, it is necessary to spend a great deal of time understanding the point of view that demands that evidence in the first place. If that point of view is still inchoate, despite claims by some of its protagonists, it is perhaps too early to expect much in the way of evidential materials to derive from it. In our view, this means that one cannot 'choose' evolutionary psychology as a perspective to consider in our review of the 'sciences of choice', since it is far from clear what one would see from this perspective, let alone choose what types of choice one could analyse thereby.

6

MODELLING CHOICE

In this chapter, we examine some of the other ways in which the 'science of choice' is conducted. We are especially interested here in the way in which different kinds of models and methods get used. Methodologies vary, of course, for any number of reasons. Approaches drift in and out of fashion. Conceptions of the 'problem' to be investigated and the appropriate way of investigating it alter over time. Philosophical perspectives evolve, and there are shifts in the boundaries of a discipline that affect methodological views, and so on. This is dramatically shown in the case of new imaging technology which purports to reimagine what 'brain science' might be. All of this brings to mind the (supposed) adage of John Maynard Keynes that, 'When the facts change, I change my mind.'

In short, changes in the pecking order brought about by new insights and, to a degree, by challenges from other disciplines inevitably affect our view of how data might be collected, analysed and theorised about. None of this changes the fundamental claim we have been elaborating, that there is an intimate and intrinsic connection between starting premises and the evidence that pertains to those premises. Nor does it mean that some shifts in the type of evidence that can be collected affect or reshape, to some degree, these starting premises. What we hope to have shown already, though, is that these premises still remain just that, starting points, ways of commencing, and, to the extent that this is so, one always has to be careful about what one expects from any inquiry. One always has to delimit what one starts with so as to allow attention elsewhere; what one starts with somehow become the unexamined phenomena, the price paid for being able to undertake research. Keynes's adage needs altering to 'When I find new facts, I need new places to view them from.'

In this chapter, we discuss three particular techniques for data capturing and explore what they can see – what they provide for their starting premises. We shall also comment on how these techniques might affect the premises that motivated their use. The first of these techniques is modelling in economics and, in particular, the modelling of what gets called the Prisoner's Dilemma. This is a way of capturing certain sorts of logical, rational action-type reasoning behaviours where the trick is to factor in more than one actor. Here we will remark on the use of this technique in the home discipline of economics, while pushing our inquiries into this discipline a little further than we did in chapters 2 and 3. We then look at an evolution of the Prisoner's Dilemma-type techniques in what has come to be called game theory. This turns out to be an approach that allows mathematical rendering of the logical outcomes of joint or multi-person interactions, if those actions can be supposed as 'rational'. It is of interest not only to economics but to other disciplines too, including philosophy and cognitive science. As we shall note, a temptation with this technique is to keep extending its scope to include activities where the starting premise, that they are to be characterised as 'rational', has not necessarily been secured. Indeed, the technique can run roughshod over starting premises and empirical matters alike. This does not mean that the technique is flawed, but, as with all techniques, it needs to be handled judiciously. We end with a sketch of Bayesian statistical approaches, a method which presupposes that probability can be used in massively evidential ways. Here too, there is an issue of scope: that some behaviours can be seen to be sensibly described or explained through probabilistic techniques doesn't mean that *all* behaviours can. This holds true if this technique is to capture 'choice' or decision-making as much as it does for other kinds of human activities. One of the special problems of handling Bayesian techniques, however, is that ascertaining where such distinctions occur can be very hard to see in the evidence that the technique itself provides. For one thing, Bayesian statistics are very complex and equally hard to understand; for another, this approach, like game theory, can become greedy as regards what its outputs imply, allowing those easily enamoured with the technique to lose sight of the range of activities over which it is not so effective. The problem for the Bayesian perspective turns out to be related not to what it can explain, then, but to those matters of choice it cannot explain.

Economic models and the Prisoner's Dilemma

It is entirely unoriginal to argue that classical economics derived its methodologies and methods from what is called the 'positivist' tradition. Successive social science textbooks have rather obfuscated the meaning of this label, and, in sociology at least, it has been reduced to a sneer word. In its proper form, traceable to the likes of Auguste Comte and John Stuart Mill, it refers to a specific commitment to the primacy of experience and to a very particular conception of what 'science' is. It thus rejects any *a priori* or metaphysical truths and insists on a commitment to something that looks like objective data. Without unnecessarily complicating the issue, it is normally thought that the ideal method of the natural sciences is the experimental method. The fact that it is impossible to carry out genuinely experimental manipulation of human behaviour – that it is either or both practically and ethically impossible to rearrange parts of people's actual lives so as to meet the demanding requirements of experiments – does not necessarily lead to the conclusion that the method is therefore inapplicable. On the contrary, the statistical manipulation of data can be used as an analogical form of the strict requirements for experiment proper. Of course, experimentation takes many forms, and we discuss some of them below. By the same token, the kinds of statistical technique that can act as a surrogate vary – from articulating the inner logic of modelled behaviour (to which we now turn) to balancing the weight of likely evidence about 'facts' (which we address with regard to Bayesian statistics).

A significant part of the debates we are reviewing has to do with the nature and value of modelling. Modelling is now increasingly common not just in economics but in psychology and sociology, among many other disciplines, although without question it is a sine qua non of economics. Leijonhufvud (1973), whom we mentioned very early on for his mocking of the caste system of the 'Econs' in the opening chapter, goes on to make some observations about the basis for caste allocation and the pecking orders to be observed among this tribe, noting that:

> The dominant feature, which makes status relations among the Econ of uniquely interest to the serious student, is the way that status is tied to the manufacture of certain types of implements, called 'modls'. The status of the adult male is determined by his skill at making the 'modl' of his 'field'. The facts a) that the Econ are highly status-motivated, b) that status is only to be achieved by making 'modls', and c) that most of these 'modls' seem of little or no practical use, probably accounts for the backwardness and abject cultural poverty of the tribe. (1973: 328)

Such caste considerations are not unique to economics, and pecking orders are arguably one of the few human universals (at least in academic life). Even so, the idea that models are of little or no practical value – do not correspond in any useful way to reality – needs some investigation, not least because powerful new computational tools make such models increasingly complex and sophisticated. Mary Morgan (2012) has traced the historical evolution of the reasoning processes associated with modelling and makes an obvious but nonetheless telling point about the nature of models in economics. They are not 'just a depiction of the economy but one that [can] be manipulated, and because it [can] be manipulated, it could be reasoned with.' Models can be produced that process data that simply could not have been 'computed' before.

Nevertheless, the turn to modelling is not without problems, as controversies surrounding climate models attest. We do not see ourselves in the camp of 'climate change deniers', but models do not only predict the direction of a change, they predict the amount. The idea that we can predict with certainty the amount of temperature change that will occur in the world over an extended interval is, frankly, absurd. What we can say, with a great deal of certainty, is that there is a direction to temperature change, that we are fairly certain that we know what is causing it, and – within a certain range of uncertainty – have some idea about the amount of change we might expect over, say, the next fifty years.

Underpinning some part of the above arguments, as we have tried to show in the previous chapter, is the vexed problem of descriptive versus normative conceptions of economic behaviour. In the former, no account of motive is necessary, since behaviour can be understood purely formally as utility maximising. An extreme example of such a view is that of Cameron (2002: 5):

> we might say that economics analyses human choices under scarcity regardless of whether explicit movement of money or operation of markets is involved. Therefore, as engaging in anything seen to be sin is an act of choice, it can be subject to the logic of choice in the economic model. Movements of money and the machinations of markets simply represent the formation of institutions which are collective goods that enhance individual welfare. Churches, families, charities and so on are simply alternative means of doing this. They are not a species of supra-rational emanation which must be taken as given or delegated to some expert from another discipline for inspection. Thus economics becomes an analysis of how institutions form from the collective attempt to maximize utility.

The point of Cameron's work on the 'economics of sin' is precisely that immorality and deviance can be understood through the economic lens just as much as normatively compliant behaviour. We do not need to identify special motives to explain why some people and not others are active sinners; all sorts of activities can be explained in one and the same way, which is on the basis of 'incentives'. In the normative conception, motivation takes a much more central role and the difficult questions have to do with the sources of motivation. Some economists believe that even this can be formally modelled through game-theoretic mechanisms dealing in trust and reputation. Others, like Sen, as we saw in chapter 3, have a quasi-sociological view. Sociological and economic rational choice views, then, share a commitment to some kind of modelling, but this disguises a range of concerns: What is the model for? Is it expected to approximate (closely or otherwise) reality? Are its parameters merely assumed or empirically founded? What gaps might there be in the data modelled?

Behaviour and hypothesised models

Of specific concern is the *kind* of model, abstraction or idealisation in question. Thus, there are statistical models which attempt to explain *post hoc* existing and large-scale economic tendencies; there are models which attempt to project the simplified assumptions embedded in them into the future – predictive models – and then there is a third class – those which draw on experimental (real or, from the German, *Gedankenexperiment*) conclusions in order to make claims about real-world behaviour. O'Connor refers to the *Gedanken* (thought) experiment as the 'trolley method', apparently after Foot (1978). Singer (2011) has succinctly called this approach 'trolleyology'. O'Connor is a moral philosopher who rejects what he calls a 'quasi-scientific' approach to moral philosophising. Now, we have no particular interest in moral philosophy, but part of O'Connor's argument is germane to the problem of the hypothetical experiment like the Prisoner's Dilemma. Since the idea of the experimental method is that an experiment tests a hypothesis, seeks to identify data which will definitively speak for or against an empirical claim, we must, if we are to avoid confusions, explain what we mean by 'hypothetical experiments'. Let us say that there is a claim as to how people will behave in a particular kind of situation, whether they will or will not deliberately sacrifice the life of some small number of individuals to save the lives of a greater number. It is easy to see why we can't set up proper experiments to determine what people would do in such circumstances – we can't allow a bunch of undergraduates to be pulling levers or turning switches in ways that may result in the killing of a greater or lesser number of people. What do we do instead? As O'Connor puts it, in his critique of the widespread and growing use of 'trolley cases', he proceeds by 'discussing the use of trolley problems by Frances Kamm, which offer perhaps the most extreme instance of treating imaginary hypothetical cases as the raw data for a quasi-scientific approach to ethics' (2012: 243).

Effectively, we present people with a hypothetical situation. The 'trolley' problem refers to a thought experiment whereby, after his brakes fail, the driver of a tram/trolley is forced to make a choice such that he can either do nothing, stay on the line, and kill five people who are tied to the track or make an active decision to switch to a spur and thereby kill one (also tied to the track). There are many versions of the problem, all designed to show that our responses to these dilemmas vary according to some specific features. Thus and for instance, it would be suggested that most of us would accept that there is a moral justification for killing one rather than five people, but, confronted with a slightly different problem, that of the 'fat man on the footbridge', we might take a different decision. In the 'fat man' problem, we are invited actively to throw the fat man off the bridge in order to save lives. It seems that most of us have a different view of whether it is acceptable to kill the fat man rather than, as in the first case, 'let him die'. Be that as it may, the trolley experiment, because it is in certain ways strategically connected to the concerns of moral philosophers, has become a model for other experiments, its original form being varied and elaborated in all sorts of ways to sharpen the 'intuitions' of philosophers, which explains the in-joke of the title 'trolleyology'.

To be fair, the use of such experiments is not to predict what people would actually do in the event of such (highly unlikely) situations but is meant to play much the same part that modelling does in economics, which is to single out the elements that might be involved in actual cases, to see whether, for example, people ordinarily make a moral difference between 'killing someone' and 'letting them die', and the assumption is that what people say they will do, just as much as their actually doing what they say they will do, can evidence the fact that they recognise such a difference.

This is not to say that circumstances cannot arise where real and serious dilemmas of this kind follow, and choices have to be made.[1] The core of 'trolley' method approaches is the claim that they usefully allow abstraction from real-life cases. In this respect, of course, they have much in common with economic modelling; and, after all,

---

[1] Edmonds (2014) provides an excellent account of the dilemmas in question and the historical context in which trolleyology arose.

a moral choice is a choice like any other. The point, however, is that such abstractions must entail the removal of *irrelevant* factors so as to clarify the role of the relevant. As Wood argues, in the context of moral problems, the difficulty is that 'Trolley problems seem . . . to abstract not from what is irrelevant, but from what is morally vital about all the situations that most resemble them in real life (2011: 82).'

Shue (2006) makes a further distinction, between abstraction and idealisation, claiming that abstraction 'removes dirt' while idealization 'adds shine'. O'Neill, with specific reference to rational choice views, points out: 'if human beings are assumed to have capacities and capabilities for rational choice or self-sufficiency or independence from others that are evidently not achieved by many or even by any actual human beings, the result is not mere abstraction; it is idealization' (1996: 41).

Now this is quite an important distinction. Shue is concerned with policy arguments about the legitimacy of using torture and about the use of examples in the argument. Examples are idealised when they assume the most favourable conditions for the point that they are trying to make, as when the argument that torture can be effective assumes that the suspect is correctly identified, that the suspect will easily yield to mistreatment, and so on. The examples are abstract when they are constructed in ways which show a lack of familiarity with or attention to the realistic requirements of using, in the relevant case, torture to urgently avert a catastrophe – as where it is assumed that the torturer is experienced, for example, and therefore more likely effective. Torturers require a supporting organisation to train and supervise them, for example.

As a result, arguments which are meant to justify the use of torture in a very special and rare case really require that torture be a regular and much more widely legitimated activity. The point is that such 'experiments' can be set up in such a way as to remove many of the things from their constituent scenarios that in practice would be relevant to weighing up the issues involved in a decision. O'Connor again:

> Trolley scenarios are rigidly framed so as to exclude all sorts of possibilities that an averagely empathetic and otherwise cognitively unimpaired rescuer should feel morally obligated to consider. It is no exaggeration, I believe, to say that the trolley method as one comes across it nowadays in practically any moral philosophy journal, and increasingly also in the cognitive sciences, would not exist without the stipulation that the rescuer can act only in strictly specified ways. (2012: 246)

Game theory

To reiterate, none of the above indicates that thought experiments (or any other kind of experiment) cannot be illuminating. Of course they can. Exactly what is being illuminated, however, always needs to be borne in mind. We now take a look at game theory, its foundations, and the different kinds of claim that can be made for it.

The first and most obvious form of experimentation associated with theories of choice and rationality is so-called game theory. Game theory has a number of forms and at least two different purposes, as Henrich et al. point out:

> game theory consists of two different enterprises: (1) using games as a language or taxonomy to parse the social world; and (2) deriving precise predictions about how players will play in a game by assuming that players maximise expected 'utility' (personal valuation) of consequences, plan ahead, and form beliefs about other players' likely actions. The second enterprise dominates game theory textbooks and journals. (2004: 57)

If the second of these two possibilities describes what experimental economists are up to, then of course it does not require any strong real-world assumptions. This is important. We do not have to assume that these game behaviours closely describe anything that happens in real life. Again, as Henrich et al. state: 'Experimental economists are usually interested initially in interactions among anonymous agents who play once, for real money, without communicating. This stark situation is not used because it is lifelike (it's not). It is used as a benchmark from which the effects of playing repeatedly, communicating, knowing who the other player is, and so forth, can be measured by comparison' (ibid.: 58). And by far its most famous exemplar is the 'Prisoner's Dilemma', as we shall see.

Before that, however, we should say something about the foundations of game theory. It is generally agreed that the inspiration for the development of game theory comes from the work of, firstly, Von Neumann and Morgenstern (1944) and, then, John Nash (1950). The fundamental assumption in Nash's 'solution' was that players in a particular kind of game will maximise their strategies, choosing the ones that are optimal for them, *when they bear in mind what their opponent is likely to do*, and in such a way that the 'solution' will tend towards an equilibrium where no one can rationally improve their chances any more (which is why this is called the 'Nash equilibrium'). There are effectively two kinds of strategy, the 'pure' and the 'mixed'. The latter is the most interesting because it describes a degree of randomness in one's moves. The player may opt among various choices specifically because she or he wants to avoid letting the other player or players know what their move is likely to be next time and will make decisions based on that. Put simply, at the point of equilibrium, each player's strategy is optimal, as rational as it can be, in the sense that one's 'payoff' will be at a maximum as long as the strategies of others do not change (but not optimal in any other sense).

It is important to remember that the kind of game in which Nash was initially interested was the 'one-time', non-cooperative game – i.e., where only one's own possible advantage is at stake. Moreover, the games in question had to have a finite set of possible moves. Where Von Neumann and Morgenstern had limited their conclusions to so-called zero-sum games – games where optimum strategies mean that no one can win (think tic-tac-toe) – Nash aimed to show that, in any game meeting the criteria outlined above (non-cooperative, finite set of moves), there must exist a point where there is an equilibrium. As a rule of thumb, it is suggested that a way of testing for this equilibrium is to reveal to players what the choices of others actually are and ask if that results in a change of strategy. If it does not, then we have a Nash equilibrium.

Now, we should be clear that the 'Nash equilibrium' is a mathematical concept and, in and of itself, predicts nothing about what people might do in real situations – that connection between this account and real action needs to be made outside the maths. In each game of the type he describes, there must be an equilibrium point, and his equations prove it. This is the crux of the matter, however: can we predict that behaviour will approach the Nash equilibrium (or equilibria, if there is more than one) and, if so, in what circumstances? Of course, since then, any number of experimental set-ups have been designed to test whether actual behaviour approaches the equilibrium point. Whether the concept of the Nash equilibrium holds for other types of game has been the subject of much investigation, and game theorists have, for instance, looked at what happens when the game is repeated over and over, what happens when a single game forms part of a larger one, and what happens when players have imperfect information with which to assess their choices. It has been shown that there can be more than one Nash equilibrium in a variety of different types of game (such as the 'Stag Hunt', mentioned below); and that some assumptions might be misleading (e.g., the idea that 'one-shot' or one-time games could predict outcomes over a sequence of games). Indeed, following Nash's initial claims, it was later accepted that these varying conditions meant that, for instance, game theory needed to deal with sequential games.

Types of game and types of human conduct

There are, then, different kinds of game. A number of games describe these variations well. The first and best known is the one we have already mentioned – the Prisoner's Dilemma game. Interestingly, the origins of the Prisoner's Dilemma lie in a game that was actually played (see Morgan, 2012: 345) in or around 1950 at the RAND Corporation. This game has a very simple setup, which goes as follows:

> Two partners in crime are held in separate cells. They are not allowed to communicate with each other. Each is made an offer which goes:
>
> • if you rat on the other criminal, and he says nothing, you go free and he gets ten years;
> • if you both stay quiet, you both get six months;
> • if you both rat on each other, you both get five years.

The importance of the Prisoner's Dilemma lies in what it tells us about cooperation and competition (or non-cooperation). Our choices may, on the one hand, lead us – in the way predicted by neoclassical economics to act competitively (to 'defect', in the game theory jargon) or they may lead us to cooperate. The result, as Morgan says (ibid.: 354–5), was something of a problem for economics because the experimental behaviour differs from what neoclassical economics might predict. In early versions of rational choice theory, the selfishness of individual choice was explained by the fact that it was the best strategy. The problem lies in the fact that what appears to be a 'best strategy' for the individual leads to an outcome which is not optimal for that individual. In the game, if one player alone decreases the level of cooperation (defects) then that person will be better off, but, if both do, then both are worse off. Statistically, the vast number of people opt to rat on their partner despite the fact that the 'rational' decision is to cooperate ('rational' in the sense that it leads to the best outcome for both players). The basic structure of the Prisoner's Dilemma game, then, deals with options and payoffs, and, as Kreps (1990b) points out, 'While the story is fanciful, the basic structure of options and payoffs that characterise this game occur over and over again in economics.' As he further notes: 'the point of game theory is to help economists understand and predict what will happen in economic contexts' (1990a: 7). He goes on, however, to point out that what to 'understand and predict' might mean is open to various interpretations.

Of course, it may well be that the conditions of the game lead to a particular outcome. The Prisoner's Dilemma, as described above, is an example of a 'strategic form game' in which each player knows what their own options are and what the payoffs of each choice are. 'Extensive form games' vary the conditions in a number of ways. They might, for instance, vary the order or the timing of choices or restrict what kind of information each player has. Perhaps if the game were to be repeated, or if it were to be set up with different conditions, an optimal outcome might be found in which the equilibrium point involves cooperation rather than non-cooperation. Robert Axelrod (1986), for instance, set up Prisoner's Dilemma experiments in which the game is played over and over, for a fixed number of times. The optimum strategy turns out to be so-called tit for tat. Somewhat surprisingly, when the game is played over and over, the simplest strategy – cooperate the first time round and then do what your partner did the move before – is by far the most successful over a long period of time.

Axelrod came to suggest a number of conditions were necessary for a given strategy to be successful under these conditions, and these include:

- being nice;
- not being the first to cheat, or 'defect', is a good strategy in repeating Prisoner's Dilemma games;
- retaliating;
- however, blind optimism does not work: retaliation is sometimes necessary. Always cooperate is a poor strategy since nasty strategies will always outdo it;
- forgiving;
- being non-envious;
- not being explicitly competitive is a good strategy.

Thus, it appears that, under certain conditions, cooperation can in fact be a rational decision. In any case, at least for economists, the value of the games depends on the degree to which their conditions describe real-world conditions. If they can be said to do so, then they have an obvious predictive value at some level. Whether they do or not remains somewhat controversial. Huck (2004: xi) has summed up the problem as follows:

[from the late 1970s] . . . there was a chasm – between the beauty and elegance of the theory of games on the one hand, and the dour facts of behaviour observed in games on the other. In between: a void. In the decades that followed, the economics literature slowly started filling this gap. Evolutionary game theory, preference evolution, learning models, models of bounded rationality with and without optimization, and, of course, more and more systematic experimental evidence – all these approaches flourished, competing with as well as complementing each other. Yet, compared to other fields, progress has not been particularly fast and the task before us is still immense. The task is, of course, to understand behaviour, and understanding is not easy. Life between hyperrationality on the one hand and simple facts on the other is not easy. There are no fixed axioms, and there is no fast-track methodology.

Classic versions of game theory did not seem to have an awful lot to do with the real circumstances of people's behaviour, and one of the reasons is that, as situations unfold, we seem to change our preferences. They might evolve. In other words, if it is true that we learn about our situations over time (information gets added in, as Bayesian statistics would have it) then perhaps we can construct experiments which demonstrate what difference that makes. These experiments have indeed become more common and constitute an evolution of game theory.

A vast number of games exploring different conditions under which choice behaviour might be examined are being investigated. They include the 'Stag Hunt' (which seems to originate with Jean-Jacques Rousseau); the 'Dictator game'; the 'Trust' game; the 'Ultimatum' game; the 'Volunteer's Dilemma', and so on. The point about all these variants is that they change the conditions under which games operate, and thus different forms of optimal 'solution' result, with different degrees of 'cooperation' versus 'defection'.[2]

The simplest form of game, sometimes called an 'ultimatum game', demonstrates something of the way in which conditions can be varied. An ultimatum game is one in which two persons bargain only to the extent that one person makes a 'take it or leave it' offer. Experimentally, a standard method is to give a sum of money to one person (say $10) and ask them to make an offer to a second person, such that, if the second person accepts the offer, they get to share

---

[2] The Stanford online *Encyclopedia of Philosophy* gives a nice summary of the different kinds of condition which turn out to be relevant (http://plato.stanford.edu/entries/game-theory/).

the money, but, if the second person rejects the offer, they both get nothing. There is a certain consistency to the results, in that typically the offer is slightly less than $5 and is accepted 90 per cent of the time. Offers of $2 or less are rejected 50 per cent of the time. This suggests some kind of 'fairness' mechanism is in play in addition to the 'pure' rationality that game theory would predict (game theory predicts that all the power lies with the person making the first offer, and thus the second person should accept anything, no matter how small, in preference to receiving nothing at all, though it is clear that the person receiving the offer can screw the first party over).

Ultimatum games, on the face of it, are a test of Stigler's hypothesis that, when self-interest and ethical values are in conflict, self-interest will win. A version of the ultimatum game is the 'dictator' game, in which only the offer is made – there is no opportunity to reject it. The theory is that dictator games give us an opportunity to distinguish between altruism and fear of rejection as motives for a particular offer (i.e., a 'fair' offer might be made for both these reasons but in the dictator game the fear motive is removed). Dictator games appear to show that fear is more important than fairness as a motive. So-called trust games are versions of dictator games. In a trust game, an investor has to decide how much capital to give the dictator – trusting that there will be a return on the investment (usually, under the terms of the game, the investor is told they can expect a return of some kind). The dictator has to decide how much money to return. Trust is measured by how much money is lent, and trustworthiness by how much is paid back. Trust games have been significant, originally in economics, because they appear to show how trust reduces transaction costs. Trust, unlike legal protection, costs little or nothing. Trust has an evident connection to the concept of social capital, reviewed in chapter 4, and we say more about this in the context of choice in the Internet age in the next chapter.

Games and ordinary life

All such games are extremely controversial, largely because results seem to vary, as do the reasons posited for variation. As with any experiments of this kind, though, the biggest problem is that of the 'demand conditions' of the experiments. That is, subjects have to decide what they consider the point of the experiment to be, and their decisions will be substantially informed by the way in which the game is set up. We should also point out that game theory does not necessarily depend on rationality in its strictest sense for predictable outcomes. Although it predicts optimising strategies, it would in principle be just as useful if it could demonstrate regular deviations from them. Game theory, then, is not at all incompatible with behavioural psychology. Camerer (2003), for instance, inserts the idea of behavioural game theory by incorporating other assumptions, such as emotion, limited foresight, mistakes, and so on.

Two issues arise from this, in our view. The first is whether this mathematical abstraction actually tells us how people go about playing games and, rather more importantly, whether it tells us anything about situations which might not normally be thought of as being 'games' at all. There is no doubt that, at one point, there was a significant divergence between theoretical elegance and real situations.

Krebs defended game theoretical outcomes in the following way: 'I contend that the major successes have come primarily from formalizing common-sense intuition in ways that allow analysts to see how such situations can be applied in fresh contexts and permit analysts to explore intuition in and extend it to slightly more complex formulations of situations' (1990b: 109). He goes on to argue:

> [game theory] . . . contributes a) a unified language for comparing and contrasting common-sense intuitions in different contexts . . . b) the ability to push intuitions into slightly more complex contexts . . .; and c) the means of checking on the logical consistency of specific insights and . . . a way of thinking through logically which of our conclusions may change drastically with small changes in the assumptions. (Ibid. 110)

Now, all this is perfectly plausible (and is very similar to arguments that can be made on behalf of the economists' 'unrealistic' models). If we can successfully identify the conditions which pertain in a game and identify that similar conditions pertain in the real world (as long as we are careful not to move from simple contexts to much more complex ones) then some useful predictions might result. Game theoretical models are predicated on particular assumptions about rationality, assumptions which – as we have seen – are more sophisticated than, and challenge, neoclassical assumptions about the rational man by making individual choices conditional on the expected responses of others. Of course, and as we have been at pains to point out, modest theories can give successful, if modest, results.

At the point where theories about human behaviour can be tempted into becoming 'greedy' – where they seek to answer all questions in terms of their preferred theoretical lens, regardless of the overall quality or range of the evidence on which they are drawing – their value starts to become questionable. That game theory helps economists identify the conditions which pertain in certain situations, compare them to other related situations, and make modest predictions about them all is not in doubt. But advocates of game theory are often tempted to claim it can be deployed to much more dramatic effect in areas such as evolutionary psychology – in this view, game theory is meant to explain some of the motivations behind change. But, as we saw in the previous chapter, the evoking of the term 'evolution' is rarely combined with a thought-out and evidence-based explanation as regards what in particular is being accounted for. This holds as true for game theory as it does for meme theory – one needs to know what aspects of human choice and action are to be thus explained. Or are the claims nothing more than very high-level abstractions?

Whether game theory can consistently and with any degree of accuracy predict the outcome of hugely complex events we also doubt – international affairs comes to mind, since this is often a claim that game theorists make (and has a long-standing history; see Snidal, 1985). The issue here is not that such matters cannot be fathomed; nor is it the case that this method might help cast the phenomena in a new light. But this comes at a price, which has to do with what is particular about this method. It functions by simplifying the important property of events, their complexity, into gaming rationalities, and as it does so it treats rationalities as calculative. Sometimes this might be sensible, since these rationalities are at work, but this method cannot uncover other forms of motivations, where game-like reasoning isn't applicable and where the complexities of the interaction may not be best rendered thus. One might say that diplomats would like international relations to have calculative forms, but one doesn't need to know much history to see that there is fog in diplomacy as there is in war. Calculative rationalities may be sought for but rarely achieved. Game theory might be a good tool for teaching undergraduates a sensibility to international relations, but it can't really claim extensive verisimilitude with the way the world functions. Some situations, we suggest, are simply not best explained by game rationalities or by their implied opposite, irrationalities – by reference to calculation of one sort or another.

What we are noting is that one trouble with the game theory technique is that it offers a way in which it appears that nearly all activities can be rendered within its lights. Indeed, one comes to the situation where one feels obliged to doubt whether game theory can tell us much at all about 'human nature', if only because enterprises of that sort – seeking all-encompassing accounts – are always fraught with the problem of reducing what the scope of that labelling might be and dealing with the temptation towards 'greed' to which we are alluding. The term 'human nature' is often used in everyday affairs to excuse a behaviour that seems irrational, for example; within academic philosophy, by way of contrast, it is used as a battle cry for conceptual clarification that entails taking the implied universalism of the word 'nature' out altogether. The former, everyday usage emphasises nature as a cause to be accepted, the latter, academic view, a term that must be abandoned (see, for example, Sandis and Cain, 2012). When it is used by game theorists, meanwhile, it seems to imply some essence to which a human can be reduced – hence the allusion to evolution mentioned above. What we are saying is that the term is far too troubling to be used precisely. Certainly no amount of modelling will produce a choice between the vernacular and the arcane use of concepts such as 'human nature'; there is no Nash equilibrium as regards words.

We might approach this more concretely. So, an evident feature of the kind of experimentation described above is that it yields up numbers. As with Bayesian reasoning, for example, which deals explicitly with subjective knowledge, any kind of information can, in principle, be turned into a set of numbers. Whether the numbers correspond to anything in reality is a different question. The fact that our choices can, in Bayesian terms, be defined according to scales which range between 0 and 1 and spell out a degree of certainty does not mean that somewhere in our heads we are calculating a probability, nor does it mean that numerals are best at characterising the 'knowledge' in question. This too is like nature – too vast and open a category for this to apply in all cases. Likewise with the game theoretical account; its value (and its value can be great) is all too often occluded by the exaggerated claims made for it.

Simplifying the world

One might say, in summary, that game theory is a version of the simplifying strategies that economists have always used, given additional force by the mathematics associated with it. It is predicated on some heuristics about 'rationality' and the way rationality impinges – at least to some extent – on our choices. It might provide us with a picture of decision-making strategies in the market place (and other clearly structured environments where 'calculativeness' is the *modus operandi*). We have no reason to doubt this.

Methodologically, game theory relies mainly on experimental tests of what is predicted in the models. A vast number of experiments have been conducted, and we have mentioned only a few. Crawford argues:

> behaviour in games is notoriously sensitive to details of the environment, so that strategic models carry an informational burden, which is often compounded in the field by an inability to observe all relevant variables ... For many questions [experimental data are] the most important source of empirical information we have and ... are unlikely to be less reliable than casual empiricism or introspection. (Cited in Camerer, 2003: 4)

He goes on to suggest that the power of game theory lies in 'its generality and mathematical precision'. It is general in the sense that it describes all competitive games and precise in the sense that, applied to economic context, it can determine pricing behaviour with a degree of accuracy. Playing competitive games, in this view, is a matter of determining optimal strategies, which seems broadly uncontroversial, bordering even on a tautology.

As Morgan points out, however, the issue is one of typicality. Almost by definition, the more that new and different games are generated, the less 'typical' the cases that they describe. She argues:

> The question for game theorists, as Sutton so bluntly stated "In explaining everything, have we explained nothing? What do these models exclude?" ... With every economic situation potentially matched by more than one candidate model from game theory, and with individual rationality being compatible with many different equilibrium outcomes, the possibilities for using game theory for explanations in terms of types of situation – the middle level explanatory power of situational analysis – is lost. Explanatory breadth, obtained by the development of further typical cases ... appears to have drowned in a sea of one-off individual cases and anecdotes. (2012: 371–2)

Vatnik makes some other observations:

> The Game in GT [game theory] is an idealized concept. Some of the assumptions can – and should be – argued against. The number of agents in any game is assumed to be finite and a finite number of steps is mostly incorporated into the assumptions. Omissions are not treated as acts (though negative ones). All agents are negligible in their relationship to others (have no discernible influence on them) – yet are influenced by them (their strategies are not – but the specific moves that they select

are). Many of the problems are linked to the variant of rationality used in GT. (2009: 176–7)

So, the question is not whether game theory actually has some useful applications, for, in those situations where it is reasonable to assume that the conditions of the game look rather like conditions in the real world, it seems that it does. At the same time, the idea that game theoretical experiments are useful for 'many' questions inevitably leads us to wonder, 'what questions?' Secondly, methodological comparisons which limit us to introspection or 'casual' empiricism rather understate the possibility of alternative approaches.

With respect to the first point, what is critically important is the degree to which game theory can be usefully applied outside the clearly structured contexts in which strategy is evidently a major feature of the task at hand and how the degrees of complexity that might be involved are to be calculated. Thus and for instance, game theory is, as far as we know and for the most part, a fairly accurate predictor of behaviour at auctions and in other 'bidding' contexts (indeed, Robert Auman received the Nobel Prize in 2005 for work on this.)

Having said that, a 1991 auction of broadband spectrum in the USA was something of a disaster for the US government when the auction raised only $14 million instead of the $1.8 billion expected. The reason, at least partly, seems to have been that there was collusion among the bidders (see Vatnik, 2009: 184). Put simply, a 'non-cooperative game' does not very adequately model a real-world situation where it turns out that some of the players are cooperating, albeit illegally.

The final issue we should mention here is the degree to which conditions alter. Much of the economic bargaining process, until the last ten years or so, was conducted in a face-to-face context. The Internet has radically altered that, insofar as we now buy and sell online without ever meeting the people we are buying from or selling to. Under these conditions, other issues come to the fore, issues such as trust and reputation (see, e.g., Bolton et al., 2004a, 2004b), and it is not at all clear that game theoretic assumptions adequately capture what is happening in these situations. Such matters, of course, speak to the problem of motivation and whether we might have a whole variety of reasons to trust or not to trust another person when making decisions about a transaction – a whole variety of experiences which might affect our decisions, and so on.

In sum, and in keeping with our overall theme, what is at stake here is the relationship between a theoretical standpoint (in this case, game theory), the methods chosen to assess its accuracy (in this case, experimental), and what reasonable limits we can place on the kinds of explanation they might provide – the standpoint and the method. It is one thing to assert that the Prisoner's Dilemma gives us a more or less accurate picture of choice behaviour in non-cooperative scenarios with finite choices to be made between a limited number of actors, and quite another to suggest, as evolutionary psychologists do, that it opens a window onto the changing shape of the human – our minds, our bodies and our societies. This too is what we can read in various accounts of game theory. Such outlandish suggestions are precisely what Brannigan (2004) cautions against when he describes the way in which the social science experiment is used to make huge and often unsubstantiated claims about such world-historical events as the concentration camps in the Second World War. Experiments are useful only if they are generalizable to some degree. If game theory answers 'many questions', then it is only reasonable to ask what questions it doesn't answer and where we should draw the line. Without such a demarcation one begins to feel seasick.

Bayesian modelling

If game theory has to do with strategy, then another technique and starting position focuses on the knowledge and beliefs that motivate strategy. The use of Bayesian modelling in choice scenarios is one such. It is important, we feel, to distinguish knowledge from beliefs in this context, as we will outline below. Bayes's theorem concerns how our knowledge and beliefs are updated as new knowledge comes along. Put as crudely as possible, we start with some kind of belief about the likelihood of something happening, then we get new evidence about that event, and the consequence is that our estimate of the event is improved; our belief becomes more knowledgeable, one might say.

Bayes famously used the example of trying to find the location of a ball on a table by dropping a series of balls on a table after it. With each ball, once we are told it is to the left or right of the original, we are able to get a better and better estimate of where the original ball is. How does this work? After the second ball is dropped, if we are told that it is to the left of the original ball, we can guess that the original is on the right side of the table (note that we may not be correct). If another ball is dropped and we are told again that it is on the left of the original then we can be even more sure that our original is on the right side of the table. With each successive ball, we get a better and better sense of where the original ball must be. We are effectively making a series of estimates which get more reliable as new information is added in.

Although it seems that Bayes did not follow up his initial intuitions on these concerns, others after him did so quite extensively. Laplace, in France, was one (see McGrayne, 2012, for a fuller account of the history of the theorem). He used this insight to show that there was a universal tendency for more boys to be born in a population than girls. His colleague Bouvard used it to calculate the masses of Jupiter and Saturn (basing his calculations on a number of different observations that had previously been made). Laplace was able to give the theorem a mathematical foundation, which is basically that the probability of an initial hypothesis C, given that we have a certain amount of evidence I for it, is the same as (equals) our initial estimate of the probability multiplied by the probability of evidence I divided by the sum of the probabilities of the data in all possible outcomes.

To non-statisticians this sounds rather complicated, but we can examine it through a well-known example used by Yudkowsky to demonstrate its somewhat counter-intuitive consequences:

> 1 per cent of women at age forty who participate in routine screening have breast cancer. 80 per cent of women with breast cancer will get positive mammographies. 9.6 per cent of women without breast cancer will also get positive mammographies. A woman in this age group had a positive mammography in a routine screening. What is the probability that she actually has breast cancer?

The correct answer (perhaps astonishingly for those unfamiliar with such a procedure) is 7.8 per cent, obtained in the following way. Out of 10,000 women, 100 have breast cancer (initial hypothesis); 80 of those 100 have positive mammographies (evidence). From the same 10,000 women, 9,900 will not have breast cancer and, of those 9,900 women, 950 will also get positive mammographies. This makes the total number of women with positive mammographies 950 + 80, or 1,030. Of those 1,030 women with positive mammographies, 80 will have cancer. Expressed as a proportion (of the possible outcomes), this is 80/1,030 or 0.07767 or 7.8 per cent.[3]

What we should take from this is not merely the output but how it is suggestive that, in ordinary life, people typically make the mistake of replacing one piece of information with another without the benefit of such calculation. That is, they begin with the information that, say, 1 per cent of women of a certain age have breast cancer,

---

[3] E. S. Yudkowski, An intuitive explanation of Bayes' theorem, http://yudkowsky.net/rational/bayes.

but they then incorrectly replace that information with the fact that 80 per cent of women who actually have cancer get positive results from mammography. But 'the probability that a woman with a positive mammography has breast cancer' is entirely different from 'the probability that a woman with breast cancer has a positive mammography'. Put simply, to find the correct answer one needs to use *all three* of the pieces of information that are at hand.

The general proposition goes like this. We can begin with a statistical *fact* of some kind and describe a probability for it. This is called the prior probability (but this need not be objectively derived – it might be a guess, a belief or an 'expert opinion'). We might subsequently run a test, or collect, or get access to some other evidence. With this, we can update our statistical analysis on the basis of this second tranche of information. It is important to bear in mind that the updated statistical probability (usually called a conditional probability) *still depends on the prior probability* but is now improved on the basis of the new evidence. To put it another way, Bayesian analysis (as it has come to be refined over the years since Bayes himself toyed with the idea) allows for a dynamic updating of statistical information.

Considered purely as a statistical mechanism, Bayes's theorem has proved very useful in areas such as evidence-based medicine (though also sometimes controversially). Bayesianism (in its so-called subjectivist version) is an alternative to so-called frequentist approaches to probability. Frequentism was an early attempt to define probability in such a way that it avoided circularity. The difficulty in definition goes like this: 'the probability of outcome A is the number of times A occurs as a fraction of the total number of times an experiment is repeated, as long as each occurrence is mutually exclusive and equally likely.' The problem is that 'equally likely' is a probabilistic concept being used to define probability. The definition is circular. Frequentism gets away from this by defining probabilities purely and simply in terms of the number of times thing A occurs over time, assuming that any single event occurs randomly. It is usually described as involving 'inverse probability', so called because it refers to inferring backwards from the data to the parameter, or from effects to causes.

Put another way, we can have a distribution of some kind in actual fact, and from this we can infer what the probability might be (we toss a coin over and over again and the results tend towards 50 per cent). This is distinct from, and the converse of, starting with a probability and deducing from it the probability of contingent events. An inverse probability approach, then, has to do with updating degrees of beliefs in propositions by use of probability theory, and in particular Bayes's theorem, to learn from experience and data. This has dominated the topics of Bayesian thinking for most of the century. Bayes's theorem, then, can be applied to objective statistical information so as to demonstrate the effects of updated statistical *facts*.

However, the strict version of Bayes's theorem (the Bayesian interpretation) defines probability in terms of degrees of updated *belief or knowledge* about a certain hypothesis. Distinctions can be made between the probabilities of things and the probabilities of our beliefs about things – an allusion to the distinction between belief and knowledge with which we started this section, though at this point in our discussions these categories get sublimated into a new one, 'the subjective'. It is subjective because it involves assigning prior probabilities to events (which may or may not be accurate) and then reassigning probabilities on the basis of updated *beliefs or knowledge* and thus altering the beliefs/knowledge.

The most famous example is the so-called Monty Hall problem (after a games show host). The Monty Hall problem goes as follows. A contestant is asked to pick one of three doors. Behind one of the doors is a car, and there is nothing behind the other two. The contestant chooses a door but does not open it. Monty then opens one of the other doors to reveal nothing there. The contestant is then invited either to keep to his first choice or to switch to the other possibility. Intuitively, we feel that it will make no difference to his probability of being right but, according to Bayes's theorem (and it has been tested empirically), it does. How can this be? This is because, when the host opens one of the doors that the contestant did *not* select and reveals nothing, *we assume* that the probabilities have shifted. There is, we think, a 50–50 chance that the car lies behind one of the two remaining doors. This is in fact wrong. A better way to think of this is in accordance with Bayes's theorem – that new information has been added to the system. The new information has to do with the behaviour of the games host. The mistake we make (and that made by the person doing the choosing on the show) is the assumption that the host will open one of the doors at random, but he will not. He *has* to open an empty door. *The host has knowledge of where the car is and avoids it* (note that the Monty Hall problem is predicated on what the host knows – this is extremely important. If the host did not know which door held the car, this would not work).

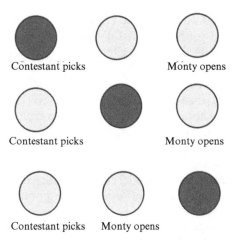

Figure 1: Using this diagram, it is easy enough to see that, if the contestant changes his or her mind, there are two chances of being right, whereas if not, there is only one chance.

Beliefs, probables

We can see where some of the problems arise, however, when Bayesian analysis is applied to beliefs rather than objective probabilities. It lies in the choice of the prior probabilities. While Bayes's theorem is internally consistent and will result in valid probabilities, given the accuracy of our initial assumptions, we cannot always be sure these assumptions are correct. That is, the difficulties lie in how we initially come by the data that we use as our prior probability. Bayesian reasoning predicts that useful information can be derived about events merely on the back of our knowledge and beliefs. One doesn't need to concur with this. Those from the classical frequentist point of view would deny it.

A way of putting the argument in question would be to say that Bayes's theorem cannot produce results that are any less reliable than the initial (prior) assumptions upon which it is built, but the opposite – that is to say, greater reliability of outputs – is not guaranteed.

At root, disagreements about the value of Bayesian work lie, firstly, in this issue, namely whether we can rely on prior probabilities. But they also have to do with what is particular in our topic, and this turns out to be just as important (and related to this first problem), and that is whether human beings actually think this way. Expert systems and other applications based on algorithmic applications of Bayes's theorem may not be based on the way in which experts, or indeed any other kind of human being, actually think and work and yet be 'successful' – do what the system needs to do according to its designers. Clearly, the idea that statistical methods of this kind are 'naturally' superior to other techniques, some of which might be deployed by people in relation to decision-making (especially when the decision-makers are experts) is not exactly proven – it is not certain what those other techniques are. To be sure, there is some evidence that, where problems are bounded, Bayesian methods are reliable, but immense problems arise when they are not. One good example of this is the so-called black swan event in economics. That is, models have predicted the extremely rare nature of certain kinds of event very poorly (see Taleb, 2004).

Another way of exploring this issue is to note that Bayesianism is an approach which is based on the idea that beliefs can be statistically assessed. This is quite a simple idea. Instead of assuming that one either believes or doesn't believe something, one can argue that beliefs come in varying degrees of strength. Moreover, if that is true, the degree to which one believes something may be subject to change as new evidence becomes available. Joyce (2004) gives the (fairly obvious) example of the decisions a gambler might make when betting on a horserace. That is, a gambler may well bet on a horse priced at 4–1 in a given race but be much more unwilling to bet on it at even money, reflecting a certain amount of confidence in the outcome, but no more. It is abundantly clear that we do, often, have at least approximate notions of 'value' when we make decisions about outcomes. At the same time, it is equally clear that these assessments can be wildly inaccurate. One of the authors has spent many hours at racecourses around Great Britain watching 'punters', as they are called, make what look like ridiculous decisions, sometimes fuelled by alcohol or attracted by a particular name, jockey, trainer, or what have you. People happily buy lottery tickets in Britain despite the statistical fact that the chances of winning the first prize are somewhat less (apparently) than the odds of being struck by lightning twice in a lifetime. Bayes's theorem, however, is not designed to test whether people actually behave in rational ways or not. Statisticians, like the rest of us, know that the wellsprings of our behaviour *in reality* may be very complex.

In addition to the self-evident fact that we have different degrees of belief, we can also (according to Bayesians) argue that people have conditional beliefs. In other words, we might believe certain things because we take for granted that other things are true. Critical to the Bayesian view is that we can measure the strength both of the initial beliefs we have and of the conditional beliefs that follow from them. There is a philosophical issue here. Either we can measure the strength of these beliefs – i.e., use a metric to place these beliefs on a scale (which we obviously can, albeit with no guarantee that our measurements mean very much) – or we can believe that people themselves actually enlist mathematical procedures when 'believing' in something. The latter seems, to us, implausible.

For the most part, Bayesian statisticians adopt the former approach. Beliefs can be placed on a scale which represents our confidence in certain outcomes. We must also assume, in this view, that our beliefs, if they can be said to be rational, must be consistent with the laws of probability. One of the earliest philosophical proponents of Bayesian thinking was F. P. Ramsey (1931). Ramsey wanted to show that if someone's beliefs are inconsistent with the laws of probability then they are being *practically irrational*. This argument has become known as the Dutch book argument. A Dutch book is more or less the same thing as what bookmakers in the UK call an 'overround' book. What it means is that, if his book is over-round, a bookmaker should make a profit in any given horserace, whichever horse wins. A Dutch book is a more general statement of the same thing. The bookmaker, in Bayesian terms, is setting the 'subjective probability' of a particular horse winning, which in the vernacular we call the 'odds'. The punter is free to choose whichever horse he or she wishes in the race, but the bookmaker, as long as he can calculate the subjective probabilities and make them add up to more than 100 per cent, should always win. It would follow that, if we were to behave like bookmakers whenever we make a decision (or, at least, whenever we make an economic decision), we would never willingly choose to make ourselves worse off than we need to be. This is what, in Bayesian terms, is called 'coherence'. We will never knowingly (and without constraint) make a choice which would leave us worse off in all possible circumstances than another choice.

But whether or not one can extend this basic tenet to non-economic decisions depends on the extent to which one believes certain other hypotheses. The first is whether one believes that, in all cases, we make choices that best fulfil our desires. This raises a wholly new question, which is whether there is any empirical evidence that shows that we are consistently motivated by self-interest, and, if so, where those motives come from. All the empirical evidence from behavioural psychology (dubious though some of it might be), what we know about our (often unreasonable) habits, the influence of our emotions and values, and so on, would suggest we cannot in fact make this assumption about human behaviour in reality as a whole but only as regards quite prescribed contexts.

Associated with this is another assumption – that we are calculating, or at least estimating, what our maximum subjective utility will be. Again, whether we are actually doing this all the time is up for grabs – clearly it is sometimes the case but clearly, too, not always.

The Bayesian perspective as a theory of learning

In a sense, it doesn't matter in any case, since Bayes's theorem is not testing actual behaviour. It sets out to test what the conditional probabilities of certain events will be if and only if actors actually do behave in accordance with those principles of rationality. It is a test, if you like, of good, rational reasons, not of what our reasons actually are – at least in some versions. Ramsey argued that the strength of our beliefs acted causally on action, a form of pragmatism. Our beliefs are identified through nothing more than our actions.

Bayesian theory, let us remind ourselves, deals with subjective probabilities. Our beliefs are just that: beliefs. They do not necessarily coincide with any objective facts. However, our confidence in an event reflects what we think we know, and any additional knowledge will change our degree of confidence. Hence, Bayesian theory gives us an account of incremental belief – how much we believe in a particular outcome as new (relevant) evidence is added to our prior beliefs. When seen this way, Bayesian theory is a *theory of learning*. Learning is nothing more or less than belief revision. Our initial belief (the prior belief, as Bayesians term it) comes about for any number of possible reasons, but the revision (which Bayesians call the posterior belief) is inferred from subsequent information. Total confidence in something has to be a function of our relative confidence in all possible (relevant) events. Now, it has been pointed out that if one applies Bayesian principles strictly – i.e., if one believes that it actually describes the way people come to believe various things rather than being just a convenient statistical device for estimating likelihoods – then it justifies any number of quite ridiculous beliefs. Joyce (2004: 149), for instance, points out that, if we apply this subjectivism strictly, it

allows a person to draw almost any conclusion on the basis of almost any evidence as long as she starts out with suitable prior beliefs. There are, for example, probabilistically consistent priors that make the existence of statues on Easter Island evidence for the conclusion that Martians built the Pyramids, or that count peyote-induced belief changes as learning experiences. By allowing such absurdities, Bayesianism seems to say that what it makes sense to believe, and what counts as evidence for what, is 'all just a matter of opinion.'

Conclusion

Of course, when put thus, it is no wonder that defenders of Bayes say that such criticisms are silly. These criticisms deny the capacity of those deploying the technique to make sensible judgements about their starting evidence. That the approach could be seen to justify the existence of Martians doesn't invalidate the approach itself; it only suggests the foolishness of some of those who use the technique.

But it cannot be denied that the value of Bayesian theory seems to lie in the degree to which beliefs, both prior and posterior, can be thought of as reliable. Savage and de Finetti (see Savage, 1971; de Finetti, 1970; Efron, 1986), for instance, argue that, even if the prior belief is fundamentally unreliable, progressive new information will make it as it were 'less unreliable' or, to put it the other way, more reliable, and the more information we have, the more reliable our estimates will be – even if we started with something ludicrous. Moreover, if two different people start with very different assumptions, the introduction of new, reliable evidence ought to bring their estimates closer and closer together – but if both started with poor information this isn't guaranteed. It seems pretty obvious that, if prior information and posterior information are both unreliable and/or inaccurate, any resulting estimate will also be more or less useless. Actual accuracy matters from start to end; subjecting information to Bayesian techniques can't alter that.

This may be true. But, in any case, there may be a bigger issue, and this has to do with the relationship between this theory and how people themselves reason. According to Joyce, the philosopher Ramsey recognised this when he started thinking about Bayes in the 1920s, and it is what led him to his notion of coherence. One of the problems he reflected on, and which is seldom mentioned in this context, is whether one can assume that the human mind works as if it were Bayesian. Do people collect information about beliefs and treat them as if they can be assessed in terms of reliability, for example? Ramsey, as we saw, treated this as merely a question of pragmatics. People do this for practical reasons or, rather, they act in a way that, on balance (given all the things they decide), proves beneficial for them.

Part of the problem here that Ramsey didn't really address is that knowledge or belief is not simply a cargo, stuff to be imbibed by the senses and then weighed and acted upon. For one thing, and as the critics of behavioural psychological experiments show, if knowledge provides the basis for people's decisions, the actual choices they make change according to the way in which the conditions in which those decisions are described also change. This holds true even when the decisions in question might seem, at some reductive and apparently objective level, identical. Hence, what turns out to be locally pragmatic needs unpacking. To ask someone to 'press' a button that appears to apply electric current to a subject in an 'experiment' for some psychologists entails the same decision as happens when someone is asked to 'press' the gas release button in a gas chamber. But the context makes the content that drives that act different, though the act is, in some lights, the same – and the differences in the two instances of pressing a button mentioned in the previous sentence need no adumbrating.

What beliefs and knowledge might be is not merely a question of taxonomy – 'they believed this, they had this knowledge' – it is not a cargo, as we say. It is not simply a question of whether knowledge (or information; they are interchangeable here) is good or bad. Meaning, purpose, sense, context, accountability, have a relationship to knowledge and belief and much else besides. This applies most emphatically to human affairs – it may well not matter when Bayesian techniques are used in other contexts. To make predictions about ecology, for example, does not require some claims about how the reasoning of the creatures being modelled account to themselves for the model. But this reflexivity, if that is the word, is essential to human conduct and hence makes the problem of 'meaning' so important to any attempt to characterise human conduct. This is why the philosopher Wittgenstein, who began to think about this topic at the same time as Ramsey, came to conclude (in his *Philosophical Investigations*, 1953) that one needs to look carefully at what it means when people use the term 'information' in their everyday language. His examination of these *practices* suggests that this use is intended to create a distancing from various kinds of authority, a delimiting of the claims that pertain to the word. To have information does not lead to certain outcomes, certain kinds of acts; it can allow the expression of an 'opinion'. 'I have information to that effect' is a statement of ambiguity, a lack of assurance, after all. One needs to be much clearer, then, about the nature of the thing that is assumed to turn the wheel in the Bayesian view of the human; even basic categories such as belief, knowledge and information are ambiguous.

Having said all this, there is something that many from the Bayesian view, and this derives in large part from Ramsey, profess about human affairs that gives their technique especial merit. Let us approach this in a roundabout way. Bayesian methods can be thought of as 'decision theoretic' insofar as they attempt to put decision-making on a different footing to the kind of thinking about choice that we typically associate with, for example, everyday life. This is not only a contrast but can require a recasting of the ways that choice is self-consciously made when people learn about and start to use Bayesian techniques. As we have noted, one of the features of Bayesian reasoning is that it is relatively abstract and can be extremely difficult to comprehend. This has consequences. As Chernoff suggests: 'Once sociologists and physicians have learned about significance levels well enough to use them, a major reorganization of the thought processes is required to adapt to decision-theoretic or Bayesian analysis. Guttman . . . has railed for years about the stargazing habits (associated with significance levels .01 and .05) of his fellow sociologists (1986: 5).' That is, non-experts should be extremely cautious about statistical information they don't always understand, and equally cautious about its results. That this is so suggests that ordinary thinking is essentially different from Bayesian. But many with the Bayesian view believe otherwise. Or rather they think their technique characterises how the mind works. This is what Ramsey came to believe, as we noted. It is this that leads to the coherence principle. People's reasoning produces, in effect, the *same* outcomes as Bayesian processes – choices are somehow balanced, cohered.

It is here, we feel, that the most worrying problem resides. The coherence principle in Bayesianism is no more or less than an assumption about rationality. For it to have value in a science of choice we would have to accept not merely that the mind works like a machine learning engine, which is itself by no means established, but we would also have to agree that there is some kind of causal relationship between belief and action, and that this relationship has the probability nexus of Bayes. But this may be little more than a methodological assumption, a starting place. Indeed it might be a reasonable one. But, as yet, it is not something that has been subject to investigation that can prove this. Studies might (sometimes) show that the outputs of the brain's processing are consistent with a Bayesian process or that a bunch of choices that a person makes might on balance produce a better outcome for themselves when sequentially ordered, and this too might suggest that their choice-making is Bayesian. But that is not the same thing as a proof. That is an *as if* argument.

In any case, there is no reason (so to speak) that one should assume that actions are caused in every instance, that our choices are the results of inputs that lead to outputs, however optimised. This too is a starting assumption, not something that has been proved. Though some philosophers who have taken to causal explanations like converts to a religion say it must be so (as does, for example, Davidson in his famous 1963 paper 'Actions, reasons, and causes', about which we shall say more in the final chapter), one doesn't have to.

After all, not all reasons have to lead to an act. Nor for that matter is having 'a reason to act' the same as having a 'cause to act'. When we choose something, it might have made sense in some instances to say that we had a cause, but in others that might not adequately describe the nature of the act in question. Besides, to assume that all acts have a cause is to confuse the courtroom for everyday life. People have to offer reasons for their acts in courts of law because some of their acts in particular seem peculiar – the ones the court is focusing on. In this view, reasons are only those things that account for acts which are not common or easily accountable. When put thus, one can begin to see that many actions in everyday life might have no reasons behind them. And, indeed, this is very much the character of everyday understanding – one doesn't need a reason to be, say, a mother or a father, just as one doesn't need a reason to breathe. One can ask for reasons for these things, but this is not doing anything other than behaving peculiarly in and of itself, since it implies that the one doing the asking is odd – that they are someone who does not know what defines a father, for example.

The issues being alluded to here might seem rather opaque, little more than a philosophical 'play' with words. But, as should be evident from our still incomplete explorations, methods such as game theory and Bayesian statistics offer ways of bypassing some of the difficulties associated with meaning, with language, with description and accounts, and so forth. They don't, in themselves, answer all of them. Some of the questions that arise ironically do so when one examines what these theories presuppose.

The coherence principle is one of these. It is not an empirically evidenced claim, though perhaps one day it will be. At the moment it is just a starting place, something chosen so as to allow a focus elsewhere, namely on examining the materials of human choice in terms of ever increasing degrees of certainty. Bayes offers a technique that allows researchers to assert with confidence that increasing amounts of information, some belief or fact, may alter the kinds of decision we choose to make. That is, even so, a long way from explaining why people choose what they wish to do with those facts, unless, of course, one likes to think that that choice, or rationality, is itself Bayesian.

7

A NEW PLACE OF CHOICE: THE INTERNET

The various arguments considered so far, like those to come, are exercised by the question of human nature. Is there one? Do all human beings share the same fundamental characteristics, the same basic mental and behavioural proclivities? The 'universalist' interpretation of 'economic man' is understood to suggest that they do, that we are all basically maximising creatures, and that differences between people is due to the application of the same basic structure of cost–benefit reasoning. Sociobiologists and evolutionary psychologists are sympathetic to a similarly universalising view, though they begin (or end) not with economic actions but with the fact that human beings are a biological species. Nevertheless, that there are various answers to what are the common and universal characteristics of the human hasn't stopped people wanting to add further perspectives on what might be the 'essential' underneath the 'misinterpretations'. Nor does it preclude people from observing that the changing landscape of the modern world is both uncovering some of these basic and universal characteristics and allowing them to flower in new ways. This recasts what human nature might be.

Some such claims are made in relation to the Internet (and the World Wide Web – we shall use these terms interchangeably here). It hardly needs saying that the very rapid development of this infrastructure and the technologies associated with it has been accompanied by no little hype. It is often asserted, for instance, that we now have a generation of people, *generation X*, who act in very different ways from those who have gone before – the *baby boomers*, say. Such, apparently, is their facility with new technology that these people are not merely a generation but part of the *net generation* (Tapscott, 2009) or *digital natives* (Palfrey and Gasser, 2008). Some even call them *netizens* (see, e.g., Hauben and Hauben, 1997). Whatever the name, the world is going to be like nothing we have seen before – and as a result we are going to be different too (Rifkin, 2015).

As we have already seen, no one ever sank into obscurity by making excessive claims; quite the reverse. Dizzying excesses not-withstanding, what is evidently true is that the Internet has done several useful things for people engaged in making choices (if that is what they do). Partly this has to do with a change that has been occurring for a century and more: a change that has altered the balance of human productivity away from things – cars, boats and planes, crudely speaking – towards information production and use. The Internet has been able to build on this long-term shift. With this technology, the time (or effort) required to investigate matters relating to information has been massively reduced: it is now at everyone's 'fingertips'. Given that choices – many of them, if not all – are based on information, then, the Internet must be affecting the way people make choices. And this, in turn, 'must be' affecting people engaged in making choices.

These changes might be slightly different from what one would think straight away, however, and the evidence one might need to use to answer how much the Internet may be changing things might be difficult to find (or simply difficult to interpret).

For example, Weiss and Weiss have argued that 'rationality' is compromised in real life by the fact that people might change their minds several times during the course of their decision-making process. As they put it: 'fast changing considerations are a crucial element in the evaluation of decision options. The momentary salience attached to a consequence can change with current, often fleeting circumstances. An option that would usually be rejected can quickly become too tempting to resist' (2012: 173). If this is the case, the speed with which the Internet and its associated technologies offer choice might also affect our rationality. Consider how search engines construct empirically grounded models of the consumer using, for instance, Clickstream data. With the analysis of this data – leaving aside for the moment what this might entail – what is available to be chosen can alter each time the user clicks on a target provided by a search engine. According to Bucklin et al. (2002), this results in the choice being qualitatively different from choice in the 'real world' (see also Van Den Poel and Buckin, 2005). It is, indeed, 'an evolving series of interrelated choices, where both consumer and marketer can play a role in shaping the context of subsequent choice events depending on the outcome of earlier encounters' (ibid.: 3). When commentators say that Internet choice behaviour is dynamic, in other words, they might not quite realise that, in some lights, changing circumstances can compromise rational action – rational choice online will be worse if Weiss and Weiss's argument about real-world rationality is right. Of course, this begs the question of how one would know what is good choice and what is bad; to say rationality is compromised is somewhat vacuous without some instances that show (or measure) what a good choice is.

For another example, the Internet has democratised the avail-ability of information and so allowed people to choose information without reference to (old) institutional and market frameworks and systems of status. If true, this comes with certain costs, not least to the authority of some interests. Academics, for example, can feel aggrieved that the blogosphere creates a challenge to their authori-tative pronouncements. More or less anyone on the Web can now be a knowledge producer, and, as a consequence, institutional status as professor of or expert in 'such and such' no longer matters so much when people go to the Web to find things out.

It might not only be academics who lose their status. Consider family life and the status of parents vis-à-vis their offspring. It had been argued with regard to market choices before the World Wide Web emerged that 'market mavens' were influential in the consumer choices of others, and this was predicated on their superior informa-tion (or knowledge, if you prefer) of the market (Feick and Price, 1987). According to Belch, Krentler and Willis-Flurry (2005), it is teenagers who are now the mavens – since it is they who are the users and gatekeepers of the Internet in most households. So mums and dads lose their status just like professors. We are now all in the hands of the amateur bloggers and holiday-seeking teenagers.

Of course, we are not saying that this is so; we are trying to suggest that how the Internet affects choice may not be as it seems. And we are saying that claims which follow on from arguments about choice – claims about, for example, human nature made visible through choices of various kinds – might also not be so easily discerned. How one might judge these matters is also to be done with evidence and not with grand, often rather sweeping arguments. Take the latter study of mavens. It suggests a rather big shift in social roles. But the study was conducted using 167 parent–teen pairs. No infor-mation, however, is given about what kind of teenagers and parents they might be, other than their degree of Internet use. One market action – the selection of vacations – was measured. No attempt was made to see whether this choice was representative of family choice rather than being a peculiarly collaborative affair, where handling the desires of teenagers might be the central problem. Nor did the study consider whether this kind of role shift persists over time. There is disparity, in other words, between a modest piece of research and the claims derived. This doesn't mean that the claim that teenagers are now market mavens is wrong; it means that one cannot judge simply on that basis.

In short, there is no doubt that the development of the Internet has vastly increased the amount of information to be found and the speed with which one can find it. Although there might be issues to do with information overload (not to mention relevance), what is required to choose – to inform choice – is now almost certainly somewhere on the Internet. The question, though, is what difference it makes to choice and how one would evidence this.

Information and human nature

Of course, as so often, the use of words such as 'might', 'may' and 'could' in academic discourse can make effects seem much more threatening than they actually are, as the example of mavens suggests (just as a sense of threat is created in Pariser's much cited book *The Filter Bubble*, 2011), which purports to offer a critical assessment of the role of capitalism in this). Leaving aside the question of whether all the claims made about the effect of the Internet hold water, what seems certain is that there are two basic ones. On the one hand, *we* are altering and, on the other, what we choose is being modelled and better *captured* (indeed, it is now almost predictable). There are other claims, as our preamble above noted, but these seem the two salient ones.

As to the first, the argument seems to be that, with the reduction on the constraints on information production and use, the diminishing cost of producing and consuming information, and so forth, we are coming to choose with less regard to our own rational self-interest. This isn't the maven argument; we are not simply choosing for others by substituting their needs for our own. Rather, and instead, we are beginning to show (in our choices) more concern for others.

According to some, it is through or with the Internet that this aspect of human nature is coming more to the fore. We choose no longer what is in our own self-interest alone. This isn't the claim that Sen makes, as discussed in chapter 4. He says that people have always combined an altruistic element in their calculations. Here we are saying that the balance of their concerns is altering towards emphasising the interests of the Other, and it is the Internet that is allowing this; it is, as it were, fostering altruism.

Take, for example, Yokai Benkler, and the claims put forward in his book *The Wealth of Networks* (2006) (see also his *The Penguin and the Leviathan*, 2011). There one finds several illustrations of how the Internet has seemingly changed what people can do and how, more especially, it allows people to act in ways that emphasise their altruism. As a consequence their choices are altering, too. Two examples are, we feel, the most important in his book. Both highlight interesting aspects of human nature and aspects of social institutions – related to how people are organised or self-organise and how these organisations reflect self-interest or altruism. The examples relate to open source programming and Wikipedia.

Benkler explains that the idea behind making coding practice a freely undertaken, collaborative enterprise, making it open source, stems from when Richard Stallman, an MIT researcher, started working on a non-proprietary operating system in 1984. Stallman 'wanted a world in which software enabled people to use information freely, where no one would have to ask permissions to change the software they use to fit their needs or to share it with a friend for whom it would be helpful' (2006: 64). However, the freedom to share and make one's own software implies, in Benkler's view, general principles that, if undertaken on a massive scale would be fundamentally incompatible with the principles that underlie the existing mode of software production. This relies on property rights and markets. In order for there to be a market in the uses of software – for Microsoft to sell its software, for example – owners of that code must be able (and we use Benkler's words here) to 'make the software unavailable to people who need it' (ibid.: 65). This is an obtuse way of saying that one can only sell something if people can't get that thing for free. To ensure that a 'marketless software' could be developed, then, Stallman wrote his code under a licence he devised, one that allowed anyone to copy, distribute and modify that code in whatever way they pleased but which had a curious claim within it: it required that, 'if the person who modified the software then distributed it, he or she must do so under the "exact same conditions" that he had distributed the software in the first place' (ibid.). This licence became the General Public License or GPL.[1] This is the essential organisational feature of open source programming – the licence that appends it. With this, whatever code is written is in effect common property. One cannot sell such

---

[1] As Benkler himself admits, the GNU GPL licence entails a kind of 'jujitsu move': with it Stallman asserts his own copyright like any 'owning capitalist' might do but forces all those downstream users of his code – his product – to make any contributions they make (to the software, to Stallman's product) available to everyone else thereafter. Thus Stallman used ownership and its protections – licensing procedures – to make his product free.

property; indeed it even becomes doubtful to think of saying this code has any value – it cannot be priced. But of course, and as we shall see, this type of code became enormously valuable.

However, the creation of this licence may have led to nothing, according to Benkler. For one thing, Stallman himself was not much of a code writer, so the operating system (OS) he wrote was not likely to get taken up by others – it wasn't that useful for anything. However, Linus Torvalds took up the development of a crucial part of the operating system, the kernel, and this turned the OS into something that was potentially really useful – indeed, so much so that the resulting version of Stallman's OS got taken up very widely. The kernel came to be called Linux. Indeed, since the time that Stallman first introduced the idea of GPL, open source coding has become commonplace, with Linux being the exemplar – this particular OS now being constituted by millions of lines of code, and with thousands of individuals contributing to it. In fact, Linux has a role on providing basic tools for the Internet right the way through to today – in Web servers, email servers and much else – most notably Android phones, the kernel of which is written in Linux.

The important point Benkler wants to make does not have to do with operating systems, however; what is important to him are the forms of social arrangement manifest in open source production and what this in turn says about the creatures that write the code – the human actors behind Linux and suchlike. In Benkler's view, this social structure is flat – or certainly flatter than has existed with other code-writing efforts. It is also flexible, with ease of access and departure for any individual as they see fit. This structure can accommodate more than simply, say, a three-person connection – the originating code writer perhaps, a user who identifies a bug, and a third coder who then fixes the first person's code (and hence the bug). It can expand to include much greater numbers of people – indeed hundreds if not thousands in the case of Linux.

Though Benkler admits that the social organisation of code-writing in the Linux kernel might not be completely flat – there are considerations relating to expertise and status that make it somewhat hierarchical, with some coders having more authority than others and some code lines being more protected than others. The key thing, though, is the orientation of all those who contribute to a common order. In this credo, if that is the word, all participants are, in theory at least, equal to all others. This is the philosophy behind the practice, the ideology that guides it all. According to Benkler (2006: 66–7), the development of Linux crystallised a model of software production fundamentally different from that which preceded it.

This new form of organisation is given a more pure or perfect form in the production and maintenance of Wikipedia, Benkler suggests. Wikipedia isn't merely an online encyclopedia but shows how the Internet, when combined with the right tools and ideology, articulates the new form presaged by Stallman's work. Wikipedia thrives because of particular social norms, ones that echo open source programming: there is no elaborate software-controlled access and editing capabilities; it is generally open to anyone to edit. The bottom line: it depends upon a self-conscious use of open discourse usually aimed at consensus: the project is 'substantially more social, more human, and intensively discourse and trust based' (Benkler 2006: 72). These features have been used by millions. Wikipedia is not an obscure product by some band of philanthropists. It's a mass product, a hugely popular, very commonly used information resource. This scale of use is proof, according to Benkler, that, with the Internet, the way the world functions can alter: 'It suggests that the networked environment makes possible a new modality of organising production: radically decentralised, collaborative, and nonproprietary; based on sharing resources and outputs among widely distributed, loosely connected individuals who cooperate with each other without relying on either market signals or managerial commands' (ibid.: 61).

This credo, this new way of working, Benkler calls 'commons-based production'. It is not merely that the Internet opens up possibilities – it is that the possibilities allow people to do what before would have been too costly to them. They can behave as they would without artificial constraints, without worrying about time, effort or managers. A particular release is from the pernicious effect of monetised media: The 'constraints that had previously affected information production are weakened; what was controlled by media powers and corrupted by the mass media through the influence of money, no longer applies' (Benkler 2006: 11). As a result, people can act more naturally and, for Benkler, this means with greater interest in others; they can behave with more altruism in their spirits.

Choice and human nature

So what has this to do with choice, beyond the obvious fact that people choose to contribute to Wikipedia or to code under the GLP licence? One thing is clear: the institutional frameworks of collaboration and production have altered. These are demonstrable facts. But what is also claimed is that, once these new social structures appear, some aspect of human nature manifests itself. Put simply, rational self-interest cannot any longer be held to be the prime motivating force for human choices;[2] something social seems to be manifest too. Instead of the rational actor implied (or made explicit) in their social relations that has gone before, there are collaborative forms and mutually beneficial behaviours. Commons-based production reflects an essential altruism. This must be the case, Benkler is arguing, if Wikipedia and open source programing are of the scale that they have reached; it is their success which is an index of the former.

Before we say anything about whether one can accept this apparent relationship, let us say something more about what this altruism might be. Benkler himself uses various synonyms for the basic idea of altruism, such as collaborativeness and cooperativeness. He tries to illustrate these somewhat general words with reference to things such as 'how things are done in the home', in friendship, even the kinds of behaviour one might find in an elevator: these are behaviours where people would think nothing of saying, 'Here, let me lend you a hand', he explains (2006: 463).

Benkler doesn't claim to have uncovered such altruistic actions. They already exist in elevator behaviours. Rather, he thinks he has identified a combination of factors coalescing on the Internet in a way that allows these occasional acts of altruism to manifest themselves more extensively and frequently. These forms are to be found in the new social and organisational forms represented by open source programming and Wikipedia: in them one can see digitally enabled altruism. This foreshadows what will be, so Benkler wants to argue.

One can hardly doubt that altruism and collaborativeness (and a sense of the convivial) are characteristic of social practices entailed in the production of Wikipedia, just as they are, for that matter, in open source programming. Whether it is correct to say that this is representative of a more widespread form of action is another thing. Whether one would willingly contrast this with other behaviours that are self-interested is also a different matter. Simply suggesting that there might be a move towards something that might be characterised as altruistic, and implying that such behaviour has been rare, is not proving the case Benkler wants to make.

One question here is whether Wiki behaviours stand as proof of something greater – that, with time, with enhancement in the technologies of the Internet, and with changes in regulatory and institutional structures, these sorts of collaborative forms of action

---

[2] Benkler addresses this in an online paper, 'Law, policy, and cooperation', www. benkler.org/Benkler_Law%20Policy%20Cooperation%2004.pdf.

will become more widespread. To succeed here they will have to displace authority arrangements and commercial transactions.[3] On this front, Benkler does admit that previously dominant structures – particularly related to monetised media systems – might resist and negate any effort to create free distribution of otherwise commercially valuable information, and indeed that is what we see in the attempts to control what Internet service providers allow their users to see.[4]

In any case, these resistances are not just to alternative institutional forms – a battle between selling code for cash and giving code for free – it is also a battle over what people become: cynical creatures who can only imagine themselves as rationally self-interested, and thus who choose accordingly, or creatures who naturally blossom in the community of sharing. Benkler offers very little evidence that the expressions of altruism manifest in open source programming are representative of something that will become more widespread. He simply assumes that this must be the case. He assumes the reader will think so too.

From claims to evidence

What is clear is that Benkler is making some very general claims about the wellsprings of human behaviour. He uses evidence about quite particular socially organised phenomena to make connections to those wellsprings. We have tried to stress in previous chapters how concepts such as 'self-interest' and 'altruism' are seldom carefully applied. They are sometimes used, quite casually, as contrast classes when trying to account for choices that seem distinct. Often

---

[3] Of course, Benkler's work argues primarily about the production of information, but we also need to consider its consumption, for there evidence seems to point in a different direction. Rational self-interest seems to describe the practice of illegal downloading quite accurately, although mediated by other factors, as Higgins (2007) tries to show. Why pay for something if you can get it for nothing? There is no need for altruism.

[4] An interesting war of escalation is taking place such that each attempt to exercise such control is accompanied (very quickly) by the publishing of methods to avoid it. The Pirate Bay, for instance, issued PirateBrowser on 10 August 2013. This circumvents countries which block the site. According to Wikipedia, it had been downloaded 2,500,000 times by October of that year. Any number of relatively effective workarounds currently exist, including so-called virtual private networks (VPNs). Are the media organisations being rational in pursuing the selling objectives, given that payment can be avoided through new mediations on the Internet such as Pirate Bay? The answer is yes, if the effects are to prevent a significant proportion (and not all) users from utilising illegal sites. We, like everyone else, currently have no real idea who will win this war.

altruistic choices are seen as the opposite of rational, when the latter is assumed to be the same as self-interest, for example. In other words, self-interest turns out to be a proxy for rational while altruism turns out to be a proxy for anti-rational. Similarly here: we might have some sloppy definitions. Is it right to say that writing code under the GPL licence is altruistic and that to do so for, say, Microsoft is not? As it happens, once the GPL licence has been applied to some piece of code, all the code that touches that becomes subject to the same licensing. As a result one cannot do otherwise even if one wanted – one has to share. Thereafter, one could not be rationally self-interested if one wanted. So is it right to say that the GPL licence creates altruism or imposes it?

Besides, it is not clear what relation there is between the worlds of Wikipedia and open source programming (so to speak) and other contexts. If one behaves altruistically in one setting, does it affect how one acts elsewhere? Even more prosaically, doesn't context alter with time? Is an action at one moment in time the same as it is at some later date? As just mentioned, the GPL licence affects what is entered into a code base after the licence has been applied; what might have been an altruistic act at first is not thereafter so easily labelled – the context has altered.

In any case, how does one recognise altruism? Is choosing a present for another an altruistic act? Or is that the case only if one doesn't calculate what the recipient might give in return? Is friendship altruistic? Of course one can offer answers here, but the point is that one might need to clarify claims and what might be particular about actions and contexts.

Part of the problem in assessing what Benkler is claiming is that much is left unsaid in his book; by that we don't mean that he avoids issues. It is rather that some of his views seem so basic to his position that it is not at all clear that he recognises how consequential they are. It is worth pausing for a moment to consider his understanding of communication between people in this regard. In his view, it is 'the most basic unit of social existence' (2006: 464). His attempts to describe and explicate the elemental features of communication are redolent, at least to us, of economists' attempts to treat communication as much like any other commodity, something to be exchanged and processed. And one of the reasons why economists like this view is that it avoids the problem of context. Communication is an exchange wherever it occurs. Where sociologists, by way of contrast, have at least some commitment to the idea of context, economists are much more prone to look for the universal.

Given its importance in Benkler's understanding of humans, it is not surprising he has quite a lot to say:

First there is an initial utterance of a humanly meaningful statement . . . Second, there is a separate function of mapping the initial utterances on a knowledge map. In particular, some utterance must be understood as 'relevant' in some sense, and 'credible'. Relevance is a subjective question of mapping an utterance on the conceptual map of a given user seeking information for a particular purpose defined by that individual . . . Credibility is a question of quality by some objective measure that the individual adopts as appropriate for the purposes of evaluating a given utterance . . . Finally, there is the function of distribution, or how one takes an utterance produced by one person and distributes it to other people who find it credible and relevant. (2006: 68)

This characterisation of communicative behaviour seems to point away from home life or politeness in an elevator. But it might tell us something about the tacit features of Benkler's thinking and hence his claims.

The characterisation Benkler emphasises is a particular view of the human where information is a kind of currency and the dialogues between people are information exchange economies that produce 'calculated outcomes'. Thus, if this holds true, when people are being altruistic when engaging in a communications economy, presumably they are choosing to be so through some calculative measures. They don't do it instinctively, but instrumentally. Yet if this is the case then one might start wondering about what kind of altruism Benkler has in mind. It turns out, we are seeing, that the individual he assumes provides content for Wikipedia and codes under the GPL licence calculates the outcomes of their actions. Is this then the kind of altruism that all the readers of his book have in their mind when he describes holding an elevator door open? For now we see that, in Benkler's view, people don't just do this to be kind, but because they judge it will be beneficial for them. Of course, Benkler doesn't say how this benefit will arise, though one can easily imagine what such kinds of instrumental measures might be: if one is nice to a neighbour they might feed the cats when one is away.

To be sure, some kinds of behaviour can be said to be calculative, and indeed some forms of communicative act have the form that Benkler describes. One need think only of communications in military organisations. But if one focuses carefully on communication one would baulk at the suggestion that this is a helpful or even barely adequate way of characterising 'the most basic unit of human affairs' *across the board*. As one of us has written elsewhere (R. H. R. Harper, *Texture: Human Expression in the Age of Communications*

Overload, MIT Press, 2011), to treat acts of communication in this way takes many of the uniquely human aspects of those actions out of them, rendering acts of friendship and honour, the skills of business presentations, education practice and political speechmaking (among other things) as all the same – merely attempts to relay content, as economic acts of a kind.

We remind the reader of O'Connor's observations about 'trolleyology' in moral philosophy, for they have exactly the same force: we are left wondering how well thought out are attempts to relate evidential instances of conduct to a broader and, in this case, tacit notion of the actions described. Trolleyology can take the phenomenon of choice out of its natural place and thus can tell us little about choices in the real world. Benkler's notion of human communication suffers, we feel, from a similar problem: it takes the diversity of communication out and leaves merely an economy. Behaving altruistically in that context has a very particular feel about it.

From altruism to prediction from personality

We should not deny the fact that Benkler's case is a hard one to put together. We should not deny either his frankness: he admits that his evidence may not be all it needs to be. He says he is only giving 'existence proofs' – proofs that there might be evidence. What we are saying, though, is that he does seem to be presupposing that the concept of rationality associated with the humans in his picture captures the general rationality of existing society. It is this which enables him to see the behavioural features that the Internet sometimes seems to produce as a radical alternative to what is already in place. In our view, however, he marries particularising examples (from the Internet) with generalisations about human nature that allow him to make rather grander claims than are warranted.

This brings us back not just to the science of choice but to how it is often the case that, when attempts are made to capture choice, this is done through combining various assumptions and starting places, as well as emphasis on particular topics. We have been reviewing the idea that the intersection of new technology and altruistic instincts is changing the choices we make, such that the competiveness associated with rational choice may be becoming less evident. We have been seeing, too, how this may produce new collaborative forms of human affiliation. We have expressed some doubts about the selectivity of the evidence which supports such views.

Nevertheless, part of the appeal of new ways of defining, exploring and, in this case, accounting for the shaping of choice is, as so often in the human and social sciences, that they end up offering promissory notes. We see in Benkler not proofs but pointers, possibilities, an implied hope that more sophisticated scientific understanding of how people make decisions and the relationship between this and new technologically mediated behaviours will emerge.

Starting from a different place

If it is the case that Benkler starts to struggle over his definitions of human nature, it might be that other attempts to understand the shaping of that nature by the Internet have more success. One way of doing so is by starting with fixed and sure definitions of the creature doing the choosing.

There are many such studies. There has been quite a lot of research on the relationship between people's online behaviour as a function, for instance, of their expressed preferences for other factors – such as demographic ones (see, for example, Baglioni et al. 2003; De Bock and Van Den Poel, 2010; Hu et al. 2007; Murray and Durrell, 1999; Weber and Jaimes, 2011). Others investigate the connection between personality and choice. Amichai-Hamburger (2009), Amichai-Hamburger and Vinitzky (2010), Golbeck et al. (2011), Gosling et al. (2011), Ross et al. (2009) and Correa et al. (2010) all link personality and social network profiles. Most of these studies are small in scale.

Kosinski et al.'s 'Manifestation of user personality' (2014) is different in offering an analysis of personality factors that uses large data-sets. Here the claim is made that one can determine someone's personality from what they say about themselves on their Facebook profile and the digital traces of their actions on the Web, notably their 'Likes' on Facebook. The prospect seems exciting. If we can find links between psychological characteristics (which might dispose people towards one kind of choice or another) and choice behaviour on the Internet, we have the possibility that we can manage the supply of information in such a way as to strongly 'nudge' behaviour – and hence control choice. On the way to doing so, we will have understood choice better too.

But is that right? To understand this one has to look at the premises of this work, its starting assumptions and the methods that ensue. What we find is that these are quite different from those deployed by Benkler, one consequence of which is that it makes comparison of the outputs of the two quite difficult. But putting them alongside one another can help show their essential shapes, and this can allow us to see how their differences are not confined to findings; the human creature that is the subject of the research is quite dissimilar too.

Kosinski and his colleagues present a view from social psychology, and it is that discipline's concepts and methods that are key to understanding the claims that they articulate. The basic idea is to construct a view of the human (and human action) that can allow an evaluation in terms of causal factors related to personality type. The authors show how the balance of these factors in any particular instance of a personality is manifest in Web behaviours, in particular in the patterns of action to be found on Facebook, evidenced in the use of 'Likes', when combined with analysis of the digital footprint that people make as they navigate around various Web pages.

They claim, more especially, that there is a predictable relationship between personality attributes along with such things as whether a person is black or white in skin colour, gay or straight in sexual orientation, or Democrat or Republican in political allegiance, and how they manifest in their Liking behaviours and other related activities. It is even claimed that degree of 'intelligence' can be captured through an analysis of the relationship between Likes, website selection and personality. In sum, and put simply, 'Likes' are an index of the factors that can be said to determine or cause personality to have the form it does. People's choice of Likes and their selection of Web pages are effects of these common causes which can be identified in the profiles people present on their Facebook pages.

No one is going to question that people are to an extent predictable, nor question whether one can estimate people's choices from their personal characteristics, but the expectation of a beefed-up science of choice would be that it would enable much more determinate and exact prediction – better than common sense, in other words. The fact that Kosinski and his colleagues can claim to have found some general associations between some broad attributes of persons and some equally broad proclivities to do things is no particular surprise to anyone – though, as often with statistical studies, the plausibility of their findings are convincing less because they have been produced through extensive statistical work than because they fit with our pre-existing understandings of how 'what people are like' connects with 'what they do'.

More particularly, Kosinski et al. claim that one can independently check an individual's statements about their political preferences, sexual orientation, and so forth, by 'scraping' their Facebook profile and their website navigation traces. They compared the analysis of that action to a sample set of 'objective' data about personality, gathered from 58,000 people who filled out an online psychometric test voluntarily. This data is organised in fairly predictable ways according to measurable factors such as extraversion, agreeableness, conscientiousness, neuroticism, and openness to experience.[5] Kosinski et al. argue (see also Bachrach et al., 2012) that, correlating this survey sample – big as it is – with the even bigger data-set from Facebook and website activity (350,000 users) more generally, these personality constructs can provide accurate predictions of the kind of websites one chooses to visit as well as such matters as the size and density of one's social network, the number of uploaded photographs and the number of group memberships. Best accuracy in these studies is provided by measures of extraversion, although other traits are supposedly significant. Moreover, the authors claim measurement of these activities on Facebook is predictive of personality traits. The nature of their findings is summed up as follows:

> Extraverts tend to be more outgoing, friendly, and socially active. They are usually energetic and talkative, do not mind being the centre of attention, and make new friends more easily. Introverts are more likely to be solitary or reserved and seek environments characterized by lower levels of external stimulation. Our results show that extraverts are more likely to reach out and interact with other people on Facebook. (Kosinksi et al., 2014: 370)

Evaluating the causalities of personality

This seems very persuasive – the numbers are large, the statistics advanced, the links appealing to common sense (the analysis sounds right). But one can put the findings more simply: what this research is saying is that people who are outgoing and friendly tend to be more outgoing and friendly on Facebook than they are elsewhere in their lives. The supposed importance of this research is that, if one can infer personality types from Facebook and other website behaviour, then one can direct the resulting insights towards the personalisation of websites or to algorithms for recommending websites. But, in our view, the necessity for the intervening variable of personality as described or rendered in the research is not really explained or justified. It is not difficult to imagine that people who like one kind of website or some features of it may also like other,

---

[5] The so-called big five personality traits and hence the five-factor model – see the 'NEO Personality Inventory' (e.g., Goldberg, 1993).

similar websites or features. What exactly does personality analysis add to this?

The promissory character of research in the human and social sciences suggests both practical potential and significant progress in those sciences themselves – the current deliverances of research may yield only relatively commonplace observations – but the promise is that the further development of theory and method will deliver much more surprising findings. We have – arguably ad nauseam – pointed to the way that enthusiastic advocates of particular approaches in the human and social science disciplines pay little attention to the serious objections which circulate within their own or other disciplines to the acceptability of both their theoretical ideas and their empirical investigations.

For example, is the factor analysis of personality uncontroversial across relevant disciplines? No. Block (1995), for instance, points to the problems associated with this technique, including 'questionable conceptual and methodological assumptions'. One does not have to be a critic of psychology to be a critic of the five-factor model. Eysenck (1992) has pointed out, for instance, that it has no theoretical underpinnings, being merely a statistical construct. A more profound critique (unsurprisingly, largely ignored) comes from philosophy. Hence, Davenport (1998: 2) remarks that the 'naturalising move remains untenable as it stands, because it forgets the crucial point that "what is known", allegedly, about human nature and personality in psychology depends on interpretation of the data, and on preconceived hypotheses about what variables are relevant in constructing explanations, that are coloured through and through by vocabulary, associations and assumptions (often unrecognised).'

From the point of view of such critics, psychology is simply begging the questions they would ask. For it has already decided that personality can be captured in factorial structures and so sees investigation into its nature as merely a problem in the methodology of measurement. It seldom if ever questions whether the term itself has any real corollary in our (mental) life. As Davenport says, 'since most of the questions that form the basis of the factorial analyses yielding the traits and types focus so much on differences in styles of behavior and subjective preference (i.e. judgments that do not imply any evaluative or objective claim on the agreement of others), do these resulting typologies really measure [personality] at all?' (1998: 7).

The way in which Kosinski and his colleagues try to identify the manifestations of personality in Internet users' behaviour depends not only on their data collection and analysis methods but upon their acceptance of the debatable (because much debated) idea that psychology is methodologically solipsistic – it identifies the bona fide properties of an individual's psychology as those characteristics which are intrinsic to that individual and are possessed by that individual independently of external and contextual effect or input. This treatment thus excludes the possibility that among the things that massively influence people's real-world behaviour is the behaviour of others (interactional matters).

It is not surprising to find, then, that Kosinski and his colleagues select their subjects' online behaviour in the websites they visit and in their Facebook activity as cogent evidence of their personality because the activities in question (Web page selection and Facebook postings) are 'to a large extent a private activity; relationships between website choices and personality might be unaffected by peer pressure and the tendency to present oneself in a positive manner' (2014: 358). Thus, 'personality' by methodological fiat has nothing to do with sensitivity to the influence of others. Similarly, while the contents of 'Facebook Status Updates, uploaded pictures or the choice of Facebook Likes might carry an element of self enhancement, the frequencies and distribution of Liking behaviour, number of uploaded photos or extent of Friendship network are less likely to be affected by users' conscious attempts to control their image' (ibid.). In short, these activities offer an 'unbiased insight into users' personalities' (ibid.) if one accepts that personality has to be treated individualistically, as the property of a solipsistic soul – one who lives alone.

As we've suggested, there are, in other parts of psychology and in other relevant disciplines, very different ideas about how the idea of personality is to be construed. We can use a fairly crude contrast to show the distance between different conceptions of personality that can find strong supporting arguments, a contrast between personality as an intrinsic and unvarying attribute that can only be picked out by being isolated from the noise-making influence of others and a view of personality as something which is performed, where the circumstances in which people find themselves and their relation to social roles and to other people combine to form the way each individual behaves. Kosinski et al. evidently hold unquestioningly to the former view and therefore methodologically elect to disregard just those things that those favouring the performative conception would regard as essential to understanding the phenomena in question.

Choosing the creature that makes the choice

The important point here is not whether one is right or wrong but how views about these matters are consequential on arguments about choice and choosing. The Kosinski view is methodologically individualist. Personality is stable and something that individuals have, and it influences their behaviour (at least when their behaviour is not subject to the influence of others). This has one odd consequence that leads us back to Benkler. From Kosinki et al.'s view, one can hardly imagine how the changes in motivation at which Benkler points could be grasped, let alone measured. Benkler wants to claim that changes in the ways people are connected to each other influence what they are like in respect of how they choose to act in regard to other people. He wants to look at social capital and its consequences, whereas Kosinki et al.'s approach depends on consideration of others being excluded. Consequent on the latter is doubt about the relevance of social capital to any explanation, let alone allowing it to effect profound changes in the way people behave. Their method is designed to demonstrate that the view implicit in Benkler's work is wrong, or simply to exclude any considerations or materials relevant to it.

Or rather, from Kosinski et al.'s view, people may have reasons for their choices, but these are not the ones they think they have. They are the 'real reasons' that people are unaware of. Now, this is something of a philosophical issue and alludes to contrasts we have made before in relation to other perspectives on choice. Leaving aside the fact the evidence in Kosinkli et al.'s study was garnered from the Internet, the general features of this view are commonplace in psychology, as we saw in previous chapters. In this discipline, a distinction is often made between the reasons people offer and 'scientific truth' about reasons. We see here a continuing theme, then – causal explanations or statistical models show little or no interest in what people understand themselves to be doing when they choose something and how they might account for this.

In and of itself, of course, this contrast between people's reasons and reasons that science uncovers matters only to those who live in the academic disciplines. Our concern is – to some extent – more prosaic, at the moment at least. It is, do we really believe that understanding what people do with the Internet is best arrived at through measures of personality? Or, as a radical alternative, might we learn more about the real world by treating the phenomenon at hand differently? If one assumed that the reasons people themselves have are in part constitutive of the actions that they undertake, then instead of ignoring those reasons they would be part of the phenomenon

described. At the moment (just wait), we are not expressing a preference for a more 'anthropological' (or sociological) view so much as
making a contrast and suggesting what might be a measure to apply
for judging between the compared techniques. It may be that there is
indeed merit in this more descriptive approach, one that makes people's reasons part of the thing that is captured or, rather, treats those
reasons as essentially constitutive of the phenomenon at hand. We
won't say anything more about that now as it will be the theme of
our concluding remarks. We raise it now since the contrast between
that approach, albeit briefly characterised, and those which claim
more 'causalist' explanations that imply a notion of science is clear.

Before we get to that, however, what should be obvious is the
following distinctions even within these 'causalist' views. If traditional economics turns away from those reasons and seeks instead
a wholly new set of explanations based simply on what can justifiably be said about the use of money, and if behavioural economics
seeks to combine those views with what it claims are experimentally uncovered truths about motive and calculation, then it seems
psychology of the sort we have just been discussing is offering yet
a third view. This recasts the specificities of human action in generalised terms that are somehow and nevertheless resonating with
the language of the individual reflection: reasoning and choice are
nothing if not evocative of the subjective, the perspectival and the
cultural. And yet the psychological perspective would seem to want
to ignore, and even, in some cases, dismiss a priori as simply misguided, how people themselves understand their reasons for doing
things and claim to replace them with a different notion of what
governs behaviour.

Choice within or outside the Internet

Regardless, we must not forget that our theme is 'choice' and
how best to understand it. Because there is a substantial literature
dealing with the transformative power of the Internet in relation to
our decision-making behaviour, we have looked at a small part of
it to understand its foundations. We find that, despite the fact that
the Internet is, in some views, radically transformative, the same
basic concepts and methods turn out to be suitable for analysing it.
Whatever the change, the methodological concerns of the individual
discipline drive the analysis. Little or nothing of the real world
intrudes.

Part of the difficulties one has with Kosinski et al.'s account is
that, from the view of everyday understanding, many other forms

of relation and connection between reasons and causes and actions are possible than is encompassed in their analysis. The big five traits of personality seem a much reduced set of possible connections between what people do and how it might be understood. Why not seven traits, or a hundred and seven? The only answer – and we cannot stress enough how flimsy such a base might be – is that various measures of these traits show a certain correlation with other traits, so they can be (unproblematically) grouped together. Kosinski et al.'s research (it seems as if we are picking on them, but our observations are aimed at all experimental research of this kind) is meant to uncover features of the world of human affairs through 'scientific' technique, but instead it seems to traduce the conceptual apparatus of that world. It offers, in our opinion, a poor picture of what might be inferred when someone 'Likes' a posting or a comment on Facebook. From the view of the science of choice, the psychology of personality traits looks a very impoverished path indeed.

We might make one final observation about the findings we discuss above, which is that they are not necessarily that startling. Extroverts have more communication online. Brighter people are more likely to 'Like' references to 'science'.[6] A liking for guns appears to correlate with lower levels of schooling. We could go on, but the more or less obvious nature of these results is seldom remarked upon, and certainly, when claims are made concerning their usefulness, few critics have challenged their assertions.

If people need information in order to make decisions, then we need some evidence which tells us what stocks of knowledge people presumably have and how they deploy these in order to make decisions. That the relevant knowledge is most usefully encapsulated in personality profiles seems to us to be intuitively unlikely. There are much better ways of figuring out what people know and what they do with that knowledge. Sociologists and social economists have dealt with this, as we have seen, through the notion of social capital. As it happens, there is a great deal of research on just this topic: the emergence of what has come to be called Web Science reflects an enthusiasm for the idea of 'social capital'. A close examination of this new domain will show, however, that much of it is concerned with what we noted above are revealed preferences – with doings rather than reasonings. The relation to these doings and various definitions of social capital are often rather opaque, too, and sometimes remote from our concerns. Much of this simply describes

---

[6] And, we might note in passing from our own experience, to websites such as 'I f*****g hate pseudoscience'.

social capital and says less about how it might be a resource for choice.

Some research is more ambitious in its claims about how prediction of individual choice can be made and can matter. Goel et al.'s 'Predicting consumer behavior with Web Search' (2010) explains that much of the research examining how information circulates – flows might be a better word – on the Internet focuses on how that circulation – its speed, scale and topic – provides a powerful and quite accurate lens on the current state of human affairs in general, on trends in the economy, for example, on political fears that are arising, and so on. But they go on to argue that traces of Internet action, related to both the information people know and share and what actions seem related, can be used to predict human behaviour and choice in particular. Again, though, the examples they present to show this are rather prosaic and intuitively persuasive, relating to the movies people choose to see or the computer games they choose to buy, but this should not distract from the importance of what they are claiming.

More particularly, they examine whether there is a relation between search engine queries and actual instances of non-Web-related behaviour thereafter. They find that there is a correlation between the fact of people searching for a movie and actual attendance at a movie theatre within a few days of the search – particularly for weekends. They find also that there is a correlation between this and the scale of advertising for a movie. Perhaps unsurprisingly, knowing about a movie will affect the likelihood that someone will make a search query about it, and thus in turn choose a movie theatre to see it. But they also note that there is a demonstrable difference between the predictive powers of using traces of search for movies to predict actions and other kinds of searches and possible actions that might result. In the case of music, for example, there is a weak connection between a search for a pop song in the charts and the likelihood that that song will then be purchased, even if that purchase is online. This is because of the distinctive nature of the phenomenon in question. When someone searches for a pop song by name, they might actually be searching for the singer of the song, or they may be searching for the album of which it is a part; they may even be searching for the movie that the song is related to. Pop songs can be an index of something else, in other words; indeed they often are, as the data shows. Though movie searches can be a route to find out about such things as the producer or the actors involved, most often this is not so. It is the movie itself the searcher is seeking – this is what the data shows.

What Goel et al. propose, then, is that the kind of things people search for and the kinds of decisions they make as a result of those searches is dependent upon the kinds of things in question and the kinds of activities those things imply. To search for a movie that is subject to a media blitz is most probably because the person who is making the search is wondering whether to see the movie. It is hardly surprising therefore that a measure of this intention – i.e., a search query – is indeed reflected in the numbers of people going to the cinema thereafter. With pop music it is different: pop songs are not just things to listen to or to buy; they are gateways to other things, to albums, for example, to genres of music, even to pictures of pop stars and YouTube videos. The thing itself unpacks into different orders of possible acts and, as a result, predicting which of those acts ensues after those things have been searched for is more difficult.

Conclusion

And thus it is that, if Goel et al. are right that people search for movies when their attention to the movie launch has been cultivated by advertising, one should not be surprised that, once cultivated, people are more likely to choose to go to the cinema. One wants to say that this seems an odd way to justify the claim that new methods and novel data from the Internet are allowing a science of choice to emerge. For one can hardly be delighted at the results being reported – at the acts that are being described. One would be more interested if it was the case that Goel and his colleagues found that there *wasn't* a correlation between search and action in regard to movies. Some aspects of the affairs of the world are intrinsically predictable; but saying this is not saying anything new. That this is so allows people to build technologies that exploit this fact. Our puzzle has more to do with the academic 'gloss' over things that look intuitively obvious if one knows the world one is talking about. It is not news to a sixteen-year-old boy that he may want to know more about a Spiderman or X-Men movie before deciding whether to go and see it. Those of us who have long forgotten what it is like to be sixteen may need to investigate further.

Just as one should not forget the obvious truth that search engines as such are remarkable instances of technologies that rely on some of the predictable forms of human affairs in ways that exploits that for further benefit, so the 'discoveries' of these authors reflect domains where one can expect to find predictable behaviours. But one can always exploit that and get some leverage from it. As Kosinski et al. point out, advertisers find a great deal of appeal in being able to quantify the likelihood that those of Republican sympathy like guns. Ordinary everyday knowledge of typical patterns of behaviour is not sufficient to justify (it is assumed) and make accountable their investment of large sums in advertising. It is not simply that numbers and statistics can provide a sheen where common sense seems pallid and uninteresting; they provide precision and calculable criteria that can be used to judge value – or, at least, they seem to.

Whether the accretion of figures and tables of statistics provides any greater insight into 'decision-making' or 'choosing' behaviour is altogether another thing. As we have tried to make clear in this chapter, one of the problems that the science of choice has to solve is how to distinguish those instances of choice- and decision-making which look predictable, and which thus reflect a world well known already, and those cases where the reasons for choices and the form of those choices are far from expected. The science needs to offer new insights and maybe some startling discoveries. It needs to show that people choose in ways that are not always expected and for reasons that are not familiar.

Again, we need to clarify. We are noting (as we have throughout the book) that people for the most part know pretty well why they choose to do one thing over another, or at least they are easily able when asked to provide accounts as to why they preferred one thing over another. In that sense, they have knowledge of their reasons. The problem lies in the diversity of human experience when the reasons people have can turn out to be diverse, often remarkably so. What is blindingly obvious to one group of people as 'reasons to choose thus' may be utterly unfamiliar to another, who have, for whatever reason, a view that leads them to choose in other ways. We should add that we are not talking about gross relativism here or indeed differences that might shock: we are alluding to how it can be that one group of people like to see a film while others prefer to read a book, yet others to do nothing at all. There are reasons for all these choices, even if, from the view of one, the actions of another set of people can seem odd, at least different.

In short, while it is clear that there are good grounds for the excitement generated around models of preference and degrees of 'rationality' or 'bias', for game theoretic models of decision-making and their use in technology design, and for the development of psychological models of reason and rationality through experiment and abstraction, it is also clear that there is a need for careful reflection. As we have been at pains to point out, the different disciplines continue to pursue approaches built on quite orthodox conceptual foundations, even when new techniques are applied. Over-claiming, as we see it, continues to be rife, and many of the lessons learned long ago about the nature of human action are either ignored or reinvented under other names. Similarly, distinctions need to be made between pragmatic insights and use and the more delicate claims appropriate in science and in evidence-based humanities.

8

REASONS IN ACTION: FROM PHILOSOPHY TO AN ANTHROPOLOGY OF CHOICE

One of the themes which has divided protagonists in discussions about choice has to do with the reasons people 'have'. No one will deny that people do give reasons for what they do, that they will offer grounds for what they have done or that they will offer reasons for what they intend to do. They might even say that they have 'no reason' for some particular act; they 'just did it', they might explain. However, a division emerges in response to the question of whether this use of reasons shows that people do in fact know why they are acting as they do. If it does, then a scientific explanation for what they do would be superfluous. On the other hand, it could be that their use of reasons doesn't adequately explain their behaviour. Many think it is for science to decide whether individuals genuinely understand the nature of their own actions, though there is then strong disagreement over what science is expected to show in this regard (or what, some might claim, science does show). Whether users have reasons or not doesn't matter, in this view.

Some argue, from this perspective, that 'folk' understandings are just unscientific, meaning that there is no room for them in a scientific explanation of human behaviour – this is effectively what neuropsychologists as well as sociobiologists and evolutionary psychologists are forcefully arguing. Others within the human and social sciences might agree that 'folk' understandings would not fit into that kind of science, but think this is only because there is something wrong with the way in which the idea of science is being applied. Many suppose that scientific explanations are essentially causal and, in this view, people's reasons can only play a part in scientific explanations of behaviour if those reasons are the true causes of actions. If they are, then these reasons can be included among proper scientific explanations. If not, they must be eliminated and explanations cast without reference to these folk terms.

Yet another possibility, we believe, is that reasons can also be thought of as non-causal kinds of explanation – which does challenge the idea that explanation is *always* and *only* a matter of identifying causes. 'Giving reasons' offers a different kind of explanation than 'giving a cause', as the philosopher Davidson (1963) noted. The continuing dispute over whether reasons are causes looms large in this chapter because it is a strategic one in relation to the divisive question of whether and how far the science of choice is a genuine science, when what is meant by that is an investigation into causality.[1] An alternative approach to understanding human activity – and hence choice – might treat reasons as sometimes explanatory, sometimes causal and sometimes descriptive. In this latter view, the ways in which people talk about and orient to reasons in their affairs makes reasons so defined different to the 'reasons' one might find in inquiries into non-human phenomena. Key to this is the apparently simple distinction that human action articulates ideas in ways that don't happen in relation to other behaviours – ant behaviour, say.

What this simple view might hide, however, is that the relation between actions and reasons may be delicate and at times opaque, an intersection or weaving of causal, descriptive and explanatory formulations. Moreover, this is also a concern of those using these formulations and a resource for the exploration of such formulations by those watching or seeking accounts for that behaviour (collaborators, say). It will be a concern as well to those wanting to do a 'science' of it. This in turn points towards the function of everyday language, with its enormously rich and powerful vocabularies, both as topic and resource in the lived world of reasons and in attempts to characterise and explain that world from without – scientifically, say, or simply empirically.

It is hardly surprising, then, that this view needs careful handling. It turns out that the relationship between ideas and action is as heterogeneous, complex and evolving as language itself. As Wittgenstein (1953) noted long ago, one should think of language not as a tidy system but more like a city, an entity with some apparent structure and patterns but with older, prior patterns and logics still present in parts, while new ones can be seen to be appearing even as one looks. In other respects, a city lacks order or structure, seeming more an aggregation of once separate and essentially dissimilar parts. After all, this is indeed probably how many cities actually emerged: a confluence of once separated villages whose growth resulted in their merging into some mass. Wittgenstein is saying that the city landscape is, if you like, ragged, and in this

---

[1] This is not to deny the possibility that science may explore other kinds of relations – but for the purposes of this chapter this rather brute description of science will do.

respect it is just like language; so it is with the relationship between ideas and actions – we are saying that it is ragged too. One shouldn't expect systematicity here, only at best a partial coherence.[2]

Different ways of characterising and explaining reasons and choice will be bound to the tropes and concepts one can find in everyday language, some of which are systematic to some degree and others less so. We have seen already one such trope: the notion that there is a scientific type of explanation about human reasons. Perhaps this derives from our occasional desire to seek 'real reasons' behind the reasons our friends present and with which we are unsatisfied. Similarly, one can sometimes doubt one's own reasons and, as we noted in the preamble to this book, blame 'human nature' – here too we can see the desire for something other than one's common reasons. And, certainly, we can see in our everyday management of reasons and the choices that result a nuance can sometimes be applied. If, on occasion, we want a view that provides reasons that compete with and in the end are assumed to be better than *our own*, folkish reasons, at other times we seek ways of combining some of the reasons people have, some of our folk wisdom about causes, with *scientific accounts*. But, of course, sometimes another trope is deployed to say 'an end to it', 'it cannot be explained'. The language of reasons is indeed subtle.

Types of account

There are obviously many other accounts of choice on offer, and not just the scientific versus the folk. Nor does one need to claim that they all derive equally somehow from everyday discourse. If we can see in some accounts a battle between science and folk knowledge, in others we can see a different sort of contrast or pairing: one such is the notion that the relationship between the physical (action) and the 'mental' (intention) is a connection that needs unpacking or specifying to explain the reasons-for-action. This evokes the often deployed everyday formulation that one doesn't know what goes on inside 'another's head'. As we have seen, one solution to the question of what motivates human beings and accounts for

---

[2] Some philosophers find this possibility deeply repugnant, holding that ideas 'must be' consistent: in their view they cannot be otherwise if ideas are said to be logical (see McDowell, 1994). Our point is that this logic may be contextually defined, with the relations between ideas and action reflecting the domain in question and not some super-arching or Kantian system of logic. That, at least, is our reading of Wittgenstein's notion of language. It is also evidenced by empirical studies, as we shall see later in the chapter.

their behaviour is that 'they' (the human creatures) can be deemed motivated by 'rationality', a rationality to be found in that location, the head. This is the central premise of much economic theorising, as we have seen; as it happens, we also saw that economists themselves don't express much interest in elaborating upon this notion, being rather more interested in the consequences this presupposed rationality has on the economy. The head is of no interest to them; spending is. One might say the wallet is the place that economists look into.

In a loose sense, the philosopher Thomas Hobbes can be thought of as the first holder of the 'rationality' view one finds in economics, and of course he argued this long before economics became a professional discipline. He ascribed (in *Leviathan*) self-interest as the motivation of all people. Hobbes saw choice as a matter of (mentally) weighing on scales, such that what is weighed on the scales are the different means to achieve our current desires (Hobbes, [1651] 1999). This solves the goals and means problem by saying that *inside the head* is a rationality engine or machine. Even so, and as Hobbes himself noted, there is still a tension between this and morality, a problem that current economists reflect upon (see Peter and Schmid's (2007b) discussion of Sen, as well as our discussions in chapter 4). Morals have a different relation to motives than do strictly calculative, self-interested reasons; it is quite perplexing to imagine what would be a morality machine, for example, irrespective of whether it is in the head or elsewhere.[3]

Another of these tropes we have reviewed is the Cartesian formulation that the relation between body and mind is itself a 'problem' – that this connection is opaque. This idea remains influential (not least in cognitive science), though in terms of the opposition between planning and execution rather than in its initial Cartesian form. It can be summarily expressed as the idea that one formulates intentions (and accumulates knowledge of the world) 'in one's mind' and then designs plans to realise those intentions in the 'external world' by acting according to the pre-formed plan. One consequence of this view, this trope, as we are calling it,[4] is that deliberative reason-

---

[3] Though some current philosophers seek to do so. Consider, for example, Gilbert and her book *Joint Commitment* (2014) or Setiya's *Reasons without Rationalism* (2007). One may juxtapose their views with Clark's notions of extended cognition (2003) – morals, like computation, are to be found 'outside' as well as in the head, in Clark's view.

[4] The philosopher of action Lilian O'Brian calls this trope a 'term of the philosopher's art'. It sounds less offensive to the discipline, one imagines, though, as should be clear, we are not wanting to imply anything other than a relationship between ways of speaking and topics of inquiry. See O'Brian (2015: 72–3).

ing (conscious or unconscious) must precede action – i.e., moving one's body (normally called 'volitionism'). This in turn points to the notion that one must be able to cause one's body to move in accord with the plan. Of course this is certainly something one occasionally describes and feels in everyday life, but it is not the usual way of formulating what we do. One lifts one's arm; one doesn't think 'to do it' before one does it except in exceptional circumstances – such as when a doctor asks one to.[5]

Gilbert Ryle offered one of the most sustained attempts to demolish this view of human mentality, pointing out *inter alia* that it leads to a homuncular fallacy and infinite regress (i.e., that we need a 'little man' in our heads to direct matters, and he, of course, needs a little man in his). It equally locates 'agency' in the mental space alone and not in the action that follows (Ryle, 1949). Subsequent to Ryle, others have proposed that this problem can be avoided through a modular conception of the mind. In this view, they assume that many mental process are hardwired into the brain and suppose that certain kinds of mental process are distributed across different 'locations' within it. What persists, though, is a view that a truly scientific explanation of action (what is external, outside) is dependent on what goes on in the mind/brain (inside), requiring us to look 'inwards' – to make some sense of mental states and characterise them in some functional or other hierarchical way. As Stout (2005: 11) points out, this has been the foundational assumption of Artificial Intelligence for many years, although other models (such as connectionism) imply other kinds of mental arrangement.[6].All of these, in various ways, elaborate on the basic Cartesian trope – the inner and the outer.

In earlier chapters we have discussed other views too. Our purpose in this, our final chapter, is to review two more. This isn't simply to be comprehensive; these last have an especially important connection to the everyday language of reasons. The first we will look at is

---

[5] Though, as it happens, there has been a debate about just this topic and free will. Some neuroscientists have shown that there is a demonstrable change of the brain that occurs before an arm moves, and this change state occurs before a change state occurs in the area of the brain purportedly responsible for conscious articulation. This is proof, they think, that there is no such thing as free will. Even as regards moving an arm, one's consciousness of it is subordinate to some prior cause. Of course, whether the imaging evidence shows just this or whether this evidence has anything to do with a concept such as free will is beyond the scope of our concerns.
[6] Connectionism, briefly, treats learning on a stochastic basis – connections between neurons are made and remade in the brain on the basis of success or failure in accomplishing tasks, thus increasing reliability. Such a view makes the connectivity of neurons in the brain the fundamental explanatory factor and treats representations as derivative phenomena.

from philosophy. This discipline has been the locus of long-standing – if sporadic – arguments over whether reasons are causes of actions and indeed what are reasons in the general (if not causes). Key to these debates has been the relationship between the vernacular and the analytical, between the philosopher's tidy accounts of reasons and reasons in everyday life.

The second relates in part to the outcome (or echoes – they are not always linear connections) of these debates (which have pointed directly to a programme of inquiries into everyday reasoning), which makes the vernacular of 'doing' reasons (as it were) the topic of inquiry. The approach we shall sketch is undertaken under a variety of auspices – empirical philosophy, sociology, computer supported cooperative work and elsewhere – though we shall label it the 'anthropology of choice'. As far as we are aware, this was first coined by the Oxford philosopher P. M. S. Hacker (2007), though he was pointing towards a direction of inquiries rather than labelling a corpus of existing findings. When we consider this view and present examples of what it looks like, we will do so not with a mind to say that this ought to be the character of a science of choice, but that this is a way forward if that science is interested in the ways that reasons are constitutive of social action, what people do together knowingly and intentionally. As we have seen, this is not necessarily what all sciences of choice want to do and certainly begs the question of whether science is the right label or *modus operandi* for such inquiries. But, that said, we do hope that, as the reader reaches this point in the book, they will see that such an approach will have merits; the question is whether those merits fit their own concerns, whatever they might be. After all, and as should be clear, economists don't need to look at everyday reasons to make their inquiries. There is no need for them to look at practical reasoning. But, for other views, such an interest might well be 'on topic'.

A philosophical approach to choice

At the outset of the book, we asked the question 'What does it mean to make a choice?' In contrast to Hobbes's view we have just noted, we can now see that this is a more complex issue than it might seem. The philosopher Holton remarks: 'choice comes when the question of what to do arises. Often in our day-to-day activities that question never arises at all. "Operations of thought," wrote Whitehead [1911: 46], "are like cavalry charges in a battle – they are strictly limited in number, they require fresh horses, and must only be made at decisive moments"' (2006: 3). The point applies not just to single choices but to choice considered as being part of episodes of deliberative reasoning. Provided that we are experienced actors, carrying out courses of action need not always involve active deliberation, even in difficult or challenging situations. Thus it is wrong to assume we are always making choices every time we do something or when we undertake a set of things in which choice is but a component.

We need to recognise too that there are types of relation to action – to episodes, if you like – that mean that different participants will have different relations to choice. Gary Klein, in his study of various kinds of experts (nurses, fire commanders, missile operators, etc.), writes:

> We asked people to tell us about their hardest cases, thinking that these would show the most decision making. But where were the decisions? The commander sees a vertical fire and knows just what to do . . . He never seems to decide anything. He is not comparing a favorite option to another option, as the two-option hypothesis suggests. He is not comparing anything. Experienced actors frequently just know what to do. (1999: 16)

Klein argues that his subjects use a number of methods to arrive at this knowledge, the most important of which involves a form of stereotyping: new situations are recognised as similar to situations that have been encountered before, and so the actor knows what to do on the basis of what worked in the past. Standardly, then, the question of what to do does not arise. When it does, this is because some special feature obtains. Choices arise when the world is unusual, then, not as part of normal affairs.

Leaving these detailed claims aside, what is being said, in other words, and what we noted at the very outset of this book, is that, for a great deal of the time, people may not be making choices at all. In the light of comments by Holton and, following on from that, Klein, we are entitled to ask, if people can give reasons for their actions, does that mean they made a choice? Not always, we are saying. One might suggest that this is, if you like, a problem of language – we need to be very clear as to what we mean when we say that someone has made a choice, for there is a difference between adopting a course of action and making a deliberative selection of that action that entails 'choice'. And, on top of this, there are a range of ways in which it makes sense to talk of a choice that colours the role of our reasoning (and hence a process that can lead to our choices). We can ask someone what choice they made and they might offer a description of one to help our understanding, but they might feel themselves that they made no choice – like Klein's experts, they might know what they are doing so well that no choices need to be made.

Reasons and choice

All of these arguments about, and the jostling for, a new science of choice have been undertaken with underpinnings of just these kinds – underpinnings to do with language, about how people invoke choice to help communicate to others, at other times act as if choice is made but without thinking of themselves as having made a choice, and how it is that one can describe an activity as a series of choices without necessarily claiming that such choices have been made consciously, or even made by the 'rational' individual at all. It might simply be a way of characterising what is seen from, let us say, a third-person point of view.

Often such underpinnings are recognised, but often without all the nuance we have just noted. Sometimes these nuances show themselves in varied ways. In philosophy, for example, the idea that reasons are causes (and nothing else) has altered its shape even over the comparatively recent history of the discipline. Up until the mid-1960s, for example, various philosophers associated – in different ways – with Wittgenstein's later philosophy insisted that reasons are not causes, partly on the basis that some usage of the language of causes was actually descriptive. Here, a cause is invoked to help describe an action, and thus, in the view current at that time, this meant that one should prohibit coining the term 'cause' as something like a cause in the natural sciences. Its descriptive function in human affairs made it different. This came to be called 'the logical connection' argument.

This was bound also to a recognition, deriving from Hume, that it was very difficult to distinguish causes from effects in human affairs. The great Scottish philosopher had argued in *A Treatise on Human Nature* ([1739–40] 1974) that a cause and its effect, to be 'truly' cause and effect, must be logically independent, since they mutually identify an entirely contingent, non-necessary connection or relation. One can only establish that some event is the cause of another event by empirical investigation when the event and the cause are evidently distinct phenomena. The cause of the disease of cholera cannot be logically derived from a description of the disease, for example. With reasons and actions in human affairs the situation is different – one can say an individual is moody and that describes his actions; it also implies its causes – 'he was moody so he acted that way'.

While this seems simple and obvious – identifying a reason nominates or implies the action that will follow from it – that this makes understanding human affairs different from other kinds of inquiry is not so obvious. But it does so, in this view, because of the way that we use language to identify a reason by reference to the action itself. This is not just a claim about peculiar causes that control human action. For this view turns around a claim about how language is intrinsic to human action, whereas this is not the case in relation to other phenomena. Planets do not talk to each other, for example, though of course 'they' exert an influence on each other, through gravity, say. People do, and as they do they cast their respective actions in patterns of description that define causes while they describe reasons. Humans are nothing if not in the business of telling each other what they are about.

This leads to an interesting problem, or at least a problem to those with a philosophical bent. If reasons in human affairs are not causes, then what are they? Ordinary people can, obviously, be asked for explanations of their actions, and they will often give them to us: 'Why were you crossing the road?' 'I wanted to get to the bread shop', and so forth. In knowing this, the same people can offer explanations for other people's actions, too. And so, if asked, 'Why is he crossing the road?', they can reply, 'Because he's going to the bread shop.' These are the tellings we allude to above, the kinds of exchanges that illustrate explanation by giving reasons. It is a common occurrence in everyday life – an essential feature, one might even say. And though one could characterise these as causes giving reasons in the vernacular of ordinary affairs, the early view on reasons and causes said that they are not the kind of reasons that would satisfy science. This is because they are not causes as independent of effect. They describe a logical connection, not a causal one.

This view has a number of consequences. One, as we say, is that the standard notion of what a scientific explanation might be does not apply for human affairs. But a riposte to this is twofold. First, why should one deny that scientific explanation has a role here? Surely one might presuppose that it will, and the task is to identify what real reasons are – maybe they are not as described in the everyday language of reasons, but perhaps one might come up with a new language that does afford this. If one has faith in science, it behoves us to get around the logical connection problem and invent this language (this is Dennett's move, as we saw in chapter 5). Another response, one that ultimately leads to a much stickier set of issues, holds that some of the ways people account for their behaviour do point to real causes, even if the way that people construct their accounts suggests that cause and effect are not separate. In other words, the logical connection argument might occlude the possibility that 'underneath a description' might lie true facts – real causes. Or, to put this another way, some of the causes described in the language of reasons might be found to be real causes despite their conflation into description relations.

Types of reason as culture

At this point there are, broadly speaking, two ways forward echoing these rebuttals. One entails a claim about types of human rationality and, in turn, to some kind of comparative view. In this perspective, some people's accounts about the reasons and causes of their actions may be dismissed, since they don't have real understanding. This has to do with people's cultural stock of knowledge and, relatedly, their mental apparatus. Others' views are, however, better, truer. Some people have progressed in their knowledge of reasons, others have not. Science is of course the ultimate form of reasoning – the view to progress, so to speak. The general presumption of this take on reasons is that reasons can be, as it were, measured, such that some can be described as less rational than others, some more rational. This, in turn, leads to claims about the people who hold good or bad reasons, rational or irrational reasons, and the cultures they are part of; it implies, too, a relationship between mental capacities and functioning as such. More to the point, this view hopes simply to bypass the logical connection argument by invoking some notion of rationality that is based on real causes. Descriptions and understanding of reasons can simply be wrong, their logical connectedness notwithstanding, and this reflects irrationality. But real rationality, proper ways of seeing what causes action, is possible.

It is worth quickly sketching out the sorts of claims that derive from this view, since it allows us to recapitulate some of the arguments we have presented in previous chapters. It also sets up some of the difficulties the other way forward entails (a view which we have yet to define).

This first view can be illustrated by a summary of a long-standing argument (across several of the social sciences) about witchcraft.[7] Most of these debates focus on an example drawn from a study of

---

[7] Just to illustrate the currency of these issues, at the time of writing, an issue of *Rationality and Society* features yet another article (Leeson, 2014) on the practice of consulting oracles among the African tribe that has been the central example for this discussion since the 1930s.

the Azande people in what is today Kenya. The Azande practise witchcraft. Now, leaving aside what that entails precisely (i.e., the magic itself or who the Azande are), this has led some people to argue that Azande reasoning is irrational. This is a judgement made in terms of rationality as a matter of the 'objective' effectiveness of a choice of means for a given end. These people say that science shows us that magic cannot possibly work, since there is no basis in nature for expecting, say, animal sacrifices to yield sound diagnoses or predictions, any more than there is for hoping that ritual dancing and rattle shaking will stop someone dying from an illness or cause the rain to fall. This is why Azande reasoning is faulty, irrational. The people who can make this assertion do so from the comfortable position of scientific understanding.

Leaving aside the question of science versus non-science for the moment, what one needs to notice here is that arguments about particular social practices can end up pointing towards more general claims. In relation to magic, it can lead to questions about cultural capacities or cargoes and this, in turn, to assertions that some societies are more primitive than others, as are the reasoning machines that constitute those societies – people.

That this is so, that the rationalities of people and the societies they are a part of can be measured against some ideal notion of rationality, is a view that has been put forward by many. It was, for example, the view of Herbert Spencer, the great Victorian book writer on all matters sociological. It was, too, the view of J. G. Frazer, the Cambridge anthropologist who argued in *The Golden Bough* ([1890] 1998) that religious belief reflected the evolving state of the human mind. Ancient religion is, in this view, naturally replaced by science. Our manner of reasoning, as it were, becomes more rational as we come to understand the world better. This now somewhat forgotten argument can of course be applied to current understanding, where folk wisdom will gradually be replaced by science. In this view, descriptions of action that muddle cause with effect will be replaced with a better, more precise language. We saw in chapter 4 that Weber was very worried that such treatments can lead to misunderstanding the relationship between rationality and cultural know-how, making some actions seem irrational when in fact all that is being done in those actions is to deploy historically situated skills, rationalities of some kind, to put it in Weberian terms. Today, of course, suggestions that some cultures are more backward that others seem offensive, somehow more a question of moral comment than facts about cognitions. Weber's historical arguments are hardly ever revisited. Be that as it may, one should see that there are echoes of the basic perspective we have just sketched in evolutionary theories of reasoning. They can be found in Pinker's work, for example, just as they can in Dennett's. In both cases, the claim is made that various techniques of science (experimental in the case of Pinker, more conceptual in the case of Dennett) allow one to bypass the problems of vernacular language and hence the logical connection argument. 'True' language can be provided by science; with science one can get to true causes.

This view has its problems, though, and they are not to do with specifying what this future language might be. Not least, it can make understanding the reasons that people have for their actions quite difficult to grasp in the first place. Indeed, this is one of the reasons why the topic of witchcraft is so central to these debates. For the debates are not really about witchcraft – whether witchcraft is irrational or not – but whether the evoking of the term as a premise of inquiries (i.e., the term 'witchcraft') is illustrative of a conceptual starting place that can inhibit understanding of the reasoning practices purportedly the topic of inquiries. In the witchcraft case, those persons are in other cultures, but the argument applies to the examination of *any practice* in which *reasons are a part* – that is to say, when language is used both to describe the actions in question and to frame actions as 'such and such' and not something else – in sum, any human action in which language has a role. What is being argued is that coining the word 'witchcraft' is tantamount to saying those being examined don't reason properly to start off with.

To avoid this pitfall, and putting it briefly and crudely, a better procedure might be to consider the practices one observes in their own terms, including the contentious example of witchcraft. This is a good example, since it highlights how it is that, within Western culture, witchcraft is a loaded description. It might be that, from inside another culture, it has a different hue. If one is open to this, one might find that there is some point or logic to those practices described as witchcraft. And, as importantly, even if one didn't, one might be able to look with more acuity at the larger society of which they are a part. If one can look at witchcraft calmly, then so too might one look at other activities and hence the reasoning practices constitutive of them.

It is perhaps worth putting this another way. At issue here is not that spells are real or not real: the point is to get the right sense of how reasons of *various sorts* come into play in some setting such that the connections between reasons, actions and notions such as cause (as well as description, explanation, and so on) can be properly caught. The debates about magic and the reasoning of the Azande are not about witchcraft, its merits or otherwise. They are about avoiding difficulties in understanding reasons. At the very least, for all those inquiries interested in the reasons that people have (in some sense or other), it ought to be a starting assumption that those reasons, people's reasons, make some kind of sense to them and, for most of the time, can be explicated around what that sense 'is', so to speak.

Needless to say, the issues here are much more complicated than the Azande argument can allow – for one thing, it is not always clear that one has characterised another culture's practices accurately; it is even harder to see when one has done it to practices closer to home. It might well be that choosing magic and witchcraft to illustrate the problems of conceptual confusion and an inhibited capacity to see reasons is not helpful. Too much turns on witchcraft and its apparent opposite, science, to make calm reflection about understanding possible here.[8]

To be sure, the crude distinction between people's own reasons and the reasons that science offers is one that is all too easily slipped into without due care and attention, and thus it is all too often a source of such infelicities. The very evoking of science prohibits good, empirical endeavour unwittingly. As we pointed out in the introductory chapter, that everyday reasons and scientific reasons somehow echo each other does not imply that adjudicating between them is any simple matter. A science of reasons is not so readily separated from the reasons of everyday action, and efforts to find reasons that fit science in the reasons of everyday life can inhibit explication of those everyday reasons. Searching for one can come at the price of the other. It is to that very problem we now turn.

Types of reasons as material causes

As we said, there are two ripostes to the logical connection argument. The second has no truck with cultural analysis if, broadly speaking, this is what we have just considered (i.e., the reasoning of the Azande and their cultural practices). Nor is it bothered with what people might think about, their worries or concerns about magic or anything else. Although it does, as we shall see, allow that subjective reasons need to be taken account of, the reasons this second view considers and thinks really matter are of a particular order. The current philosophy of action, as it is called, holds that these reasons have material form – that they cause some observable action or, rather, that they are 'physical events'. Real reasons, in this

---

[8] This is certainly the view that Peter Winch came to after effectively commencing this topic in his book *The Idea of a Social Science* (1958).

view, are then shown in the real world. But they are also outcomes of reasons in the inner world, in the mind. Actions and mental events are, in this view, all 'material'. Reasons are psychological states; these states come before action; they cause action.

The roots for this view go back some way, to Donald Davidson in fact, to 'Actions, reasons, and causes' (1963). He wanted to get rid of the idea that there might be two different worlds – the world of humans with their language and the world of objects without words – by showing that there was only one, and that the actions of human beings can be explained according to the laws of physics just like the movements of any other body.

His is a kind of 'getting things moving' causality that involves relations between physical events. In Davidson's view, the actual movement of one's body to take an action follows from a prior physical event in one's nervous system. The sorts of things that relevantly, for Davidson's purposes, go on in your mind are the occurrence to you of beliefs and desires. Your desire here is, say (for a colourful example), for your wife to stop beating you up, and you figure that if you are divorced she won't be able to beat you up any more. So when you come to the point at which you want to put a stop to the beating, and believe you need a lawyer to do this, then the event of desiring this in *conjunction* with believing that contact with a lawyer will stop the beatings will *cause* you to pick up the phone and make an appointment. And here is the rub: how does the cause come to be a cause?

Conventional forms of psychology are keen on this way of thinking. Psychology is enamoured of the idea that our mental life is made up of goals and means – things we want to do and ways of achieving them. Davidson's account fits very neatly with this, since the positive attitude can be thought of as the 'goal' and the belief as the 'means'. Since every action contains this explanation, all actions can be explained in terms of goals and means.

Unfortunately, though one can articulate this view quite well, and Davidson's 'Actions, reasons, and causes' is treated as a momentous event in the modern philosophy of action, today this view is under assault. As Leist notes, the view is now thought of as 'portraying reasons too simply' (2007: 9). The emphasis on causality has tended to 'distort' the richness of the relationship between reasons as descriptions, reasons as explanations, and reasons as causes 'under a description'. As we note above, Davidson's view distinguishes thoughts that come to be causes from other kinds of mental landscapes, such as conjecture. It excludes, too, the role of descriptions if not as elements of causes. And, beyond this, it can come, and indeed has come, to be treated as excluding the subtle ways in which the landscape of reasons is a described outcome of everyday affairs. As we mentioned above, people are nothing if not talkers, and in their talk they describe the world of action they see around them, populating that landscape with reasons of various kinds. These reasons provide the bedrock of how choices are seen, accounted for and ignored. They also characterise relations between people and reasons: not all reasons are seen to be owned by people; some reasons are components of how the world is seen that bypasses the role of human responsibility – suggesting that 'one's genes did it' is one such move. This is what we mean when we say 'the landscape of reasons is a described outcome of everyday affairs.'

Leist (2007: 1–52) thinks that this is not what Davidson himself wanted and that, over his career, the latter sought to bring back into philosophical inquiry a sensitivity for and a concern with 'subjective reasons' – with this described outcome. But, as Sandis (forthcoming) notes, the 1963 paper ended up throwing the baby out with the bathwater. Instead of having a philosophy of action that looked at causes for action and the landscape of action described and understood through the language of reasons, it allows only causal reasons. This has had a peculiar impact on the philosophy of action ever since (see also Wiland, 2012).

For example, Gilbert explains that, subsequent to Davidson, philosophers are no longer interested in those reasons that can be defined as causes of action, since that makes those the subject of the science of psychology. If one says one is going to a swimming pool the day after tomorrow but in the end does not, then that is a fault of one's brain, of one's machinery, of no interest to philosophy. As Gilbert puts it, the person in question 'will act in error if [they] fail to go swimming' (2014: 6). The resulting space for the philosophy of action is looking at how thoughts come to be causes, when one of the concerns there has to do with finding an evidential basis. In Gilbert's case she is interested in how individual people come to see, through evidence, that others are acting in ways that show some kind of commitment, and that this commitment is also something that obliges them (i.e., causes them) to act collaboratively.[9]

The problem for philosophy is how ideas are shaped into causes. Once that shaping is done, the actual mechanics of a cause to act is no matter. In this view, the philosophy of action thus excludes a whole range of ways of thinking and describing, accounting and telling, that are evidently constitutive of the world we see

---

[9] If we leave aside what that might 'mean'. Gilbert's work points to sociology, but she strictly avoids reading any sociology, even though she admits to being inspired by Durkheim.

around us but which don't fit this model. Leist again: 'The mutual dependencies of cognition and biographical framework, the dependencies between individual and social action – these aspects are surely discussed in many disciplines ... but fatally are largely absent and systematically ignored in the philosophy of action' (2007: 39).

If economists are not interested in what goes on in people's heads, and indeed are basically interested only in what we earlier called an imagined entity, 'the market', then so too are most within the current field of the philosophy of action limited in their concerns: if ordinary people understand the world through a rich and diverse vocabulary, where reasons are complex, at times descriptive and accounting, at other times evoking casual chains, then the philosophy of action cuts out most of this from its inquiries. Its starting premises seek to remove a great deal of the world of reasons as lived in by people themselves, and the price it pays is an ever increasing attenuation between it and the felt life – the world of reasons over which people argue, dispute, reflect and reconsider. Philosophy no longer speaks to ordinary souls in the ways it once did.

Perspectives as reasonable places to look at reasons and choices

It is very important to understand that this is not meant to imply that there is anything peculiar about philosophy here – other than a claim that some philosophers have made over the years of speaking to the human predicament, in which 'reasons for action' are the cause of angst. Evidently, these claims have become increasingly spurious. Philosophers have cast out many of the reasons that cause people angst yet claim to offer guidance on that angst with reference to only a few – and, if we are to believe Leist (2007), not the most interesting ones.

That aside, what we are wanting to show is how philosophy, like the social sciences we have dealt with, undertakes its inquiries by presupposing what the phenomena of interest might be. This has all sorts of advantages, one being that it can make evidence constrained and thus tractable to particular modes of explanation – causal, as we have seen. With this, philosophy can develop appropriate methodologies – ones that allow the likes of Gilbert to remove topics from their inquiries.

All this is reasonable; after all, no method is good for all inquiries, just as no inquiries are about all evidence. All disciplines, whether they claim the nomenclature of science or, as in the case of philosophy, the humanities, need starting places, and these, we have seen, entail choices about what to look at, what to ask about the thing being examined, and what might be the kinds of answers that would derive from inquiries. We are noting that philosophy similarly limits its topics – though, as we say, many think it has become too circumspect, its narrowness a trap rather than an enabler.

We are not wanting to make big claims about philosophy here nor more generally about the philosophy of sciences in the broad; we certainly don't want to make claims that might be suggestive of, for example, Kuhn and his paradigmatic explorations. All we are trying to present is the sensibility that different disciplinary views on choice entail, and the way we have sought to do that is by looking at how they variously approach evidence, what is treated as their taken for granted assumptions about choice, and what is the question that their inquiries seek to pose given all that. There are many perspectives on choice, as we have seen. There is at least one more, and this seeks to examine reasons in their vernacular context as a topic in its own right. As we say, Hacker wants to call this approach an 'anthropology of choice', but he has no expertise on the social sciences, being by his own admission resolutely a philosopher and a philosopher alone. Be that as it may, his coining of the phrase does not claim this perspective for the discipline of anthropology. His label emphasises the topics of such inquiries: how people reason as part of their affairs, as part of the anthropology of their existence, and to the variety of such affairs, in different workplaces and countries, in different cultural settings and diverse geographies, from city to country, from work to play. Reasons are as diverse as the human world we see around us.

It is important to note that this perspective is not so much denuded of theory as it is a view with its own theoretical gambit: this holds that there might be some properties in the reasoning of the everyday that are worth examining in their own right, and that these are to be examined by looking at them within their own inter-locative frameworks – i.e., as they are spoken about and oriented to by those who use them. If economists look at the imagined market, psychologists the imagined mind mapped on the brain, and sociologists the social structures that they conceive governs individual choice, the anthropology of choice imagines that there might be demonstrable logics to everyday, vernacular reasoning. It holds that how people talk about their reasons, how they interpret and adjust them, ignoring some while invoking others at different moments in time, creates a landscape of understanding that can be seen to have systematic properties, ones that can be described and explored empirically, generating thereby the stuff that might constitute a social science, even if that social science doesn't as yet have any formal status. It is to these we now turn.

An anthropology of choice

The origins of this approach lie variously in people we have mentioned quite extensively already – Wittgenstein, for example, and Peter Winch's (1958) elaboration of that in relation to social science. It has its roots also in the philosophical work of Alfred Schutz (1962, 1964, 1966), who looked at the organisation of reasoning from a phenomenological point of view. And it has its echoes in Elizabeth Anscombe's exploration of Wittgenstein's analysis of reasons in her book *Intention* (2000). Beyond this it also has its roots in the sociology of Harold Garfinkel, who condensed many of these perspectives in his *Studies in Ethnomethodology* (1967b).

More latterly, a concern for such reasoning has its echoes in, for example, the anthropology of Tim Ingold (2012) and his desire to make the 'felt life', and the reasons that constitute the trajectories of action through that life, the centre of a new kind of anthropology, one less interested in social structural matters than hitherto and more in the reasons people have. It has further echoes in the work of Doreen Massey (2005), a human geographer who, like Ingold, wants to make how people reason important in studies of how society spaces itself.

However, both these latter authors, unlike Garfinkel, seek dialogues with their home perspectives and don't want to claim a vigorous new concern for choice and reasoning per se. Instead, they want to treat that topic within the regimes of their disciplines and their traditional topics. For Ingold, this means in terms of how reasons articulate power, for example; this is a central concern for anthropology irrespective of the role of reasons in action. For Massey, it has to do with how space allows reasons to unfold and be acted upon and thus is confined to the central topic of geography – not reasons, that is, but geometries of space between persons in which reasons can bind and separate 'spatialities'.

This desire for dialogue with their parent disciplines on the part of Ingold and Massey seems entirely merited, but it can be contrasted with the approach of Garfinkel, who came to think that his arguments might lead to a new discipline where reasons and reasoning in all their rich and ragged form would become a topic in their own right – without reference to prior disciplinary concerns. For the purposes of this book, this seems an equally reasonable thing to do. And so it is with Garfinkel that we shall start.

Though Garfinkel wanted to move into a new field, he had his disciplinary source in sociology, as we say. Key here is the presumption that people's reasons matter, that their rationalities have a relation to their choices. This still leaves much room for different ways of deploying this starting presumption. As we have seen (in chapter 4), even for quantitative sociologists such as John Goldthorpe, as a case in point, rationality can be seen as 'situationally determined'. This retains the possibility of rational action being subjectively experienced while allowing sociologists to identify (and own, if you like, by dint of expertise) the external constraints on the range of alternatives available for that rationality. Garfinkel wanted to broker this limited or constrained notion of reasons with a more philosophically inspired perspective that treated reasons as *encompassing*.

The philosophies of Wittgenstein and Elizabeth Anscombe, neither of whom were of course sociologists, hold that reasons in action are *inescapable*; in their view, reasons, rationality in the broad sense, will *always* be how action is understood. All action will fall 'under a description', they explain, and, as outlined above, this means that description of action is suffused with reasons. For Anscombe, and for Wittgenstein, reasons are not to be thought of situationally determined as a starting premise; rather, some reasons may have this character. But other reasons will not be of this form. As we remarked above, reasons can be the causes of action and sometimes the ways that action is described; but reasons can also be the account for why some action cannot be understood causally – after all, one person can say of another, 'There is no reason for what he did', and that account becomes sufficient. Nevertheless, the inexplicability of the other, one's colleague or friend, say, allows a kind of understanding – one that allows one to move on and not ask unanswerable questions. In this way, even when no reason can be avowed, reasons in this broad sense govern how people understand action. The shape of reasons in human affairs is then subtle, complex, knotted – accounting for even the ineffable.

An important feature of Wittgenstein and Anscombe's view about reasons is not just allowing this ragged heterogeneity, but that, in the normal course of events, reasons are discernible as a natural feature of making sense for people in ordinary life. Reasons and intentions are not hidden somewhere, in the head, say; they are, as it were, there to be seen, as part of the behaviour in question. Among other things, they are used to recognise that behaviour for what it is intended to achieve, as well as, for example, to characterise the persons involved in terms of motive and such (even when none can be found, as just remarked).

So, to develop this: people sometimes state intentions and follow through on them with action, and those actions can be properly (and largely unproblematically) identified/described as 'actions with intentions'. This is an empirical matter for people themselves, as it is for any disciplinary trade or empirical research endeavour that seeks to investigate them, such as an anthropology of choice. And indeed these 'rational properties' of action were fundamental to Garfinkel's inquiries in his *Studies*. He assumed that reasons were a part of the actions he observed. His view, like Wittgenstein's, is not that one can make a distinction between rational and non-rational action in one's observations but that, in the first instance, activities are organised such that they are rational and are seen to be so when one looks. One presumes they are rational from the outset. Without this being the case, Garfinkel, like Wittgenstein, is arguing that one would not be able to see the actions for what they are – as action with 'this goal' in mind, with 'these circumstances' at hand, and so on.

This doesn't mean that some actions can turn out to be more opaque and less rational than they appear at first, nor it does it deny the possibility that some actions seem inexplicable at first glance. What it does suggest is that reasoning is presumed to be a visible feature of action even though it might be hard to discern on some occasions. That reasoning is part of the action is a premise, in other words, and, much like the premises we have seen in other disciplines and perspectives, determines what is focused on.

What is different here is that these reasons are not to be investigated through contrasts with external definitions of reasons, of good and bad reasons, say. Nor does this view point towards some machinery of reasoning that might or might not work properly in some setting. One thinks of the premises of economics in the former, those of psychology in the latter. What the anthropology of choice is concerned with is reasons in all their varieties and shape – as an empirical topic in their own right without corrective, as Garfinkel himself put it.

Key here is not being tempted by unhelpful contrasts and comparisons. The Azande case comes to mind, though this is not something Garfinkel himself wrote upon. Nevertheless, he makes the same point that came out of those debates:

> a leading policy [in his approach] is to refuse serious consideration to the prevailing proposal that efficiency, efficacy, effectiveness, intelligibility, consistency, planfulness, typicality, uniformity, reproducibility of activities – i.e. that rational properties of practical activities – be assessed, recognised, categorised, described by using a rule or a standard obtained outside actual settings within which such properties are recog-

nised, used, produced and talked about by settings' members. (Garfinkel 1967b: 33)

Garfinkel doesn't want studies that compare magic and non-magic, rational and non-rational, 'the logics of the inside' with 'logics from the outside'; he simply wants studies of rationality in all its forms when these forms are part and parcel of the subject matter of the inquiries in question – studies, that is to say, of the world at large.

What is distinctive about this view is that it shares none of the disciplinary predilections discussed in previous chapters – ones that predefine the topic. It contains no assumptions about the form that rationality must take or universal properties of rationality, and it postulates no psychological processes; instead it assumes that there are reasons to be found, if one is prepared to look for them. It pre-supposes, also, that these can be found in any and all social action and interaction. Like Wittgenstein and Anscombe, then, Garfinkel starts from the assumption that reasons are in human action, and that they are says something about those reasons – they are a part of it.

Let us take a simple example, from an ordinary day in the life of an academic, to illustrate what a view of reasons would look like:

Well, I'd been thinking about buying a good coffee machine for some time, but I was a bit reluctant to spend a lot of money. We were in town one day, and I had nothing better to do so I went into [a shop] to have a look. I saw this lovely looking machine, made by [. . .], and they have a good reputation, I think . . . but then I looked at the price and it was about £1200. I remember thinking, 'Bloody hell, what do you get for that?' and I could see on the buttons that you could do expressos, cappuccinos, Americanos, and so on. I was quite tempted . . . but then the partner was standing next to me and giving me that look . . . nope, I went home without. Then, a bit later, I thought, 'I wonder if I can find something cheaper and just as good on the Web?' So, I did a bit of idle searching, and all the machines with the same kinds of button were more or less the same price, and then I saw the actual one I'd been looking at in the shop, adver-tised for £700. So I clicked on it and there it was. But it was some outlet I'd never heard of. I thought, do I trust these guys or is it a rip-off? So, I did another search, using the name of the outlet and adding words like 'scam', 'fraud', and so on, to see if there were reasons to be suspicious. Couldn't find anything and this machine was just staring at me. And then I thought, '**** it', I want that, so I clicked on 'Purchase'. It arrived the very next day. It's great. I love it. (From a telephone conversation between two friends).

Although this is only one little transcript, of a telling over a telephone, it is enough to illustrate some things about the real-world character of rationality and hence decision-making. A range of issues are in play, including some expression of an intention, some kind of deliberation, some limited forms of comparison, a concern for the time taken, a fretting about moral implications ('what would the partner think'); the example shows too how people reason about their 'unreasoned' behaviour, their impulses, just as much as they reason about the mechanics of some action and choice, how the Internet might be used (and abused), and so on.

We venture to suggest that these topics are recognisable to many people who engage in purchasing decisions – even if spending such sums on coffee machines isn't. Our point is that this transcript exemplifies Garfinkel's claim that one might look at 'real worldly' rationality and that one will find it in abundance wherever one looks. To do so one must presuppose that reasons are to be found in the action taken; that they thus partly constitute the action; and that hence they also help fabricate the sense of the action in which they are a part.

This is one of the reasons why Garfinkel likes to use the word 'member' to label people in the settings he describes:

> With respect to the problematic character of practical actions and to the practical adequacy of their enquiries, members take for granted that a member at the outset must 'know' [i.e., have a sense of] the settings in which he is to operate if his practices are to serve as measures to bring particular, located features of these settings to recognisable account. . . . Members know, require, count on and make use of this reflexivity to produce, accomplish, recognise, or demonstrate rational-adequacy-for-all-practical- purposes [in their actions]. (Garfinkel, 1967b: 8)

An anthropology of choice

In previous chapters we have looked at views that presume the universal character of information and hence the basis of reasoning, and with this presumption it follows that an 'information economy' is what is critical to decision-making. In this view, through the rational choice lens, 'knowledge' or 'information' is something to be explicitly sought to remedy a deficiency and enable the 'right' choice. We have enough of 'it', say, such that we can make an 'objectively' rational decision, or we do not have all we need and so cannot. Our choices will be rationally perfect only when we have adequate information. They might feel 'subjectively' rational if we do not, but this would be a mistake. 'Information', in this view, has what appears to be a precise and technical sense: it is what is sought in order to enable a right decision or correct choice to be made. This is quite different from the view we are outlining here, a view from the anthropology of choice.

Now, it may well be true that we can speak of 'knowledge' or 'information' as something to be explicitly sought. Thus, there will certainly be times when one speaks of the need to 'find something out', when one may indeed 'seek information' or may recognise that there are things one needs to know; it is also the case that, in ordinary circumstances, there are many other senses in which one can 'know things' or 'have' information. One of them is the ability to recognise when another (a partner, say) is becoming impatient – as in the coffee machine example above. This, in turn, relates to the way in which rights to participate in a decision can be relative to people – one's partner may not be prepared to put the time into finding out about a product, say (leaving aside their concerns for monetary value!).

We leave it to the reader to decide how many kinds of rationality, if any, are being exhibited in the example about coffee machines; as we remark, not everyone will consider paying such sums for an early morning brew. But all readers should be able to recognise that the rationality in question is closely fitted to the contingent and local features of the decision-making situation; what one might say is their endogenous arrangements – the who of it, the what that will result if the action is undertaken, as well as the desires and relative measures of value that are articulated in the chosen reasons, and so on. It is all this and more that comes to make up the gestalt of real-world decision-making. One might not buy such a machine oneself, but one can see another's reasoning here, even if it brings a smile of disbelief to one's face.

Garfinkel was obviously writing some time ago, but the approach to reasoning he outlined has been further developed over the years such that now there are various studies of reasoning of this ilk, of how people come to choose whatever it is they do from within the gestalt of their world.

Even terms that label the kinds of abstract cargoes that concern the other social sciences we have looked at have been examined from this perspective. As a case in point, Sakai, Awamura and Ikeya (2012: 1) pursue the topic of 'information' and argue that reasoning

with and through information can be understood only through the
relevant practices of those deploying the term itself:

> In our view, what remains missing . . . is an approach that seri-
> ously considers the practitioners' points of view. If we hope to
> capture the aspects of social practitioners' practices and how
> information activities are embedded in their practices, digging
> into indigenous methods that the participants use and describ-
> ing these methods from within are necessary. In other words,
> we must be able to capture the practical concern that partici-
> pants experience rather than replace it with theoretical concern.

Moreover, and as Goodwin (1994) points out, the status of information may vary even if we allow its fitting to place being the salient
move in an inquiry, when by that is meant not how information
from outside a setting is brought to bear so much as how information becomes part of a setting. Goodwin's research, as a case in
point, looks at the material practices of archaeologists and others as
they organise and display 'expert information' about their domain
– their sites in which they dig, the efforts they make to identify
the things they find, the way they eventually use those artefacts to
account for their investment in time, effort and money, and so on.

We should make the point, however, that, in the view of the
anthropology of choice, there is no need to limit the concept of
'information' to professionally acquired and deployed knowledge.
It may, for instance, be the case, as Marvin Scott intimates, that
'Information may be defined simply as what a social actor knows
about a situation' (1968: 1). If so, he argues, there may be at least
two senses in which we can speak of 'information': 'the first involves
an actor's knowledge about the overall situation; the second is what
he knows in common with other actors with whom he is in interaction' (ibid.). We might add, further, that information is typically
relevantly acquired. That is, as intentions are negotiated, adjusted
and evolved, so the relevance of information and how to use it will
be interactionally mediated, and often mediated in a relevant-to-
expressed-purpose way.

To be clear, in the anthropology of choice perspective, there
is indifference to whether the subjects in question have 'enough'
knowledge or not. Instead, the topic of interest is in how information or knowledge is made relevant in situationally specific terms.
'What we know', seen this way, is a matter of deploying both
'stocks of knowledge' and 'recipes' – ways of doing, to put it in
Schutz's (1962, 1964, 1966) terms, that allow the elaboration of an
intentional path. As the coffee example shows, practical informa-

tion handling is embedded in organisational paths, even if those paths seem evidently domestic in their form. Searching for a coffee machine was done, it would appear, from the home setting – a couch perhaps.

Now, and of course, the range of reasons, intentions and knowledge, and the occasions on which they are deployed, is obviously huge; they are doubtless varied in form too. They may consist, for instance, of knowing how to queue in a local context, how to order dinner, how to be polite, and so on. They may also consist of professional knowledge, as we have noted, while nevertheless having a local flavour.

Examples of inquiries into such reasoning practices are thus also likely to be quite diverse. Indeed, they already are. For instance, Hester and Francis (2000) look at the educational contexts, as do Iszatt-White et al. (2011); if education is commonplace, there are also studies of much more arcane matters, such as the practices of neuroscientists (Alač, 2011). Lynch, meanwhile, has looked at science, particularly bench science (Lynch, 1993), and, more recently, at the role of DNA fingerprinting in criminal investigations (Lynch et al., 2008). Here the status of such evidence as 'material to reason about' is explored through reference to the process of court interaction and decision-making. Reasoning in mathematics (Livingstone, 1986) has been looked at too, with particular regard to how proofs are done. An important feature of such proofs is precisely that they do prove, so comprehensively that it becomes hard to see how the truth could ever have been thought otherwise. According to Livingstone, what was understood before the proof is shown becomes difficult to recall thereafter in all the vitality it once had – the proof seems to rewrite history. What Livingstone points towards, then, is not just the logic of proofs, but how the reasoning constituting them affects the felt life.

For yet one last example, there is a study undertaken by one of the authors of this volume of how people use documents to reason. Harper's *Inside the IMF* (1998) is worth mentioning, since this research was undertaken under the rubric of Human Computer Interaction (a subfield of computer science) rather than, say, sociology (as the above studies were). Though it is now treated by anthropologists as 'inventing' the study of 'documentary reason' (Hull, 2012: 253), its auspices give credit to our suggestion that there is an anthropology of choice to be found that isn't to be confined to any one discipline, and certainly not to anthropology itself. It is, rather, an approach that is showing itself across the social sciences and even in some technical ones, such as computer science.

With the increased interest in choice across the board, from economics to psychology, from sociology to computer science, so the
lineaments of this approach are becoming easier to discern and,
we hope, understand. In the future, it may be that the term might
be used to self-describe research that looks at how people come to
reason, to choose, as part of their lives; one day it might be that
researchers themselves choose an anthropology of choice.

Economic reasoning as choices in action

Be that as it may, we want to conclude the book with further examination of some of those illustrative anthropology of choice studies.
We want to focus in particular on studies which are more or less
obviously to do with 'economic' contexts. The topic of these studies
will allow us to evoke the beginning of our arguments, when we
looked at the perspective of economics and how it views 'economic
reasoning'. As we saw, its interests are only in that kind of reasoning, though this discipline tends to see that reasoning well outside
of monetary affairs alone, as we found in Becker's work. Now we
can better understand why an anthropology of choice is so different from the economist's view – not necessarily better or worse,
nor more or less empirical, but of a different order in all sorts of
respects. Below, we briefly describe various studies that look at
'action to do with money': Anderson, Hughes and Sharrock's (1989)
study of management in a catering company, Harper, Randall and
Rouncefield's (2000) study of banking, Heath's study of auctions
(2013) and Crabtree and Chamberlain's investigation of a rural
market (2014). The authors were variously involved in the first
two.

We begin with Anderson, Hughes and Sharrock's book *Working
for Profit* (1989). This is a study of entrepreneurial activity, in this
case, the senior management activities of a fairly large catering
company employing more than 500 people. What motivates their
study is Garfinkel's desire to examine practical reasoning, but they
gloss this with Geertz's (1975) famous phrase about the manner of
anthropological description: Anderson et al. are after 'thick description', which, for them, is a prerequisite of answering the question
'What the devil do they think they're up to?', when the 'they' are the
managers of the firm.

The study is thus to be contrasted with those from the economics discipline (as well as management science, though we have not
presented much from that view in previous chapters), since these,
according to Anderson et al., 'seem to resist being given what we

might call an empirical reference' (1989: 11).[10] An economist might imagine that such a reference would be to, for example, calculation, how economic action is done through maths. Anderson et al. are certainly interested in the use of numbers, but they don't assume that work with numbers defines the work done in the situation they describe.

The authors of *Working for Profit* are indifferent to predefined rationalities such as those to do with the numerical treatment of the company and its performance; instead, they investigate the 'social organization of calculability' by focusing on the concerns of members of the firm, whatever they might be – from numbers to work schedules, from daily tasks to the 'annual return'. They are interested especially in how these concerns are viewed from the particular point of view of different levels of managers and staff in the company, with different concerns in the division of labour. They call this concern 'egological'. This involves not the theoretical redescription of the experience of those under investigation, but a direct account of the organization of experience as members of the company themselves account for it and orient to in their practical, choice-making actions.

Among other things, Anderson et al. note the burden and scale of what needs to be known and is known by these staff as part of their daily routines:

> When [Marx and Weber] talk about rational miserliness or work as a necessary part of life, what they miss out are the sheer capacities, absorbed busyness, skilful elan which [people, the members of the company in question, its staff] bring to their business activities . . . They cannot help themselves. They have to know how the fridges are divided up, where the keys to the safe are kept, how often the light fittings are cleaned, what size cups are used to dispense soft drinks and what items the staff are allowed to consume while on duty. They cannot stop themselves noticing who is wearing a uniform and who isn't. . . . This isn't an impersonal curiosity. They have to find out. They have to get things done. (1989: 178)

In other words, the form of rationality that one finds in a catering company is rich and detailed and can be surprisingly comprehensive even if one confines oneself to senior staff: it's not merely the

---

[10] A particular contrast they want to make is with a version of institutional economics promoted by, for example, Amitai Etzioni (1987) and which he called 'socio-economics'.

numbers in the account books these individuals reason about, it
is even whether a light bulb has been cleaned, and, if not, who will
get round to do it given workload. Rationality is ubiquitous, one
might say, or at least its concerns; but rationality is burdensome
too, a matter of light bulbs and calculating whether there is time to
change them as much as of 'doing the books' – adding entries to the
profit and loss sheets in the accounts. The vision that comes to mind
here is not just how there is so much to think about in making a
company profitable, but a cultural memory: one thinks of Victorian
capitalists, worried not just about the vast profits they were making
but about every detail and every expense – the cost of tea, the price
of shoes and the profit to be made on cotton. It turns out that this
parallel is not so unlikely, the catering company that Anderson et al.
study being in Manchester – the seat of nineteenth-century capitalism if ever there was one.

A similar study of routine work is carried out by Harper, Randall
and Rouncefield (2000), but here the domain is consumer banking –
banks on what is called the high street in the UK. These researchers
examined *inter alia* how decisions about lending to consumers are
made by bank staff. This entails looking carefully at how staff have
to learn to interpret and apply the criteria for lending in relevant
and sensible ways to some particular customer and their needs. No
consumer is like any other at first glance, but every decision needs to
abide by some kind of standard.

In the study, a series of real lending decisions are analysed. In
each case, what the authors show is the practical ways in which decisions are arrived at – sometimes in keeping with overall bank policy
and sometimes not, but always depending on a series of judgements
about the competence of the customer seeking a loan and the competence of the bank's staff at dealing with the loan system. Here the
word 'competence', as regards the customer, stands as a synonym
for their apparent reliability, their trustworthiness, and even their
communicability (i.e., how well they express their circumstances
and needs), while the competence of the staff has to do with whether
they can 'work' the system, by which is meant the computer-based
loans system.

Key to these decisions are not just characterisations of the customer but also the interactional steps required in filling out online
forms while dealing with the customer in person. Reasoning here
has to do with finding out what the customer wants and understanding what the online forms require in terms of content and
documented action. Online forms have 'gates' that have to be gone
through before a next step in the form-filling can be taken. Gates
have to do with entering financial history, for example, or to do with

income (in the past, in the present and, of course, prospectively), other debts, and so on. Putting it simply, bank staff have to converse with real persons with real financial histories (not all of which are 'good') while they 'converse' with on-line forms. It is thus they work their way through these gates.

Often these gates arise in their interaction with the computer in ways that do not 'sync' with their dialogues with the customer. Speaking and keying clash; while the data is being entered on one topic, the customer starts offering other information, not yet required.

Bank staff don't like to make customers repeat themselves, nor do they like to test their own memories but, rather, do these things as and when they have to: they need to be handled together despite how they don't fit. With practice, bank staff come to develop ways of 'reasoning through' these procedures and interactions; they do so by treating the problems they have as ones that can be solved in common ways. The result of this is that, despite the uniqueness of every customer and the invariable contingencies of every attempt to speak with a customer and enter data on the machine at the same time, bank staff typically conclude these interactions in ways that can predictably guarantee that loans will be provided. Customers become 'types' to whom the bank staff know the systems will let them grant loans; the gates can be 'worked around' in predictable and commonly known ways so that the 'yeses' are derived. Prior debts can be ignored if they can be said to have been the responsibility of a partner, say (a husband or wife, for example); incomes can be calculated without regard to costs that reduce the benefits of such incomes.

Of course, not all customers are in the end offered loans; sometimes their competence is deemed too low by the bank staff. But, in any event, it is in these ways that a socially structured world of decision-making within the bank appears, and this is one not reflected in the computer systems per se. Rather, it is articulated through the decisions the systems come to document. Bank staff work the systems; the systems do not control bank staff.

How staff do this is what these same staff view as the 'knowledge' they need to do their job. This is what they teach each other, and this is what they judge the competence of their colleagues by too; this is reasoning in action. This is how choices are made. 'By placing plans, procedures and decision making within its social and organisational context, they come to be . . . elements which enable workers to make sense of their own work and that of others and to come to a decision about future courses of action' (Harper et al., 2000: 100). The choices that result in any particular instance are treated as choices that any and all the staff would have made; what one individual chooses as the loan that is or comes to be offered is assumed to be what any competent colleague would offer too. For Harper et al., key to this is how rationality is understood as what needs to be done in the circumstances at hand, with the resources and constraints that come to define how to choose.

The business of making loans, then, is not by any means confined to some reductive financial formulas. On the contrary, 'What [the study] emphasises is the importance of seeing how and in what ways plans and procedures are interwoven into a highly variegated set of phenomena that make up the social organisation of work [people and machines]' (Harper et al., 2000: 100). As do Anderson et al., these authors stress the need for an approach which addresses the real-time, real-world of reasoning (and decision-making); researchers need to approach a setting 'independently of the preconceptions of received organisational theories and methods, being "led by the phenomena" rather than by the concerns and requirements of a particular standpoint [outside of the setting and its members]' (ibid.).

What one takes away from the study is not just a sense of the logics in action when decisions about loans are made in high-street banks, but a sense also that this decision-making may have been bound to the particularities of the time. The system gates are treated as hoops to jump through, and the staff deploy their own competencies and judgements to figure out how to do so. Presumably over time, and with changes in bank policy, these techniques of working the system would and will have evolved. How they might do so would require historical study, of course. Whether the choice-making procedures that Harper et al. observed resulted in the better portfolio of loans for the bank in the longer term is a moot point in their analysis, though in hindsight the spread and contagion of 'bad loans' that consumed high-street banking in the UK (and of course even more so in the USA) some two or three years after the study might suggest that this is so.

A more recent study, though well removed from banking or the banking crisis, is that of Heath (2013), who focuses on conduct in fine art auctions. He notes, as do all the authors above, that, typically, different disciplinary interests – economics, say, or sociology – tend to assume that there is a general order to markets of whatever kind and, as a result, scarcely ever investigate how those markets are practical concerns for those involved, concerns which presumably involve various orders of relevant and appropriate reasoning. As he points out, even economic sociology (which doesn't really have decision-making as its focus) has a specific concern, which is to relate interactional matters to a wider institutional, social and economic context rather than to investigate in any detail what those interactional matters look like in real action – in an art auction, say. As Heath explains, the kinds of study of economic action can '[stand] in marked contrast to more traditional, macro-oriented studies of economic behaviour and the social organization of markets with their emphasis on institutional forms and inter- and intra-organisational relations' (2013: 208). But they are not for the most part concerned with 'addressing the situated production of market transactions and the social interaction through which [they] are accomplished' (ibid.).

Using careful analyses of conversation and behaviour in the auction rooms captured on video, Heath is able to show how such events entail delicate and complex 'work'. Bids, 'runs', the work of auctioneers, and so on, can all be understood in sequential fashion, such that each utterance and each action can be, and indeed is, perceived in relation to the actions and utterances that are (in the main) adjacent and prior to it. At each point, the actions in question depend on understandings of the words, gestures, glances, and so on, that precede it; this is embodied work of a particular kind where the reasoning is shown and managed in the movement of the hands, the glancing of eyes. It turns out that being successful in auction, being a bidder whose bids are noted, being an auctioneer who properly sees a person making a bid, and cohering all this into a functioning event where a bidding cycle with multiple participants comes to conclusion, isn't just about arithmetic or the mental apparatus of counting (if there is such a thing); it's about a dance of bodies and minds, an orchestration of an economy of postures and promises in a particular space and time.

The simple fact that this interaction is a kind of dance is not the issue. Rather, identifying the precise way in which interactions are ordered to have this dance-like quality is. Through looking at sequential turn-taking in talk, in body movement, and so forth, Heath reveals something about the 'resources, practices and reasoning' that are brought to bear on the emerging situation by those involved – the auctioneer and bidders, as well as bystanders – all those who are not bidding in any particular instance. All choose to act and are seen to be acting in such an orchestrated manner that the dance comes into being. It is thus that auctions have the shape they do.

There is a simple point that Heath is making here, but one which is often not recognised in other accounts of economic or market activity. This has to do with what we have said above about 'reasons' as seen from without and from within. The point has to do with questions of trust, reputation, coordination, cooperation

and competition. These might seem distant from matters to do
with hand-waving and glances of the eye. But what Heath shows is
that trust and body movement, reputable auction behaviour, and
the coordination of hand waves and their acknowledgment are not
encountered and experienced separately – participants in an auction
don't look around and see a trusted competitor or otherwise; they
see this in the coordination of action – in eyes and hands, in invoked
numbers 'shouted out' or simply seen, in turns at bidding. From the
point of view of the 'member', these things, taken together, form a
gestalt: the seen and acted upon world of the auction room.

Crabtree and Chamberlain (2014), meanwhile, report a study of
the ways in which people in a small town organise the local market.
They point out that people in the market they describe (on the
Welsh borders, a remote and quite poor part of the UK) do not
always choose to orient their selling (or buying) of local goods with
reference to how those acts might be 'scaled up' to a larger, and
hence more profitable, scale. While this desire might be consistent
with orthodox assumptions about economic activity and the desire
for growth incarnate in this activity, these researchers show that
increasing volume is not particularly important for participants in
the market they are looking at; this is particularly so for vendors of
agricultural fare – meat, vegetables.

In other words, the nature of the supply chain in this context is
not to be understood merely in terms of cost-effectiveness where
scale would deliver benefits. There is instead a concern, for instance,
to ensure that local wealth is not 'leached away' by national and
international retailers and thus should be sold to other, 'local'
traders; there is a concern too that the goods sold should have that
'local' character – not only produced thereabouts but sold to local
people and at 'local rates'. There are commitments to 'organic'
produce, fair-trade ideals and local sourcing, where possible.

Of course, it might seem there is a kind of credo at play here,
an ideology that governs action in the market. But Crabtree and
Chamberlain are at pains to point out that actual decision-making
has a mundane feel about it which does not evoke these terms.
Members of this Welsh community don't think of themselves as
ideologues imposing their views on a recalcitrant world: this is
merely farmers and families 'doing the work' of being local, making
their fleeting economic transactions in ways that means the market
place has the feel it does – one that is local, that celebrates the local,
that involves this neighbour buying off that neighbour and, in turn,
selling something else to yet a third neighbour. This isn't incipient
capitalism. Nor is it some strange anthropological practice, the
ritual-like exchange that Malinowski observed in the Trobriand

Islands, for example (Malinowski, 1922). This is simply a small rural community surviving and doing so through a trope – 'being local'.

None of this negates the economic conception of the market place, one which we said, somewhat playfully, turned around an 'imagined phenomenon'. It simply has to do with seeing a market place as a real place (see Knorr-Cetina and Preda's remarks (2006) about the situatedness of market places). Be that as it may, what it does show is that empirical description can add a great deal to what is understood as the reasoning that goes into making a market, that produces or leads to the choices that are made there. As Crabtree and Chamberlain put it:

> when we turn our attention to what motivates and drives micro enterprises we find a host of local concerns that respecify 'value' as it is usually understood in economic and business discourse. The respecification is consequential. It replaces the standard economic concern with scale or growth, and the mechanisms whereby that might be affected, and puts concern on such things as community, family, sustainability, self-determinacy and self-sufficiency, quality of life and quality of product. (2014: 692)

This might suggest that Crabtree and Chamberlain have some political agenda – as if they are wanting to affect the changes that Amartya Sen seeks in economic explanation and which we discussed in chapter 4. Sen wants quality of life factors to be included in economic rationality; so do these authors. But this would be to misunderstand what Crabtree and Chamberlain are about. To be clear, their view does not seek to problematize the economic view of 'markets' (and there is an obvious difference between markets in general and a specific market). Rather, their work points to the way in which economic matters are *realised* in a local context. 'Community, family, sustainability, self-determinacy and self-sufficiency, quality of life and quality of product' (2014: 693) may be instantiations of the way in which the competition for market share is organised in this context. *How* such matters are organised in a local context, however, is precisely what this approach might offer. Sen wants such topics imposed as starting premises; Crabtree and Chamberlain discover that they are there already.

Having recounted some examples of this kind of descriptive inquiry, what we are calling an anthropology of choice, we should note that work which focuses on the close and detailed analysis of decision-making in some part of the business or financial world is not that easy to come by – though, as we pointed out, one of the authors was able to undertake a study in perhaps one of the most closely guarded settings in the financial world, the International Monetary Fund (Harper, 1998). The reasons why sites of economic action might be difficult to access are likely to be many and varied, Harper's study notwithstanding. It may be that some people are concerned that their actions won't appear 'good enough' when seen in the severe light of an expert observer. And, indeed, given our review of some of the approaches to choice and decision-making, one can readily understand why some people are resistant to being examined. Who would want a behavioural economist to observe one acting if the premise of that perspective is that people reason badly? Who would want to talk to an experimental psychologist if one knows that they think choices derive from causes that one might not understand? The same holds true for the sociological perspective too: here it is social factors that govern choice, not individual reasoning. The sensitivities that make getting access to the world difficult may then reflect the state of the current disciplines and general perception of them. These perceptions might not be entirely accurate – perhaps they might be wrong – but they may be real in their consequences nonetheless. As we say, studies of choice in the economic realm are remarkably few.

However, all of this should not constitute 'in principle' objections to studies under the auspices of an anthropology of choice. We have been illustrating what such studies of economic reasoning look like – how they characterise the shape of choice that one finds in real, 'lived' economic settings. There are, of course, many other venues for such inquiries, and the difficulties, though worrying, are in any case often merely practical – to do with the old bugbear of anthropologists (particularly), of 'getting access', of 'getting in'. But such matters need not detain us here – if there is a will, if there is a reason, such a research can be done.

Conclusion

If we now return our discussion to a more abstract level, it should be clear that we have sought to demonstrate that concepts such as 'intention', 'motive', 'reason' and 'information' are at once devices in the vernacular and deployed scientifically; the former have endogenous, practical logics of many forms and particularities, as our sketch of economic motivations suggests. When used scientifically, meanwhile, these concepts are endowed with often quite special disciplinary meanings. Our earlier chapters have looked at some of these meanings in economics, psychology, evolutionary theory, sociology, and so on.

We don't want to recapitulate those chapters now. What we do want to end on is a common misconception, we feel, about whether terms such as 'motivation' and 'reason', and hence also 'choice', can easily and readily be adopted for the vocabulary of science if the science in question is wanting to treat the use of those concepts in the vernacular setting as its topic. Many think this can be done easily; we are less confident. We think, and we believe some of our explorations above show, that this often results in muddles about how to understand the use of vernacular terms. The co-option of these terms for science makes inquiries into the ordinary, vernacular use difficult for a host of reasons.

This was certainly a concern for Wittgenstein. The main problem, in his view, was that technical usage often muddles up the phenomena which the technical term has been deployed to clarify. Take the case of the Azande: if one has a meaning for the concept of 'magic' and this gets treated as if it is technical, as the 'right' meaning irrespective of how that concept might be used in the real world, it can be hard to see practices under the auspices of magic other than through that technical rendering. If, as we saw, this view holds that magic is irrational, it becomes hard to see how practices in which the word 'magic' is deployed in vernacular ways cannot also be irrational. Putting this another way, making vernacular categories into 'technical' terms can result in those categories becoming somehow mangled, often too literal, for example, or sometimes without the subtlety and nuance that gives them power in ordinary life.

Likewise with the terms 'rationality' and 'reasoning': these can be treated as technical labels for defined actions or as categories used in and applicable to the hurly-burly of everyday life. We reported on how Harold Garfinkel began to elaborate what looking at these terms in action might look like. The language of his work can be hard but nevertheless points towards how being rational is a feature of everyday action. Rationality is presupposed in action by those involved in that action, he wanted to claim, and, given this, inquiries into rationality should not set up contrast pairs – good and bad, adequate and inadequate. Such matters are for those whose business it is in their affairs.

This does not mean that one should proscribe the use of terms that are deployed in everyday life for technical use. It means care is required. We saw in the opening chapter that economics is very interested in intention and information but that these terms describe features of the market, not properties of individual action. Though economists assume that economic actors have intention and process

information, that this is so doesn't distract from their real concern
– economists are interested not in people but in markets. However,
when such assumptions are used to make claims about the individual, the merits of the economic view can become strained. Examples
from behavioural economics showed this. Nevertheless, and as we
have just seen, there are studies of human reasoning and choice in
economic settings that report on how terms such as 'intention' and
'information' get used as a feature of the settings in question. These,
we hope we have shown, would be difficult to undertake under the
rubric of economics. We have suggested a new rubric, the anthropology of choice.

We cannot, of course, presume that 'intention in action' or the use
of 'relevant information' will be found in every possible site investigated by this new approach. The view we are ending with is simply
starting from the premise that human action can be seen as rational
and ought to be presumed as such even if in some instance it turns
out otherwise. But starting here has the great benefit of easing our
ability to see that rationality if it is there.

Nor do we wish to undervalue the difficulty of understanding
reasons and rationality, especially when it can have hugely arcane
forms. Garfinkel was very sensitive to this himself and observed that
one can rely on one's 'vulgar competence' in doing, since even the
most arcane reasoning relies upon more basic commonplace skills.
As Lynch (1993) notes in his studies of laboratory work, though the
scientific insights written up in papers might be very difficult to comprehend for a non-scientist, the skills of hand that allow scientists to
use the bench in front of them are very real worldly and common
(i.e., the stuff anyone can do when adequately enculturated).

We ought to add that we don't want the concept of 'vulgar competence' to acquire any technical sense. After all, all members of
a given culture are 'vulgarly competent' in that culture, at least in
some respects (though, as Winch (1958) points out, not in all). The
concept has appreciably more value when it comes to the selection
of data with which to show the kinds of reasoning to be found in
any setting – reasoning by professionals, say, or ordinary people
in mundane affairs. The point is that we do not necessarily need
to have recourse to a specialised professional methodology or to
a disciplinary lexicon in order to shed light on how people reason.
We need care and delicacy; we need to know what we are concerned
with and what to avoid. When we look at entrepreneurs seeking
profit, for example, we mustn't presuppose that we will find economic reasoning as economists think of it, the stuff they try and
model. We will find other orders of reasoning. Nevertheless, what
entrepreneurs achieve will certainly be of interest to economists –

but only once it has been reduced and altered into the form they prefer – one they can model with.

By way of an end to our discussion, we might recall that we started by noting that choice is something that some people have begun to claim can be explicated. The mechanics of choice can be determined, these people hold, its inner logic tamed by new forms of inquiry. What choice is and how it is done can be captured. We noted also that the ineffability of some choices has been a topic of playwrights, poets and novelists from time immemorial and that this is one reason why these claims for a new science seem so exciting.

It should be clear by now that, if it were the case that the new science of choice had achieved its ambition, much of the cultural cargo about the ineffability of choice would lose its appeal: who would be charmed by Greek plays about hubris if the cause of that hubris were not the judgement of the character but merely a function of evolutionary development, computations in the brain?

What we have seen, however, is that many of the claims that choice can be understood illustrate their arguments with accounts of human reasoning that offer massively reduced and simplified depictions, often casting the human actor who makes choices in ways that take that actor out of the ordinary life in which questions of choice (and of reasoning more generally) would have their natural place. All too often the real world is replaced with examples that are determined by what fits a method of inquiry and not by the richness of evidence from everyday life. As a consequence of this, we think that playwrights and poets have little to worry about from the science of choice. For this science is still too impoverished to replace their topic. In some respects, our inquiries have led us to think that this science won't ever do so, though in some areas a great deal has been uncovered. Much more could be if the anthropology of choice got taken up more widely, we feel. Time will tell.

And what about the reader of this book? Have we provided them with an answer to the question which animates so much of the work that we have been assessing, namely, 'Are human beings rational?' Can all their choices be understood? We have not. This is not because these are hard questions to answer, but because they can be answered with only a brief reflection on one's own and others' experience – in reference to the world they live in and understand through reasons they find there. When put thus, the answer to the question 'Are human beings rational?' is likely to be 'Pretty much but not always'. Does this mean we ordinarily think that those around us and even ourselves are always impeccably rational? 'You must be kidding' would be the proper, everyday answer.

Or, at least, we would hope that sometimes this is an answer.

But at other times we would hope something else would arise that we have not mentioned at any point in this book: a smile. It seems to us that it might well be that such an expression will come to the face of the reader when that question is put to them and they come to think about the ordinary world they live in as they go about their own business, whatever that might be, and having put this book down. As we have seen, approaches to choice are massively tied up with disciplinary views and, as a result, are often very dry. But, for anyone who lives in the real world, making choices is very much part of what makes them who they are, and laughter is very much part of all of us, even if it is in varying degrees and subject to change. But, if laughter is important, even then choice is at issue: with laughter you can often see what is in front of you – foolishness, wisdom, thoughtfulness. Yet seeing it is the hard thing to do. Our hope with this book is that we have allowed the reader to see some of the issues more clearly. Whether they can make their choices better as a result is, of course, none of our business.

References and Bibliography

Abell, P. (ed.) (1991) *Rational Choice Theory*. Aldershot: Edward Elgar.

Acquisti, A., and Grossklags, J. (2005) Privacy and rationality in individual decision making, *IEEE Security & Privacy*, 3(1): 26–33.

Alač, M. (2011) *Handling Digital Brains: A Laboratory Study of Multimodal Semiotic Interaction in the Age of Computers*. Cambridge, MA: MIT Press.

Albee, A., and Boyd, G. (1997) *Doing it Differently: Networks of Community Development Agents*. Edinburgh: Scottish Community Education Council.

Ambady, N., and Rosenthal, R. (1992) Thin slices of expressive behavior as predictors of interpersonal consequences: a meta-analysis, *Psychological Bulletin* 111(2): 256–74.

Ambady, N., Bernieri, F. J., and Richeson, J. A. (2000) Toward a histology of social behavior: judgmental accuracy from thin slices of the behavioural stream, *Advances in Experimental Social Psychology* 32: 201–71.

Amichai-Hamburger, Y. (2009) Personality, individual differences and Internet use, in *Oxford Handbook of Internet Psychology*, ed. A. N. Joinson, K. Y. A. McKenna, T. Postmes, and U.-D. Reips. Oxford: Oxford University Press.

Amichai-Hamburger, Y., and Vinitzky, G. (2010) Social network use and personality, *Computers in Human Behavior* 26(6): 1289–95.

Anand, P., Pattanaik, P., and Puppe, C. (2009) A *Handbook of Rational and Social Choice*. Oxford: Oxford University Press.

Anderson, R., Hughes, J., and Sharrock, W. W. (1989) *Working for Profit: The Social Organisation of Calculation in an Entrepreneurial Firm*. Aldershot: Avebury.

Andrejevic, M. (2013) *Infoglut: How Too Much Information is Changing the Way We Think and Know*. London: Routledge.

Anscombe, G. E. M. (1957) *Intention*, Cambridge, MA: Harvard University Press.

Anscombe, G. E. M. (2000) *Intention*. 2nd edn, Cambridge, MA: Harvard University Press.

Archer, M., and Tritter, J. (2000) *Rational Choice Theory: Resisting Colonization*. London: Routledge.

Archer, M., Bhaskar, R., Collier, A., Lawson, T., and Norrie, A. (1998) *Critical Realism: Essential Readings*. London: Routledge.

Ariely, D. (2008) *Predictably Irrational: The Hidden Forces that Shape our Decisions*. New York: HarperCollins.

Ariely, D. (2010) *The Upside of Irrationality: The Unexpected Benefits of Defying Logic at Home and Work*. New York: HarperCollins.

Arrow, K. J. (1951) *Social Choice and Individual Values*. New York: Wiley.

Asch, S. (1952) *Social Psychology*. Englewood Cliffs, NJ: Prentice-Hall.

Atlas, S. W. (2009) *Magnetic Resonance Imaging of the Brain and Spine*, Vol 1. 4th edn, Philadephia: Lippincott Williams & Wilkins.

Aue, T., Lavelle, L., and Cacioppo, J. (2009) Great expectations: what can fMRI research tell us about psychological phenomena? *International Journal of Psychophysiology* 73(1): 10–16.

Aunger, R. (2002) *The Electric Meme: A New Theory of How We Think*. New York: Free Press.

Axelrod, R. (1986) An evolutionary approach to norms, *American Political Science Review* 80(4): 1095–111.

Azmanova, A. (2012) *The Scandal of Reason: A Critical Theory of Political Judgment*. New York: Columbia University Press.

Bachrach, Y., Kosinski, M., Graepel, T., Kohli, P., and Stillwell, D. (2012) Personality and patterns of Facebook usage, *Proceedings of WebSci '12: the 4th Annual ACM Web Science Conference*. New York: ACM Press.

Baglioni, M., Ferrara, U., Romei, A., Ruggieri, S., and Turini, F. (2003) Preprocessing and mining web log data for web personalization, *AI*IA 2003: Advances in Artificial Intelligence* 2829: 237–49.

Banaji, M., and Greenwald, A. (2013) *Blindspot: Hidden Biases of Good People*. New York: Delacourt Press.

Bargh, J. A. (2006) What have we been priming all these years? On the development, mechanisms, and ecology of nonconscious social behavior, *European Journal of Social Psychology* 36: 147–68.

Bargh, J. A., Chen, M., and Burrows, L. (1996) Automaticity of social behavior: direct effects of trait construct and stereotype activation on action, *Journal of Personality and Social Psychology* 71(2): 230–44.

Baron, J., and Hannan, M. (1994) The impact of economics on contemporary sociology, *Journal of Economic Literature* 32(3): 1111–46.

Bauer, R. A. (1967) Consumer behavior as risk taking, in *Risk Taking and Information Handling in Consumer Behavior*, ed. D. F. Cox. Boston: Harvard University Press, pp. 23–33.

Baumrind, S. (1985) Research using intentional deception: ethical issues revisited, *American Psychologist* 40(2): 165–74.

Becker, G. S. (1968) Crime and punishment: an economic approach, *Journal of Political Economy* 76: 169–217.

Becker, G. S. (1996) *Accounting for Tastes*. Cambridge, MA: Harvard University Press.

Becker, K., and Stalder, F. (2009) *Deep Search: The Politics of Search beyond Google*. Piscataway, NJ: Transaction.

Belch, M., Krentler, K., and Willis- Flurry, L. (2005) Teen Internet mavens: influence in family decision making, *Journal of Business Research* 58: 569–75.

Benkler, Y. (2006) *The Wealth of Networks*. New Haven, CT: Yale University Press.

Benkler, Y. (2011) *The Penguin and the Leviathan: How Cooperation Triumphs over Self-Interest*. New York: Crown Business.

Benkler, Y. (2012) Law, policy, and cooperation, in *Government and Markets: Toward a New Theory of Regulation*, ed. E. Balleisen and D. Moss. Cambridge: Cambridge University Press; http://benkler.org/Pub.html#Cooperation.

Bennett, C. M., Baird, A. A., Miller, M. B., and Wolford, G. L. (2010) Neural correlates of interspecies perspective taking in the post-mortem Atlantic salmon: an argument for proper multiple comparisons correction, *Journal of Serendipitous and Unexpected Results* 1(1): 1–5.

Berger, J., and Offe, C. (1982) Functionalism vs. rational choice? Some questions concerning the rationality of choosing one or the other, *Theory and Society* 11(4): 521–6.

Bermudez, J. (2009) *Decision Theory and Rationality*. Oxford: Oxford University Press.

Bhaskar, R. (2011) *Reclaiming Reality: A Critical Introduction to Contemporary Philosophy*, intro. M. Hartwig. Abingdon: Routledge.

Biderman, S., and Scharfstein, B.-A. (eds) (1989) *Rationality in Question*. Leiden: Brill.

Blackburn, S. (1998) *Ruling Passions (A Theory of Practical Reason)*. Oxford: Clarendon Press.

Blackmore, S. (1999) *The Meme Machine*. Oxford: Oxford University Press.

Blau, P. (1964) *Exchange and Power in Social Life*. New York: John Wiley.

Blau, P. (1987) Microprocess and macrostructure, in *Social Exchange Theory*, ed. K. Cook. London: Sage.

Block, J. (1995) A contrarian view of the five-factor approach to personality description, *Psychological Bulletin* 117(2): 187–215.

Blossfeld, H.-P., and Prein, G. (eds) (1998) *Rational Choice Theory and Large-Scale Data Analysis*. Boulder, CO: Westview Press.

Bolton, G., Katok, E., and Ockenfels, A. (2004a) How effective are electronic reputation mechanisms? An experimental investigation, *Management Science* 50(11): 1587–602.

Bolton, G., Katok, E., and Ockenfels, A. (2004b) Trust among Internet traders: a behavioral economics approach, www.fernuni-hagen.de/PRPH/ockt.pdf.

Bond, R. (2005) Group size and conformity, *Group Processes & Intergroup Relations* 8(4): 331–54.

Borges, J. L. (1998) *On the Exactitude of Science: Collected Fictions*. New York: Penguin.

Boudon, R. (1981) *The Logic of Social Action*. London: Routledge.

Boudon, R. (2000) *The Origin of Values: Sociology and Philosophy of Beliefs*. New Brunswick, NJ: Transaction.

Boudon, R. (2003) Beyond rational choice theory, *Annual Review of Sociology* 29: 1–21.

Bourdieu, P. (1980) Le capital social: notes provisoires, *Actes de la Recherche en Sciences Sociales* 31: 2–3.

Bourdieu, P. (1986) The forms of capital, in *Handbook of Theory and Research for the Sociology of Education*, ed. J. G. Richardson. New York: Greenwood Press, pp. 241–58.

Boylan, T. A., and Gekker, R. (2009) *Economics, Rational Choice and Normative Philosophy*. London: Routledge.

Brannigan, A. (2004) *The Rise and Fall of Social Psychology*. New York: Aldine de Gruyter.

Brantingham, P. J., and Brantingham, P. L. (eds) (1981) *Environmental Criminology*. Prospect Heights, IL: Waveland Press.

Bratman, M. (1992) Shared cooperative activity, *Philosophical Review*, 101(2): 327–41.

Bratman, M. (2007) *Structures of Agency: Essays*. New York: Oxford University Press.

Breen, R. (1999) Beliefs, rational choice and Bayesian learning, *Rationality and Society* 11(4): 463–80.

Breen, R., and Goldthorpe, J. (1997) Explaining educational differentials: towards a formal rational action theory, *Rationality and Society* 9: 275–305.

Brubaker, R. (1984) *The Limits of Rationality: An Essay on the*

Social and Moral Thought of Max Weber. London: Allen & Unwin.

Bucklin, R. E., Lattin, J. M., Ansari, A., Bell, D., Coupey, E., Gupta, S., Little, J., Mela, C., Montgomery, A., and Steckel, J. (2002) Choice and the Internet: from clickstream to research stream, *Marketing Letters* 13(30: 245–58.

Burr, V. (2002) *The Person in Social Psychology*. Hove: Psychology Press.

Buskens, V. (2002) *Social Networks and Trust*. Dordrecht: Kluwer.

Byrne, D. (1998) *Complexity Theory and the Social Sciences: An Introduction*. London: Routledge.

Cabral, L. (2005) *The Economics of Trust and Reputation: A Primer*, http://pages.stern.nyu.edu/~lcabral/reputation/Reputation_June05.pdf.

Camerer, C. F. (2003) *Behavioural Game Theory: Experiments in Strategic Interaction*. Princeton, NJ: Princeton University Press.

Camerer, C. F. (2008) The case for mindful economics, in *The Foundations of Positive and Normative Economics*, ed. A. Caplin and A. Schotter. Oxford: Oxford University Press.

Camerer, C. F., and Fehr, E. (2006) When does 'economic man' dominate social behavior? *Science* 311, 47–52.

Camerer, C. F., Loewenstein, G., and Prelec, D. (2005) Neuroeconomics: how neuroscience can inform economics, *Journal of Economic Literature* 43: 9–64.

Cameron, S. (2002) *The Economics of Sin: Rational Choice or No Choice at All*. Cheltenham: Edward Elgar.

Caplin, A., and Schotter, A. (2008) *The Foundations of Positive and Normative Economics*. Oxford: Oxford University Press.

Casscells, W., Schoenberger, A., and Graboys, T. (1978) Interpretation by physicians of clinical laboratory tests, *New England Journal of Medicine* 299(18): 999–1001.

Chainey, S., and Ratcliffe, J. (2005) *GIS and Crime Mapping*. Chichester: John Wiley.

Chamberlain, A., Crabtree, A., Davis, M., Greenhalgh, C., Rodden, T., Valchovska, S., and Glover, K. (2012) Fresh and local: the rural produce market as a site for co-design, ubiquitous technological intervention and digital-economic development, *Proceedings of MUM '12*. New York: ACM.

Chan, D. K. (ed.) (2008) *Moral Psychology Today: Essays on Values, Rational Choice, and the Will*. Berlin: Springer.

Charness, G., Karni, E., and Levin, D. (2009) On the conjunction fallacy in probability judgment: new experimental evidence regarding Linda, *Games and Economic Behavior* 68: 551–6.

Chatterjee, P. (2001) Online reviews: do consumers use them?, in

NA: Advances in Consumer Research 28, ed. M. C. Gilly and J. Meyers-Levy. Valdosta, GA: Association for Consumer Research, pp. 129–33.

Chayko, M. (2008) *Portable Communities: The Social Dynamics of Online and Mobile Connectedness*. Albany: SUNY Press.

Chernoff, H. (1986) Comment [on Efron], *American Statistician* 40(1): 5–6.

Chomsky, N. (2006) *Language and Mind*. 3rd edn, Cambridge: Cambridge University Press.

Chwe, M. (2001) *Rational Ritual: Culture, Coordination, and Common Knowledge*. Princeton, NJ: Princeton University Press.

Clark, A. (2003) *Natural-Born Cyborgs: Minds, Technologies and the Future of Human Intelligence*. Oxford: Oxford University Press.

Clark, J. (ed.) (1996) *James S. Coleman*. London: Routledge Falmer.

Clarke, R. V. G., and Felson, M. (eds) (1993) *Routine Activity and Rational Choice*. New Brunswick, NJ: Transaction.

Cohen, L. E., and Felson, M. (1979) Social change and crime rate trends: a routine activity approach, *American Sociological Review* 44: 588–608.

Coleman, J. S. (1973) *The Mathematics of Collective Action*. Chicago: Aldine.

Coleman, J. S. (1986) *Individual Interests and Collective Action: Selected Essays*. Cambridge: Cambridge University Press.

Coleman, J. S. (1990) *Foundations of Social Theory*. Cambridge, MA: Harvard University Press.

Coleman, J. S., and Fararo, T. J. (eds) (1992) *Rational Choice Theory: Advocacy and Critique*. London: Sage.

Collier, P. (1998) *Social Capital and Poverty*. Washington, DC: World Bank.

Coltheart, M. (2006) Perhaps functional neuroimaging has not told us anything about the mind (so far), *Cortex* 42: 422–7.

Cook, K., and Emerson, R. (1978) Power, equity, and commitment in exchange networks, *American Sociological Review* 43: 721–39.

Correa, T., Willard Hinsley, A., and Gil de Zúñiga, H. (2010) Who interacts on the Web? The intersection of users' personality and social media use, *Computers in Human Behavior* 26(2): 247–53.

Coulter, J., and Sharrock, W. (2007) *Brain, Mind, and Human Behavior in Contemporary Cognitive Science: Critical Assessments of the Philosophy of Psychology*. Lewiston, NY: Edwin Mellen Press.

Cox, D. F. (1967) *Risk Taking and Information Handling in Consumer Behaviour*. Cambridge, MA: Harvard University Press.

Crabtree, A., and Chamberlain, A. (2014) Making it 'pay a bit better': design challenges for micro rural enterprise, in *CSCW '14:*

Proceedings of the 17th ACM Conference on Computer Supported Cooperative Work & Social Computing. New York: ACM Press, pp. 687–96.

Crowley, P. H., and Zentall, T. R. (eds) (2013) *Comparative Decision Making*. Oxford: Oxford University Press.

Danielson, P. (1998) *Modelling Rationality, Morality, and Evolution*. Oxford: Oxford University Press.

Danziger, K. (2008) *Marking the Mind: A History of Memory*. Cambridge: Cambridge University Press.

Darnton, R. (2009) *The Case for Books: Past, Present, and Future*. New York: Public Affairs.

Davenport, J. (1998) *A Philosophical Critique of Personality-Type Theory in Psychology: Esyenck, Myers-Briggs, and Jung*, http://faculty.fordham.edu/davenport/texts/Jung-MyersBriggs.pdf.

Davidson, D. (1963) Actions, reasons, and causes, *Journal of Philosophy* 60: 685–700: repr. in *Action & Events*. Oxford: Oxford University Press, 1980, pp. 3–20.

Dawes, R. M. (2001) *Everyday Irrationality: How Pseudo-Scientists, Lunatics, and the Rest of Us Systematically Fail to Think Rationally*. Boulder, CO: Westview Press.

Dawkins, R. (1989) *The Selfish Gene*. Oxford: Oxford University Press.

De Bock, K. W., and Van den Poel, D. (2010) Predicting website audience demographics for web advertising targeting using multi-website clickstream data, *Fundamenta Informaticae* 98(1): 49–70.

de Bruin, B. P. (2010) *Explaining Games: The Epistemic programme in Game Theory*. Berlin: Springer.

de Finetti, B. (1970) Logical foundations and measurement of subjective probability, *Acta Psychologica* 34: 129–45.

Dean, M. (2013) What can neuroeconomics tell us about economics (and vice versa)?, in *Comparative Decision Making*, ed. P. H. Crowley and T. R. Zentall. Oxford: Oxford University Press.

Dennett, D. (1995) *Darwin's Dangerous Idea: Evolution and the Meanings of Life*. New York: Simon & Schuster.

Dennett, D. (1996) *Kinds of Minds: Towards an Understanding of Consciousness*. London: Weidenfield & Nicolson.

Dennett, D. (1998) *Brainchildren: Essays on Designing Minds*. Harmondsworth: Penguin.

Dhongde, S., and Pattanaik, P. K. (2010) Preference, choice, and rationality: Amartya Sen's critique of the theory of rational choice in economics, in *Amartya Sen*, ed. C. Morris. Cambridge: Cambridge University Press.

Diesing, P. (1962) *Reason in Society: Five Types of Decision and their Social Conditions*. Westport, CT: Greenwood Press.

Douglas, M. (1966) Purity *and Danger: An Analysis of the Concepts of Pollution and Taboo.* London: Routledge & Kegan Paul.

Doyen, S., Klein, O., Pichon, C.-L., and Cleeremans, A. (2012) Behavioral priming: it's all in the mind, but whose mind? *PLoS One* 7(1): e29081.

Duesenberry, J. (1960) Comment on 'An economic analysis of fertility', in *Demographic and Economic Change in Developed Countries,* ed. NBER. New York: Columbia University Press, pp. 225–56.

Dunbar, R., Barrett, L., and Lycett, J. (2005) *Evolutionary Psychology: A Beginner's Guide.* Oxford: Oneworld.

Duncan, J. (2010) *How Intelligence Happens.* New Haven, CT: Yale University Press.

Dupre, J. (2001) *Human Nature and the Limits of Science.* Oxford: Clarendon Press.

Dupre, J. (2003) *Darwin's Legacy: What Evolution Means Today.* Oxford: Oxford University Press.

Durkheim, E. ([1895] 1982) *Rules of Sociological Method.* Chicago: University of Chicago Press.

Durkheim, E. ([1912] 2001) *Elementary Forms of the Religious Life,* trans. C. Cosman, ed. M. Cladis. Oxford: Oxford University Press.

Edling, C. (2000) Rational choice theory and quantitative analysis: a comment on Goldthorpe's sociological alliance, *European Sociological Review* 16(1):1–8.

Edmonds, D. (2014) *Would You Kill the Fat Man? The Trolley Problem and What your Answer Tells Us about Right and Wrong.* Princeton, NJ: Princeton University Press.

Edwards, W. (1954) *The Theory of Decision Making.* Washington, DC: American Psychological Association.

Efron, B. (1986) Why isn't everyone a Bayesian? *American Statistician* 40(1): 1–5.

Elster, J. (1985) *Making Sense of Marx.* Cambridge: Cambridge University Press.

Elster, J. (1999) *Alchemies of the Mind: Rationality and the Emotions.* Cambridge: Cambridge University Press.

Elster, J. (2000) Rationality, economy and society, in *The Cambridge Companion to Weber,* ed. S. Turner. Cambridge: Cambridge University Press.

Elster, J. (2007) *Explaining Social Behaviour: More Nuts and Bolts for the Social Sciences.* Cambridge: Cambridge University Press.

Elster, J. (2009a) *Reason and Rationality.* Princeton, NJ: Princeton University Press.

Elster, J. (2009b) *The Cement of Society.* Cambridge: Cambridge University Press.

Etzioni, A. (1987) Towards a Kantian socio-economics, *Review of Social Economy* 65: 37–42.

Eusepi, G., and Hamlin, A. (2006) *Beyond Conventional Economics: The Limits of Rational Behaviour in Political Decision Making*. Cheltenham: Edward Elgar.

Eysenck, H. (1992) Four ways five factors are *not* basic, *Personality and Individual Differences* 13(6): 667–73.

Faggini, M., and Vinci, C. (2010) *Decision Theory and Choices: A Complexity Approach*. Berlin: Springer.

Fararo, T. (1996) Foundational problems in theoretical sociology, in *James S. Coleman*, ed. J. Clark. London: Routledge Falmer.

Faulkner, P. (2014) The practical rationality of trust, *Synthese* 191: 1975–89.

Fehr, E. (2009) The economics and biology of trust, *Journal of European Economics* 7(2–3): 235–66.

Feick, L. F., and Price, L. L. (1987) The market maven: a diffuser of marketplace information, *Journal of Marketing* 51: 83–97.

Ferraro, F., Pfeffer, J., and Sutton, R. I. (2005) Economics language and assumptions: how theories can become self-fulfilling, *Academy of Management Review* 30(1): 8–24.

Fiedler, K. (1988) The dependence of the conjunction fallacy on subtle linguistic factors, *Psychological Research* 50: 123–9.

Field, A. (2001) *Altruistically Inclined?* Ann Arbor: University of Michigan Press.

Fine, B. (1980) *Economic Theory as Ideology*. London: Edward Arnold.

Fine, B. (2001) *Social Capital versus Social Theory*. London: Routledge.

Fine, B. (2010) *Theories of Social Capital: Researchers Behaving Badly*. London: Pluto Press.

Finke, R., and Stark, R. (1992) *The Churching of America, 1776–1990: Winners and Losers in our Religious Economy*. New Brunswick, NJ: Rutgers University Press.

Fodor, J. (1975) *The Language of Thought*. Cambridge, MA: Harvard University Press.

Fodor, J. (1996) Deconstructing Dennett's Darwin, *Mind and Language*, 11(3): 246–62.

Foot, P. (1978) The problem of abortion and the doctrine of the double effect, in *Virtue and Vices and Other Essays in Moral Philosophy*. Oxford: Blackwell, pp. 19–32.

Frank, R. H. (1998) *Passions within Reason: The Strategic Role of the Emotions*. New York: W. W. Norton.

Frank, R. H. (2008) *The Economic Naturalist: Why Economics Explains Almost Everything*. London: Virgin Books.

Frazer, J. G. ([1890] 1998) *The Golden Bough: A Study in Magic and Religion*. Oxford: Oxford University Press.

Freud, S. ([1900] 1913) *The Interpretation of Dreams* [*Die Traumdeutung*], trans A. Brill. New York: Macmillan.

Friedman, M. (1953) The methodology of positive economics, in M. Friedman, *Essays in Positive Economics*. Chicago: University of Chicago Press.

Gal, D. (2006) A psychological law of inertia and the illusion of loss aversion, *Judgment and Decision Making* 1(1): 23–32.

Garfinkel, H. (1967a) Good organizational reasons for 'bad' clinic records, in *Studies in Ethnomethodology*. Englewood Cliffs, NJ: Prentice-Hall.

Garfinkel, H. (1967b) *Studies in Ethnomethodology*. Englewood Cliffs, NJ: Prentice-Hall.

Geertz, C. (1975) *The Interpretation of Cultures*. London: Hutchinson.

Gert, J. (2004) *Brute Rationality: Normativity and Human Conduct*. Cambridge: Cambridge University Press.

Gigerenzer, G. (1996) On narrow norms and vague heuristics: a reply to Kahneman and Tversky, *Psychological Review* 103(3): 592–6.

Gigerenzer, G. (2002) *Reckoning with Risk: Learning to Live with Uncertainty*. London: Penguin.

Gigerenzer, G. (2007) *Gut Feelings: The Intelligence of the Unconscious*. New York: Penguin.

Gigerenzer, G. (2014) *Risk Savvy: How to Make Good Decisions*. New York: Viking Press.

Gigerenzer, G., and Selten, R. (eds) (2002a) *Bounded Rationality: The Adaptive Toolbox*. Cambridge, MA: MIT Press.

Gigerenzer, G., and Selten, R. (2002b) Rethinking rationality, in *Bounded Rationality: The Adaptive Toolbox*. Cambridge, MA: MIT Press.

Gigerenzer, G., and Sturm, T. (2012) How (far) can rationality be naturalised? *Synthese* 187: 243–68.

Gilbert, M. (1989) *On Social Facts*. New York: Routledge.

Gilbert, M. (2014) *Joint Commitment: How We Make the Social World*. Oxford: Oxford University Press.

Gilboa, I. (2010) *Rational Choice*. Cambridge, MA: MIT Press.

Gintis, H. (2009) *Game Theory Evolving: A Problem-Centered Introduction to Modelling Strategic Behaviour*. 2nd edn, Princeton, NJ: Princeton University Press.

Gladwell, M. (2005) *Blink: The Power of Thinking without Thinking*. Harmondsworth: Penguin.

Gleick, J. (2011) *The Information: A History, a Theory, a Flood*. London: HarperCollins.

Godwin, M. (1994) Meme, counter-meme, *Wired*, http://archive. wired.com/wired/archive/2.10/godwin.if_pr.html.

Goel, S., Hofman, J. M., Lahaie, S., Pennock, S. M., and Watts, D. J. (2010) Predicting consumer behavior with Web Search, *Proceedings of the National Academy of Sciences* 107: 17486–90.

Golbeck, J., Robles, C., and Turner, K. (2011) Predicting personality with social media, in *CHI '11 Extended Abstracts on Human Factors in Computing Systems*. New York: ACM Press, pp. 253–62.

Goldberg, L. R. (1993) The structure of phenotypic personality traits, *American Psychologist* 48(1): 26–34.

Goldman, A. (1986) *Epistemology and Cognition*. Cambridge, MA: Harvard University Press.

Goldstein, W. (2006) *Marx, Critical Theory and Religion: A Critique of Rational Choice Theory*. Leiden: Brill.

Goldthorpe, J. (1996a) The quantitative analysis of large-scale data-sets and rational action theory: for a sociological alliance, *European Sociological Review* 12, 109–26.

Goldthorpe, J. (1996b) *Rational Choice Theory and Large-Scale Data Analysis*. Oxford: Oxford University Press.

Goldthorpe, J. (1998) Rational action theory for sociology, *British Journal of Sociology* 49: 167–92.

Goodwin, C. (1994) Professional vision, *American Anthropologist* 96(3): 606–33.

Gosling, S. D., Augustine, A. A., and Vazire, S. (2011) Manifestations of personality in online social networks: self-reported Facebook-related behaviors and observable profile information, *Cyberpsychology, Behavior, and Social Networking* 14(9): 483–8.

Granovetter, M. (1985) Economic action and social structure: the problem of embeddedness, *American Journal of Sociology* 91: 481–510.

Green, D., and Shapiro, I. (1994) *Pathologies of Rational Choice Theory: A Critique of Applications in Political Science*. New Haven, CT: Yale University Press.

Groarke, S. (2002) Psychoanalysis and structuration theory: the social logic of identity, *Sociology* 36(3): 559–76.

Gui, B., and Sugden, R. (2005) *Economics and Social Interaction*. Cambridge: Cambridge University Press.

Gul, F., and Pesendorfer, W. (2005) The case for mindless economics, www.princeton.edu/~pesendor/mindless.pdf.

Hacker, P. M. S. (2007) *Human Nature: The Categorical Framework*. Oxford: Blackwell.

Hamilton, W. D. (1963) The evolution of altruistic behaviour, *American Naturalist* 97: 354–6.

Hamilton, W. D. (1964) The genetical evolution of social behaviour, *Journal of theoretical biology* 7: 1–52.

Hands, D. W. (2001) *Reflection without Rules: Economic Methodology and Contemporary Science Theory*. Cambridge: Cambridge University Press.

Hands, D. W. (2004) On operationalisms and economics, *Journal of Economic Issues* 38(4): 953–68.

Harford, T. (2008) *The Logic of Life: The Rational Economics of an Irrational World*. New York: Random House.

Harper, R. H. R (1998) *Inside the IMF: An Ethnography of Documents, Technology and Organisational Action*. London and San Diego: Academic Press.

Harper, R. H. R. (2011) *Texture: Human Expression in the Age of Communications Overload*. Cambridge, MA: MIT Press.

Harper, R., Randall, D., and Rouncefield, M. (2000) *Organizational Change and Retail Finance: An Ethnographic Perspective*. London: Routledge.

Harrison, R. (1979) *Rational Action: Studies in Philosophy and Science*. Cambridge: Cambridge University Press.

Hastie, R., and Dawes, R. (2010) *Rational Choice in an Uncertain World: The Psychology of Judgement and Decision-Making*. London: Sage.

Hauben, M., and Hauben, R. (1997) *Netizens: On the History and Impact of Usenet and the Internet*. Los Alamitos, CA: IEEE Computer Society Press.

Hausman, D. M. (2005) Sympathy, commitment, and preference, *Economics & Philosophy* 21(1): 33–50.

Heath, C. (2013) *The Dynamics of Auction: Social Interaction and the Sale of Fine Art and Antiques*. Cambridge: Cambridge University Press.

Heath, J. (2003) *Communicative Action and Rational Choice*. Cambridge, MA: MIT Press

Hechter, M. (1987) *Principles of Group Solidarity*. Berkeley: University of California Press.

Hechter, M., and Kanazawa, S. (1997) Sociological rational choice theory, *Annual Review of Sociology* 23: 191–214.

Heckman, J., and Neal, D. (1996) Coleman's contributions to education, in *James S. Coleman*, ed. J. Clark. London: Routledge Falmer.

Hedstrom, P. (2005) *Dissecting the Social: On the Principles of Analytic Sociology*. Cambridge: Cambridge University Press.

Hedstrom, P., and Stern, C. (2008) Rational choice and sociology, in *The New Palgrave Dictionary of Economics Online*, ed. L. Blume and S. Durlauf. 2nd edn, Basingstoke: Palgrave Macmillan.

Henrich, J., Boyd, R., Bowles, S., Camerer, C., Fehr, E., Gintis, H., and McElreath, R. (2001) In search of homo economicus: behavioral experiments in 15 small-scale societies, *American Economics Review* 91(2): 73–8.

Henrich, J., Boyd, R., Bowles, S., Camerer, C., Fehr, E., and Gintis, H. (2004) *The Foundations of Human Sociality*. Oxford: Oxford University Press.

Hertwig, R., and Gigerenzer, G. (1999) The 'conjunction fallacy' revisited: how intelligent inferences look like reasoning errors, *Journal of Behavioral Decision Making*, 12: 275–305.

Hertz, N. (2013) *Eyes Wide Open: How to Make Smart Decisions in a Confusing World*. London: HarperCollins.

Hester, S., and Francis, D. W. (2000) *Local Educational Order*. Philadelphia: John Benjamins.

Higgins, G. E. (2007) Digital piracy, self-control theory, and rational choice: an examination of the role of value, *International Journal of Cyber Criminology* 1(1): 33–55.

Hillis, K., Petit, M., and Jarrett, K. (2013) *Google and the Culture of Search*. Abingdon: Routledge.

Hobbes, T. ([1651] 1996) *Leviathan or The Matter, Forme and Power of a Common Wealth Ecclesiasticall and Civil: Revised Student Edition*, ed. R. Tuck. Cambridge: Cambridge University Press.

Hochman, G., and Yechiam, E. (2011) Loss aversion in the eye and in the heart: the autonomic nervous system's responses to losses, *Journal of Behavioral Decision Making* 24(2): 140–56.

Hodges, B., and Geyer, A. (2006) A nonconformist account of the Asch experiments: values, pragmatics and moral dilemmas, *Personality and Social Psychology Review* 10(1): 2–19.

Hollis, M. (1998) *Trust within Reason*. Cambridge: Cambridge University Press.

Hollis, M., and Nell, E. J. (1975) *Rational Economic Man*. Cambridge: Cambridge University Press.

Holton, R. (2006) The act of choice, *Philosopher's Imprint* 6(3) 1–15.

Homans, G. (1958) Social behavior as exchange, *American Journal of Sociology* 63: 597–606.

Homans, G. (1961) *Social Behavior: Its Elementary Forms*. New York: Harcourt, Brace.

Homans, G. (1964) Bringing men back in, *American Sociological Review* 29: 809–18.

Homans, G. (1969) The sociological relevance of behaviourism, in *Certainties and Doubts: Collected Papers, 1962–1985*. New Brunswick, NJ: Transaction.

Hsu, M., and Zhu, L. (2013) Ambiguous decisions in the human brain, in *Comparative Decision Making*, ed. H. Crowley and T. R. Zentall. Oxford: Oxford University Press.

Hsu, M., Bhatt, M., Adolphs, R., Tranel, D., and Camerer, C. F. (2005) Neural systems responding to degrees of uncertainty in human decision-making, *Science* 310(5754): 1680–3.

Hu, J., Zeng, H.-J., Li, H., Niu, C., and Chen, Z. (2007) Demographic prediction based on user's browsing behavior, *Proceedings of the 16th International Conference on the World Wide Web*, pp. 151–60.

Huck, S. (ed.) (2004) *Advances in Understanding Strategic Behaviour: Game Theory, Experiments and Bounded Rationality*. Basingstoke: Palgrave Macmillan.

Hull, M. (2012) Documents and bureaucracy, *Annual Review of Anthropology* 41: 251–67.

Hume, D. ([1739–40] 1974) *A Treatise on Human Nature*. 2nd edn, ed. P. Niddich. Oxford: Oxford University Press.

Iannaccone, L., Finke, R., and Stark, R. (1997) Deregulating religion: the economics of church and state, *Economic Inquiry* 35: 350–64.

Ingold, T. (2012) *Being Alive: Essays on Movement, Knowledge and Description*. Abingdon: Routledge.

Iszatt-White, M., Graham, C., Randall, D., Kelly, S., and Rouncefield, M. (2011) *Leadership in Post-Compulsory Education*. London: Continuum.

Jasso, G. (1988) Principles of theoretical analysis, *Sociological Theory* 6: 1–20.

Jeannenay, J.-N. (2007) *Google: The Myth of Universal Knowledge*. Chicago: University of Chicago Press.

Jones, S. (1992) Was there a Hawthorne effect? *American Journal of Sociology* 98(3): 451–68.

Jonsson, J. (1999) Explaining sex differences in educational choice: an empirical assessment of a rational choice model, *European Sociological Review* 15: 391–404.

Joseph, P. M., and Atlas, S. W. (2009) Artifacts in MR, in Atlas, S. W. 2009. *Magnetic Resonance Imaging of the Brain and Spine*, Vol. 1. 4th edn, Philadelphia: Lippincott Williams & Wilkins.

Joyce, J. M. (2004) Bayesianism, in *The Oxford Handbook of Rationality*, ed. A. Mele and P. Rawling. Oxford: Oxford University Press.

Kahneman, D. (2011) *Thinking, Fast and Slow*. London: Allen Lane.

Kahneman, D., Slovic, P., and Tversky, A. (1982) *Judgement under Uncertainty: Heuristics and Biases*. Cambridge: Cambridge University Press.

Kahneman, D., and Tversky, A. (1996) On the reality of cognitive illusions, *Psychological Review* 103(3): 582–91.

Kanaan, R. A., and McGuire, P. K. (2011) Conceptual challenges in the neuroimaging of psychiatric disorders, *Philosophy, Psychiatry and Psychology* 18(4): 323–32.

Kihlstrom, J. F. (2006) Does neuroscience constrain social psychological theory? *Dialogue* 21: 16–17.

King, P. (ed.) (2005) *Trusting in Reason: Martin Hollis and the Philosophy of Social Action*. London: Frank Cass.

Kiser, E., and Hechter, M. (1998) The debate on historical sociology: rational choice and its critics, *American Journal of Sociology* 104: 785–816.

Kitcher, P. (1985) *Vaulting Ambition: Sociobiology and the Quest for Human Nature*. Cambridge, MA: MIT Press.

Klein, G. A. (1999) *Sources of Power: How People Make Decisions*. Cambridge, MA: MIT Press.

Knorr-Cetina, K., and Preda, A. (2006) *The Sociology of Financial Markets*. Oxford: Oxford University Press.

Kohli, P., Bachrach, Y., Stillwell, D., Kearns, M., Herbrich, R., and Graepel, T. (2012) Colonel Blotto on Facebook: the effect of social relations on strategic interaction, *WebSci '12*: 141–50.

König, R., and Rasch, M. (eds) (2014) *Society of the Query: Reflections on Web Search*. Amsterdam: Institute of Network Cultures.

Kosinski, M., Stillwell, D., and Graepel, T. (2013) Private traits and attributes are predictable from digital records of human behavior, *Proceedings of the National Academy of Sciences* 110: 5802–5.

Kosinski, M., Bachrach, Y., Kohli, P., Stillwell, D., and Graepel, T. (2014) Manifestations of user personality in website choice and behaviour on online social networks, *Machine Learning Journal* 95(3): 357–80.

Kreps, D. (1990a) *Game Theory and Economic Modelling*. Oxford: Oxford University Press.

Kreps, D. (1990b) *A Course in Microeconomic Theory*. Princeton, NJ: Princeton University Press.

Kronfeldner, M. E. (2007) Is cultural evolution Lamarckian? *Biology and Philosophy* 22(4): 493–512.

Ku, G., Malhotra, D., and Murnighan, J. K. (2003) Towards a competitive arousal model of decision-making: a study of auction fever in live and Internet auctions, *Organizational Behavior and Human Decision Processes* 96: 89–103.

LaLancette, M.-F., and Standing, L. (1990) Asch fails again, *Social Behavior and Personality* 18(1): 7–12.

Lalich, J. (2004) *Bounded Choice: True Believers and Charismatic Cults*. Berkeley: University of California Press.

Leeson, P. T. (2014) Oracles, *Rationality and Society* 26(2): 141–69.

Leijonhufvud, A. (1973) Life among the Econ, *Western Economic Journal* 11(3): 327–37.

Leist, A. (ed.) (2007) *Action in Context*. Berlin: de Gruyter.

Levy, I. (2013) Ambiguous decisions in the human brain, in *Comparative Decision Making*, ed. P. H. Crowley and T. R. Zentall. Oxford: Oxford University Press, pp. 135–55.

Lewontin, R. (2000) *It Ain't Necessarily So: The Dream of the Human Genome and Other Illusions*. London: Granta.

Lewontin, R., Rose, S., and Kamin, L. (1984) *Not in our Genes*. New York: Pantheon Books.

Lichbach, M. (2003) *Is Rational Choice Theory All of Social Science?* Ann Arbor: University of Michigan Press.

Lindenberg, S. (1985) Rational choice and sociological theory: new pressures on economics as a social science, *Journal of Institutional and Theoretical Economics* 141: 244–55.

Lindenberg, S. (1990) Homo socio-economicus: the emergence of a general model of man in the social sciences, *Journal of Institutional and Theoretical Economics* 146: 727–48.

Livingstone, E. (1986) *The Ethnomethodological Foundations of Mathematics*. London: Routledge & Kegan Paul.

Lloyd, E. A. (2003) Violence against science: rape and evolution, in *Evolution, Gender, and Rape*, ed. C. B. Travis. Cambridge, MA: MIT Press.

Lollo, E. (2011) *Social Capital and the Capability Approach: New Answers to Old Problems*, www.happinesseconomics.net/ocs/index.php/heirs/markethappiness/paper/view/272/136.

Lollo, E. (2012) *Toward a Theory of Social Capital Definition: Its Dimensions and Resulting Social Capital Types*, http://socialeconomics.org/Papers/Lollo1C.pdf.

Loury G. C. (1977) A dynamic theory of racial income differences, in *Women, Minorities, and Employment Discrimination*, ed. P. A. Wallace and A. M. LaMond, Lexington, MA: Lexington Books, pp. 153–86.

Lovink, G. (2012) *The Society of the Query and the Googlisation of Our Lives: A Tribute to Joseph Weizenbaum*, www.zak.kit.edu/downloads/Lovink_8_fertig.pdf.

Lui, S. M., Lang, K. R., and Kwok, S. H. (2002) Participation incentive mechanisms in peer-to-peer subscription systems, *Proceedings of the 35th Hawaii International Conference on System Sciences*. Los Alamitos, CA: IEEE.

Lumsden, C. J., and Wilson, E. O. (2005) *Genes, Mind and Culture: The Coevolutionary Process*. Hackensack, NJ: World Scientific.

Lynch, M. (1993) *Scientific Practice and Ordinary Action: Ethnomethodology and Social Studies of Science*. Cambridge: Cambridge University Press.

Lynch, M., Cole, S. A., McNally, R., and Jordan, K. (2008)

Truth Machine: The Contentious History of DNA Fingerprinting. Chicago, University of Chicago Press.

McDowell, J. (1994) *Mind and World.* Cambridge, MA: Harvard University Press.

McGrayne, S. B. (2012) *The Theory That Would Not Die: How Bayes' Rule Cracked the Enigma Code, Hunted Down Russian Submarines, & Emerged Triumphant from Two Centuries of Controversy.* New Haven, CT, and London: Yale University Press.

Madrick, J. G. (2014) *Seven Bad Ideas: How Mainstream Economists Have Damaged America and the World.* New York: Alfred A. Knopf.

Malik, K. (2000) *Man, Beast and Zombie: What Science Can and Cannot Tell Us about Human Nature.* London: Phoenix Press, chaps 8 and 9.

Malinowksi, B. (1922) *Argonauts of the Western Pacific: An Account of Native Enterprise and Adventure in the Archipelagos of Melanesian New Guinea.* London: Routledge.

March, J., and Simon, H. ([1958] 1993) *Organisations.* 2nd edn, Oxford: Blackwell.

Margolis, H. (2007) *Cognition and Extended Rational Choice Theory.* London: Routledge.

Marsden, P. (2005) The sociology of James S. Coleman, *Annual Review of Sociology* 31: 1–24.

Massey, D. (2005) *For Space.* Thousand Oaks, CA: Sage.

Mayo, E. (1933) *The Human Problems of an Industrial Civilisation.* New York: Macmillan.

Mead, G. H. (1932) *Mind, Self and Society from the Standpoint of the Social Behaviourist.* Chicago: University of Chicago Press.

Mele, A., and Rawling, P. (eds) (2004) *The Oxford Handbook of Rationality.* Oxford: Oxford University Press.

Midgeley, M. (1985) *Evolution as a Religion.* London: Methuen.

Midgeley, M. (2004) *Beast and Man: The Roots of Human Nature.* London: Routledge.

Milgram, S. (1974) *Obedience to Authority.* New York: Harper & Row.

Miller, G. (2001) *The Mating Mind: How Sexual Choice Shaped the Evolution of Human Nature.* New York: Anchor Books.

Milonakis, D., and Fine, B. (2009) *From Political Economy to Economics: Method, the Social and the Historical in the Evolution of Economic Theory.* London: Routledge.

Misztal, B. (1996) *Trust in Modern Societies.* Oxford: Blackwell.

Morgan, M. S. (2012) *The World in the Model: How Economists Work And Think.* Cambridge: Cambridge University Press.

Morgan, S. L. (2002) Modeling preparatory commitment and

non-repeatable decisions: information-processing, preference formation and educational attainment, *Rationality and Society* 14: 387–429.

Morris, C. (2010) *Amartya Sen: Contemporary Philosophy in Focus.* Cambridge: Cambridge University Press.

Mosteller, F., and Moynihan, D. P. (eds) (1972) *On the Equality of Educational Opportunity.* New York: Vintage Books.

Mui, L. (2002) Notions of reputation in multi-agents systems: a review, *Proceedings of the First International Joint Conference on Autonomous Agents and Multi-Agent Systems: Part 1.* New York: ACM.

Murray, D., and Durrell, K. (2000) Inferring demographics attributes of anonymous Internet users, in *Web Usage Analysis and User Profiling.* Berlin: Springer, pp. 7–20.

Nagel, T. (1970) *The Possibility of Altruism.* Princeton, NJ: Princeton University Press.

Narayan-Parker, D., and Pritchett, L. (1997) *Cents and Sociability: Household Income and Social Capital in Rural Tanzania.* Washington, DC: World Bank.

Nash, J. F. (1950)The bargaining problem, *Econometrica: Journal of the Econometric Society* 18(2): 155–62.

Nickerson, R. (2008) *Aspects of Rationality: Reflections on What it Means to be Rational and Whether We Are.* New York: Psychology Press.

Nieuwenhuis, S., Forstmann, B., and Wagenmakers, E.-J. (2011) Erroneous analyses of interactions in neuroscience: a problem of significance, *Nature Neuroscience* 14: 1105–7.

Norkus, Z. (2000) Max Weber's interpretive sociology and rational choice approach, *Rationality and Society* 12: 259–82.

North, D. C. (1990) *Institutions, Institutional Change and Economic Performance.* Cambridge: Cambridge University Press.

North, D. C. (2005) *Understanding the Process of Economic Change.* Princeton, NJ: Princeton University Press.

Notturno, M. (1988) Truth, rationality and the situation, *Philosophy of the Social Sciences* 28(3): 400–21.

O'Brian, L. (2015) *Philosophy of Action.* Basingstoke: Palgrave.

O'Connor, J. (2012) The trolley method of moral philosophy, *Essays in Philosophy* 13: 242–55; available at: http://commons.pacificu.edu/eip/vol13/iss1/14.

O'Neill, O. (1996) *Towards Justice and Virtue: A Constructive Account of Practical Reasoning.* Cambridge: Cambridge University Press.

Orne, M. T., and Holland, C. H. (1968) On the ecological validity of laboratory deceptions, *International Journal of Psychiatry* 6: 282–93.

Orr, H. A. (2003) Darwinian storytelling, *New York Review of Books*, 27 February [review article].

Palfrey, J., and Gasser, U. (2008) *Born Digital: Understanding the First Generation of Digital Natives*. New York: Basic Books.

Pariser, E. (2011) *The Filter Bubble: What the Internet is Hiding from You*. London: Penguin.

Parsons, T. (1937) *The Structure of Social Action*. New York: Free Press.

Perrin, S., and Spencer, C. (1980) The Asch experiment: a child of its time, *Bulletin of the British Psychological Society*, 32: 405–6.

Perrin, S., and Spencer, C. (1981) Independence or conformity in the Asch experiment as a reflection of cultural and situational factors, *British Journal of Social Psychology*, 20: 205–10.

Peter, F., and Schmid, H. (eds) (2007a) *Rationality and Commitment*. Oxford: Oxford University Press.

Peter, F., and Schmid, H. (2007b) Rational fools, rational commitments, in *Rationality and Commitment*, ed. F. Peter and H. Schmid. Oxford: Oxford University Press.

Pettit, P. (2002) *Rules, Reasons, and Norms*. Oxford: Clarendon Press.

Pettit, P. (2005) Construing Sen on commitment, *Economics & Philosophy* 21: 15–32.

Pinker, S. (1997) *How The Mind Works*. London: Penguin.

Pinker, S. (2003) *The Blank Slate: The Modern Denial of Human Nature*. London: Viking Press.

Pinker, S. (2011) *The Better Angels of our Nature: Why Violence Has Declined*. New York: Viking.

Portes, A. (1998) Social capital: its origin and applications in modern sociology, *Annual Review of Sociology* 24: 1–24.

Putnam, R. D. (2000) *Bowling Alone: The Collapse and Revival of American Community*. New York: Simon & Schuster.

Putnam, R. D., Leonardi, R., and Nanetti, R. (1993) *Making Democracy Work: Civic Traditions in Modern Italy*. Princeton, NJ: Princeton University Press.

Quervain, D. J.-F. de, Fischbacher, U., Treyer, V., Schellhammer, M., Schnyder, U., Buck, A., and Fehr, E. (2004) The neural basis of altruistic punishment, *Science* 305: 1254–8.

Quine, W. V. (1951) *Two Dogmas of Empiricism*. New York: Longmans, Green.

Quine, W. V. (1960) *Word and Object*. Cambridge, MA: MIT Press.

Rainee, L., and Wellman, B. (2011) *Networked: The New Social Operating System*. Cambridge, MA: MIT Press.

Ramsey, F. P. (1931) *The Foundation of Mathematics and Other*

Logical Essays, ed. R. B. Braithwaite. London: Routledge & Kegan Paul.

Randall, D., Harper, R., and Rouncefield, M. (2007) *Fieldwork for Design*. London: Springer.

Ransom, G. (2012) Some thoughts on Hayek, Wittgenstein and how *not* to 'model' language or the price system, http://hayekcenter. org/?p=5500.

Raub, W., and Weesie, J. (1990) Reputation and efficiency in social interactions: an example of network effects, *American Journal of Sociology* 96: 626–54.

Rawls, J. (1971) *A Theory of Justice*. Cambridge, MA: Harvard University Press.

Resnick, M. (1987) *Choices: An Introduction to Decision Theory*. Minneapolis: University of Minnesota Press.

Richards, D. (1971) *A Theory of Reasons for Action*. Oxford: Oxford University Press.

Richardson, J. G. (ed.) (1990) *Handbook of Theory and Research for the Sociology of Education*. New York: Greenwood Press.

Ridley, M. (1997) *The Origins of Virtue: Human Instincts and the Evolution of Cooperation*. New York: Viking Press.

Ridley, M. (2003) *The Red Queen: Sex and the Evolution of Human Nature*. New York: Perennial.

Ridley, M. (2004) *The Agile Gene: How Nature Turns on Nurture*. New York: Perennial.

Riegelsberger, J., Sasse, A., and McCarthy, J. (2005) The mechanics of trust: a framework for research and design, *International Journal of Human–Computer Studies*, 62(3): 381–422.

Rifkin, J. (2015) *The Zero Marginal Cost Society: The Internet of Things, the Collaborative Commons, and the Eclipse of Capitalism*. New York: Palgrave Macmillan.

Rose, H., and Rose, S. (2001) *Alas Poor Darwin: Arguments against Evolutionary Psychology*. New York: Harmony Books.

Rosenthal, R., and Jackson, L. (1968) *Pygmalion in the Classroom*. New York: Holt, Rinehart & Winston.

Ross, C., Orr, E. S., Sisic, M., Arseneault, J. M., Simmering, M. G., and Orr, R. R. (2009) Personality and motivations associated with Facebook use, *Computers in Human Behavior* 25(2): 578–86.

Ross, D. (2002) Why people are atypical agents, *Philosophical Papers* 31(1): 87–116.

Ross, D. (2010) Neuroeconomics and economic methodology, http://ssrn.com/abstract=1622157.

Ross, D. (forthcoming) Psychological versus economic models of bounded rationality. *Journal of Economic Methodology*.

Rossiaud, S., and Locatelli, C. (2010) *Institutional Economics.* Polinares Working Paper no. 12.

Rubinstein, A. (2000) *Economics and Language: Five Essays.* Cambridge: Cambridge University Press.

Runciman, W. G. (1998) *The Social Animal.* Ann Arbor: University of Michigan Press.

Runciman, W. G. (2009) *A Theory of Cultural and Social Selection.* Cambridge: Cambridge University Press.

Ryle, G. (1949) *The Concept of Mind.* London: Hutchinson.

Sabel, X. (1994) Learning by monitoring: the institutions of economic development, in *Handbook of Economic Sociology*, ed. N. J. Smelser and R. Swedberg. Princeton, NJ: Princeton University Press.

Sacks, H. (1984) On doing 'being ordinary', in *Structures of Social Actions: Studies in Conversation Analysis*, ed. J. M. Atkinson and J. Heritage. Cambridge: Cambridge University Press.

Sakai, S., Awamura, N., and Ikeya, N. (2012) The practical management of information in a task management meeting: taking 'practice' seriously, *Information Research* 17(4); http://InformationR.net/ir/17-4/paper537.html.

Samuels, R., Stich, S., and Bishop, M. (2002) Ending the rationality wars: how to make disputes about human rationality disappear, in *Common Sense, Reasoning, and Rationality*, ed. R. Elio. New York: Oxford University Press.

Sandis, C. (2012) *The Things We Do and Why We Do Them.* Basingstoke: Palgrave.

Sandis, C. (forthcoming) One fell swoop: small red book historicism before and after Davidson, *Journal of the Philosophy of History.*

Sandis, C., and Cain, M. (eds) (2012) *Human Nature.* Cambridge: Cambridge University Press.

Sartre, J. P. ([1945] 2001) *The Reprieve* [*Le sursis*], Penguin, London.

Sartre, J. P. ([1949] 1999) *Iron in the Soul* [*Le Mort dans l'âme*], Pengiun, London.

Sartre, J. P. ([1945] 2009) *The Age of Reason* [*L'âge de raison*] Penguin, London.

Sassatelli, R. (2005) Trust, choice and routines, in *Trusting in Reason: Martin Hollis and the Philosophy of Social Action*, ed. P. King. London: Frank Cass.

Savage, L. J. (1971) Elicitation of personal probabilities and expectations, *Journal of the American Statistical Association* 66: 783–801.

Schutz, A. (1962) *Collected Papers*, I: *The Problem of Social Reality*, ed. M. Natanson. The Hague: Martinus Nijhoff.

Schutz, A. (1964) *Collected Papers*, II: *Studies in Social Theory*, ed. A. Broderson. The Hague: Martinus Nijhoff.

Schutz, A. (1966) *Collected Papers*, III: *Studies in Phenomenological Philosophy*, ed. I. Schutz. The Hague: Martinus Nijhoff.

Scott, M. (1968) *The Racing Game*. Chicago: Aldine.

Searle, J. (1997) *The Mystery of Consciousness*. London: Granta.

Sellen, A., and Harper, R. (2002) *The Myth of the Paperless Office*. Cambridge, MA: MIT Press.

Sen, A. (1982) *Choice, Welfare and Measurement*. Oxford: Blackwell.

Sen, A. (2003) Sraffa, Wittgenstein and Gramsci, *Journal of Economic Literature* 41: 1240–55.

Sen, S., and Lerman, D. (2007) Why are you telling me this? An examination into negative consumer reviews on the web, *Journal of Interactive Marketing* 21(4): 76–94.

Sent, E. M. (1997) Sargent versus Simon: bounded rationality unbound, *Cambridge Journal of Economics* 21: 323–38.

Setiya, K. (2007) *Reasons without Rationalism*. Princeton, NJ: Princeton University Press.

Shapiro, I. (2005) *The Flight from Reality in the Human Sciences*. Princeton, NJ: Princeton University Press.

Shenk, D. (1997) *Data Smog: Surviving the Information Glut*. San Francisco: Harper Edge.

Shue, H. (2006) Torture in dreamland: disposing of the ticking bomb, *Case Western Reserve Journal of International Law* 37: 231–9.

Silver, N. (2012) *The Signal and the Noise: The Art and Science of Prediction*. London: Penguin.

Simon, H. A. (1947) *Administrative Behaviour: A Study of Decision-Making Processes in Administrative Organization*. New York: Free Press.

Simon, H. A. (1967) *The Sciences of the Artificial*. Cambridge, MA: MIT Press.

Simon, H. A. (1990) Invariants of human behavior, *Annual Review of Psychology*, 41: 1–19.

Singer, P. (2011) *The Expanding Circle*. Princeton, NJ: Princeton University Press.

Skyrms, B. (2010) *Signals: Evolution, Learning and Information*. Oxford: Oxford University Press.

Smelser, N. J., and Swedberg, R. (1994) *Handbook of Economic Sociology*. Princeton, NJ: Princeton University Press.

Smith, M. ([1972] 2012) Equality of educational opportunity: the basic findings reconsidered, in *Agent-Based Computational Sociology*, ed. F. Squazzoni. Chichester: Wiley.

Snidal, D. (1985) The game theory of international politics, *World Politics* 38(1): 25–57.

Sober, E., and Sloan Wilson, D. (1998) *Unto Others: The Evolution and Psychology of Unselfish Behaviour.* Cambridge, MA: Harvard University Press.

Squazzoni, F. (ed.) (2012) *Agent-Based Computational Sociology.* Chichester: Wiley.

Sraffa, P. (1960) *Production of Commodities by Means of Commodities: Prelude to a Critique of Economic Theory.* Cambridge: Cambridge University Press.

Stark, R., and Finke, R. (2000) *Acts of Faith: Explaining the Human Side of Religion.* Berkeley: University of California Press.

Stout, R. (2005) *Action.* Chesham: Acumen.

Sturm, T. (2012) The 'rationality wars' in psychology: where they are and where they could go, *Inquiry: An Interdisciplinary Journal of Philosophy* 55(1): 66–81.

Suchman, L., and Wynn, E. (1984) Procedures and problems in the office, *Office: Technology and People* 2: 133–54.

Sunstein, C. R. (2014) *Why Nudge? The Politics of Libertarian Paternalism.* New Haven, CT: Yale University Press.

Swedberg, R. (1990) *Economics and Sociology.* Princeton, NJ: Princeton University Press.

Taddeo, M. (2009) Defining trust and e-trust: old theories and new problems, *International Journal of Technology and Human Interaction* 5(2): 23–35.

Taddeo, M. (2011) The role of e-trust in distributed artificial systems, in *Trust and Virtual Worlds: Contemporary Perspectives,* ed. C. Ess and M. Thorseth. New York: Peter Lang, pp. 75–88.

Taleb, N. N. (2004) *Fooled By Randomness: The Hidden Role of Chance in Life and in the Markets.* London: Texere.

Tanney, J. (2013) *Rules, Reasons, and Self-Knowledge.* Cambridge, MA: Harvard University Press.

Tapscott, D. (2009) *Grown up Digital: How the Net Generation is Changing Your World.* New York: McGraw-Hill.

Ten Have, P. (2002) The notion of member is the heart of the matter: on the role of membership knowledge in ethnomethodological inquiry, *Forum: Qualitative Social Research/Sozialforschung* 3(3); http://nbn-resolving.de/urn:nbn:de:0114-fqs0203217.

Thaler, R. (1980) Toward a positive theory of consumer choice, *Journal of Economic Behavior and Organization* 1(1): 39–60.

Thaler, R. H., and Sunstein, C. R. (2008) *Nudge: Improving Decisions about Health, Wealth and Happiness.* New Haven, CT: Yale University Press.

Thibaut, N., and Kelley, H. (1959) *The Social Psychology of Groups.* New York: Wiley.

Thornhill, R., and Palmer, C. T. (2000) *A Natural History of Rape: Biological Bases of Sexual Coercion.* Cambridge, MA: MIT Press

Tollefsen, D. (2005) Let's pretend! Children and joint action, *Philosophy of the Social Sciences* 35(1): 75–97.

Tomasello, M. (2005) Understanding and sharing intentions: the origins of cultural cognition, *Behavioral and Brain Sciences* 28(5): 675–91.

Tommasi, M., and Ierulli, K. (1995) *The Economics of Human Behaviour*. Cambridge: Cambridge University Press.

Tooby, J., and Cosmides, L. (1992) The psychological foundations of culture, in *The Adapted Mind: Evolutionary Psychology and the Generation of Culture*, ed. L. Barkow, J. Tooby and L. Cosmides. Oxford: Oxford University Press.

Travis, C. B. (2003) *Evolution, Gender and Rape*. Cambridge, MA: MIT Press.

Tudge, C. (2009) The minds of birds, in *The Secret Life of Birds*. London: Penguin, chap 9.

Turner, J. C., Hogg, M. A., Oakes, P. J., Reicher, S. D., and Wetherell, M. S. (1987) *Rediscovering the Social Group: A Self-Categorization Theory*. Oxford: Blackwell.

van Benthem , J., Gupta, A., and Pacuit, E. (eds) (2011) *Games Norms and Reasons: Logic at the Crossroads*. Berlin: Springer.

Van Den Poel, D., and Buckin, W. (2005) Predicting online purchasing behaviour, *European Journal of Operational Research* 166(2): 557–75.

Vanberg, V. J. (1994) *Rules and Choice in Economics: Economics as Social Theory*. London: Routledge.

Vatnik, X. (2009) *Facts and Fictions in the Securities Industries*. Skopje: Narcissus.

Von Neumann, J., and Morgenstern, O. (1944) *Theory of Games and Economic Behaviour*. Princeton, NJ: Princeton University Press.

Vul, E., Harris, C., Winkielman, P., and Pashler, H. (2009) Puzzlingly high correlations in fMRI studies of emotion, personality, and social cognition, *Perspectives on Psychological Science* 4(3): 274–90.

Waldron, J. (2014) It's all for your own good, *New York Review of Books*, 9 October 9, pp. 21–3 [review article].

Wason, P. C. (1966) Reasoning, in *New Horizons in Psychology*, ed. B. M. Foss. Harmondsworth: Penguin.

Watson, R. (2014) Trust in interpersonal interaction and cloud computing, in *Trust, Society and Computing*, ed. R. H. R. Harper. New York: Cambridge University Press, pp. 172–98.

Watson, R. (2009) Constitutive practices and Garfinkel's notion of trust: revisited, *Journal of Classical Sociology* 9(4): 475–99.

Watts, D. J. (2004) *Six Degrees: The Science of the Connected Age*. London: Vintage Books.

Watts, D. J. (2011) *Everything Is Obvious: Once You Know the Answer*. New York: Crown Business.

Weber, I., and Jaimes, A. (2011) Who uses web search for what? And how?, in *WSDM' 11*. New York: ACM, pp. 15–24.

Weber, M. ([1922] 1978) *Economy and Society*. Berkeley: University of California Press.

Weber, M. ([1949] 2011) *Methodology of the Social Sciences*, trans. E. Schills and H. Finch. New Brunswick, NJ: Transaction.

Weber, M. ([1905] 1930) *The Protestant Ethic and the Spirit of Capitalism*, trans. T. Parsons. London and Boston: Unwin Hyman.

Weiner, N. ([1948] 2014) *Cybernetics: Control and Communication in the Animal and the Machine*. Cambridge, MA: MIT Press.

Weiss, J. W., and Weiss, D. J. (2012) Irrational: at the moment, *Synthese* 189: 173–83.

Wellman, B., Quan Haase, A., Witte, J., and Hampton, K. (2001) Does the Internet increase, decrease, or supplement social capital? Social networks, participation, and community commitment, *American Behavioral Scientist* 45 (3): 436–55.

Whitehead, A. N. (1911) *An Introduction to Mathematics*. London: Oxford University Press.

Wiland, E. (2012) *Reasons*. London: Continuum.

Williams, M. (2000) Wittgenstein and Davidson on the sociality of language, *Journal of the Theory of Social Behaviour* 30(3): 299–318.

Williamson, O. E. (2005) Transaction cost economics, in *Handbook of New Institutional Economics*, ed. C. Ménard and M. M. Shirley. Dordrecht: Springer, pp. 41–65.

Wilson, E. O. (1975) *Sociobiology: The New Synthesis*. Cambridge, MA: Harvard University Press.

Wilson, E. O. (1996) *In Search of Nature*. Washington, DC: Island Press/Shearwater Books.

Wilson, E. O. (1998) *Consilience: The Unity of Knowledge*. New York: Alfred A. Knopf.

Wilson, T. (2002) *Strangers to Ourselves: Discovering the Adaptive Unconscious*. Cambridge, MA: Harvard University Press.

Winch, P. (1958) *The Idea of a Social Science and its Relation to Philosophy*. London: Routledge.

Wittgenstein, L. (1953) *Philosophical Investigations*. 4th edn, trans. G. E. M. Anscombe, P. M. S. Hacker and J. Schulte. Oxford: Blackwell.

Wood, A. (2011) Humanity as end in itself, in *On What Matters*, ed. D. Parfit. Oxford: Oxford University Press, Vol. 2, pp. 58–82.

Wright, E. O. (1985) *Classes*. London: Verso.

World Congress of Social Economics, www.socialeconomics.org.

Yechiam, E., and Telpaz, A. (2013) Losses induce consistency in risk taking even without loss aversion, *Journal of Behavioral Decision Making* 26(1): 31–40.

Yudkowski, E. S. (2003) *An Intuitive Explanation of Bayes' Theorem*, http://yudkowsky.net/rational/bayes.

Zablocki, B. (1996) Methodological individualism and collective behaviour, in *James S. Coleman*, ed. J. Clark. London: Routledge Falmer.

Zafirovski, M. (1999) Unification of sociological theory by the rational choice model: conceiving the relationship between economics and sociology, *Sociology* 33(3): 495–514.

Zafirovski, M. (2005) The influence of sociology on economics: selected themes and instances from classical sociological theory, *Journal of Classical Sociology* 5(2): 123–56.

Zak, P. J. (2008) The neurobiology of trust, *Scientific American*, June.

Zimbardo, P. (1972) Comment: pathology of imprisonment, *Society* 9: 4–8.

Žižek, S. (1989) *The Sublime Object of Ideology*. London: Verso.

Index